UNDERSTANDING CONTEMPORARY CHILDHOOD

From Classic Theories to Contemporary Issues

Fiona Corby and Rob Creasy

First published in Great Britain in 2026 by

Policy Press, an imprint of
Bristol University Press
University of Bristol
1-9 Old Park Hill
Bristol
BS2 8BB
UK
t: +44 (0)117 374 6645
e: bup-info@bristol.ac.uk

Details of international sales and distribution partners are available at policy.bristoluniversitypress.co.uk

© Bristol University Press 2026

DOI: 10.51952/9781447376347

British Library Cataloguing in Publication Data
A catalogue record for this book is available from the British Library

ISBN 978-1-4473-7631-6 hardcover
ISBN 978-1-4473-7632-3 paperback
ISBN 978-1-4473-7633-0 ePub
ISBN 978-1-4473-7634-7 ePdf

The right of Fiona Corby and Rob Creasy to be identified as authors of this work has been asserted by them in accordance with the Copyright, Designs and Patents Act 1988.

All rights reserved: no part of this publication may be reproduced, stored in a retrieval system, or transmitted in any form or by any means, electronic, mechanical, photocopying, recording, or otherwise without the prior permission of Bristol University Press.

Every reasonable effort has been made to obtain permission to reproduce copyrighted material. If, however, anyone knows of an oversight, please contact the publisher.

The statements and opinions contained within this publication are solely those of the authors and not of the University of Bristol or Bristol University Press. The University of Bristol and Bristol University Press disclaim responsibility for any injury to persons or property resulting from any material published in this publication.

Bristol University Press and Policy Press work to counter discrimination on grounds of gender, race, disability, age and sexuality.

Cover design: Nicky Boroweic
Front cover image: Adobe Stock/Chayon Sarker

For Hattie, Findlay and Oscar, and all the other little people negotiating a complicated world

Contents

Acknowledgements		vi
1	Introduction	1
2	The persistence of attachment and seeing children as becomings	24
3	From working to playing	40
4	Thinking about how and why we educate	59
5	How policy shapes the child's world	80
6	The landscape of childhood, or knowing and telling the truth	101
7	Living in a world of media	120
8	Gender	136
9	Thinking about outcomes and health	154
10	Children's futures and future childhoods	170
11	Tips to get higher grades	182
References		189
Index		211

Acknowledgements

Our thanks go to Jake Furby, of the York LGBT+ Forum for taking the time to meet with us and provide advice and guidance in relation to our coverage of gender and sexuality issues. Any errors are ours.

1
Introduction

> **This chapter will help you to understand:**
> - why our concern is with childhood, not children;
> - how social constructionism helps us to understand childhood;
> - how Bronfenbrenner's socio-ecological model can be used to understand the range of influences on childhood and children;
> - the concept of agency;
> - where we stand in terms of positioning our arguments.

Some initial thoughts about childhood

Our focus in writing this book is to encourage you to think about ideas relating to children but specifically to childhood and to consider that childhood has to be understood as something that exists within a context. This underpins the title, *Understanding Contemporary Childhood*, and draws attention to the idea that childhood now, in contemporary society, is likely to be understood and experienced differently when compared to previous periods but also in different countries other than the UK, where we are based.

As time moves on ideas and social practices change but sometimes ideas from the past are not so easy to shake off and this is one reason we offer the subtitle, *From Classic Theories to Contemporary Issues*. So, although we can say that there have always been children, what we understand in relation to the idea of childhood changes. Because of this we want you to consider that childhood is socially constructed rather than being in some way natural and that, similarly, it is possible to pick out a range of ideas which relate to children and which shape their childhood. As such, the context of childhood is the society in which children live and the concerns of that particular society.

Our aims in writing the book are twofold: firstly, to demonstrate the social construction of childhood, showing that childhood is not at all obvious or axiomatic; and secondly, to assist students in their studies in terms of making sense of social science approaches to studying childhood and in terms of how they approach assignments. It is maybe worth noting at this point that although childhood tends to evoke ideas about children who are quite young within contemporary society, young people are deemed to be children up to the age of 18. As such, there will be times when we refer to young people to indicate that we mean older children and/or adolescents.

Overall, we hope to encourage you to think about childhood and introduce some useful concepts which we feel have a clear place in student assignments. As with our previous textbook, *Children, Family and the State*, we will seek to show how the material within the book can be used in assignments and we will include study tips throughout the book.

We start though by saying something that we have regularly said in our classes; you don't have to accept everything that we say, you are free to argue against us, but you do have to think about it, and if you want to argue against us then you really do need to do a lot of reading in order to articulate and support your argument. Actually, if you want to do well as a student then you really have to do a lot of reading.

Study tip

Always be careful not to think that your own experiences can be generalised, and that they apply to everyone.

This is an easy trap to fall into and one we can all be guilty of. On reading applications from potential students in the early 1990s, Creasy was surprised that an applicant had been a prefect at school. This was surprising to him because he had never been to a school that had a prefect system (this was the 1960s and 1970s), though he was familiar with the term. Because of his experiences he thought that prefects belonged to a previous generation and that schools had moved on. This was a mistake.

So, your own experiences are valid, they are real, but they are not necessarily representative of what others experience or know!

At this point then let's make sure we start with the basics. We are writing from the position that there is nothing natural about childhood, it is socially constructed. But if that is the case then how is childhood socially constructed? We can start by putting forward three factors which act to shape childhood. In addition, the ways in which childhood is shaped in a general sense will have a greater or lesser bearing on how children experience their own lives. So:

- Childhood is social. It is shaped by relationships such as the family along with other people who are in a child's life, such as teachers. Sibling relationships and family position such as being the oldest or youngest child also shapes childhood.
- Childhood is cultural. Our relationships with children are shaped by cultural practices such as how society expects children to behave, what they are expected to do or how childcare is provided.
- Childhood is political. The political system that we live in draws upon social and cultural understandings and then establishes policies and legislation which reinforce a particular view of what is appropriate for children, such as compulsory education or age restrictions on what they can and cannot do.

Introduction

At this point it is worth making a clear statement so as to assert the position that we take throughout the book: we adopt the position that although there is a real biological basis which underpins the difference between children and adults, childhood can be best understood as being constructed within the interplay of the social, cultural and political forces at work within any given society. As a shorthand version of this statement, we will tend to say that childhood is social. So, and this is something that will be repeated and reiterated throughout this book, although children may represent a biological stage of development, childhood is always social. As such, childhood will shape the lived experiences of children to a much greater degree than biology. A way of accepting this concept is considering how children live their lives differently but not necessarily better or worse, depending on when they live, where they live and who they live with. To make sense of this think about childhood as the social context within which children live their lives.

Study tip

When you are writing assignments it is always helpful to be precise in stating a position in the way that we have done here. There are two aspects to this:

- Be clear, concise and precise in how you write.
- Let the reader of your work know the position that you are taking or make it clear how you are defining a key issue.

We trust that at this point you know exactly what we mean when we are referring to children and childhood.

There are real differences between children and adults which may appear to be natural and which form part of the human life cycle. If we approach children by looking at them from a biological position, we would be quite confident in saying that humans undergo a change over time and as they change, we apply descriptive terms that relate to their progress. As such we may refer to pre-adult humans as babies, infants, toddlers, children and adolescents. However, it is also fair to say that the biological differences, upon which the designation of child rests, is not sufficient to explain the social position of children or the experiences that children have. Children may be similar in age or size, but this does not mean they will be similar in how they behave, what they know and/or what they do.

This is not a new argument. Although it may appear as though children have some universal characteristic by virtue of being children, they grow up within a range of different contexts and even the boundary between child and adult changes geographically and over time (Gittins, 1998). In one sense, this reflects the concerns that some academics have with the idea of embodiment. Embodiment as an academic concern is focused upon the ways in which our real biological bodies have meaning in respect of how we negotiate the world and how we are located within it. As such there is much to be said for the idea that children's bodies are often the focus for the ways in which adults, and other children, relate to them. However, a concern with embodiment itself is not sufficient for understanding contemporary childhood.

So, to be clear, we are certainly not denying a biological reality to children. What we want you to consider though is that humans do not experience their development in a vacuum. Humans always develop within social settings, and we are very confident in saying that the social settings that are experienced have greater or lesser degrees of influence over the lives of children and young people.

Starting to think about differences

We start this section by reiterating the point that was made earlier, that childhood is not as obvious as it may appear. If you consult a dictionary, you will not find a meaningful definition of childhood that can be applied to the society that you live in, never mind all societies and all cultures. Childhood can differ greatly and will mean different things in different contexts. The *Collins English Dictionary* identifies childhood as being 'the period of life before puberty'. This is neither accurate, nor a very useful definition. For example, if a child hits puberty at age ten, what does that mean in terms of their status in our society? Does starting puberty define the end of childhood? Does it make them an adult?

Study tip

Avoid putting dictionary definitions in your assignments. The example here demonstrates there are limitations to dictionary definitions, especially when you are writing assignments that are focused on social science. So, if you are seeking to define childhood in your assignments, stay focused on the types of definitions that you will find in social science texts.

What is apparent is that we may find it fairly easy to identify children as a biological and/or developmental stage in human life, but what we understand as childhood is nowhere near as clear. Smith (2010) asks the question, is there 'a universal child?'. By this he is asking, does childhood, in any way, have common or similar attributes for all children? Is childhood similar for boys and girls, for rich and poor, for children of different ethnicities, even for children today as for children from previous generations? In considering this though it may be useful to take into account the idea of intersectionality. When we say that Smith's ideas about a universal child ask us to consider differences between children it is important to acknowledge that although children may have different characteristics they should not be understood as having one dominant characteristic.

Note

As a concept, intersectionality encourages thinking about how different characteristics, such as social class, gender, ethnicity, disability and so on, may intersect in respect of any individual's life. For example, being female in UK society means experiencing certain disadvantages because of sexism and discrimination but being female and being disabled or belonging to a minority ethnic group would introduce other disadvantages. In that sense intersectionality reflects the complexity of social life and points to the way that structures of power and privilege can be experienced differently as social characteristics combine, (Hill Collins and Bilge, 2016).

In addition, Gittins (2009) comments that as adults our ideas about childhood reflect our own experiences and that these are filtered through our memories. Gittins also notes that memory is reconstructed through re-remembering as well as through discussion with others that may have been part of that memory, such as parents, siblings and others. What this means is that our memories may not be accurate. Alongside this we may often come across the idea that we are who we are because of our childhood experiences, our formative years. This suggests that our character, sometimes even our successes or failures, are the consequences of previous experiences. Yet people with similar experiences are not all the same. Our past may have some influence over us, but it does not determine who we are.

Another key issue is that childhood is often portrayed as a state of incompleteness. Children are seen as developing, or working towards, becoming an adult, and therefore they are viewed as important in what they will become rather than in terms of what they are or who they are as a child.

Note

In respect of childhood, two contrasting notions are very important in shaping how we interact with, and provide for, children. We see children either as:

- becomings; we view them in terms of what they will be in the future; or,
- beings; we see them as what they are now.

Both are important to a social understanding of childhood and will be discussed much more fully later.

The idea of stages of development has become deeply embedded within social ideas about children and it is common to hear of children being in a particular stage of development and developing towards the next stage. This is summed up by the term ages and stages. There is a sort of commonsense aspect to this because our own experiences, either as a child, or with children, inform our understanding of the ways in which children develop. As children develop, we see that they become more able, or more capable, of understanding and doing things and this is often linked to the age of the child. It is maybe because of this experience that we often find this ages and stages approaches to understanding children as helpful in making sense of children and childhood. It seems like common sense. However, we have to make a distinction here between children and childhood.

Note

Children refers to humans who have not yet achieved adulthood. Children are individuals in a particular stage of biological development, but this is very general in relation to their specific age; for example, not all five-year-olds are at the exact same stage of development.

Childhood refers to the wider social context which shapes how we understand, interact with and provide for children. As such, childhood is social; it is the context within which children live. In this context we may have specific expectations of how children behave, such as understanding how to behave or what to do in specific situations.

What we will demonstrate throughout this book is that the lived experiences of children are significantly influenced by the way in which childhood shapes what is normal, possible and/or expected.

We have already stated that childhood is a social construct. What we mean by this is that childhood is a concept rather than something which is real and fixed. We will offer a critical view of childhood to explain how what we know about children and childhood is the product of social relationships, structures and power. It is this which makes it sociological. Although we favour a sociological approach we will also draw upon other academic disciplines at times.

Traditionally, sociology wasn't too concerned about childhood. More recent sociological approaches, however, have considered how society shapes an understanding of childhood. As such we can consider how children can be seen as social actors. This means that children interact with the world around them in their own right and, as such, they should be seen as active in their own lives. This fits with the idea of how children are able to have a voice. The idea of the child having a voice has become an important part of professional practice with children but is a quite recent development resulting from the United Nations Convention on the Rights of the Child, which we will discuss further, later.

We will also discuss later how different societies construct childhood as well as how a range of factors, such as gender, socio-economic group, ethnicity and other issues, impact on what childhood is. In doing so, it can be seen how individual children within any given society are likely to experience childhood differently but also that children in different social groups will have their childhoods shaped differently.

The idea of what childhood is, or should be, often becomes a highly contested issue. In saying this we mean that there are many different ideas and theories about childhood. These ideas and theories come to shape discourses about childhood, some of which dominate our understanding. We will explain discourse in Chapter 2.

Alongside ideas about children's development is an increased concern with children's education. The development of education policy compels children to be educated and determines what they will learn about, as well as how they will be taught at times. Think about how, at different times in history, we have provided different types of education for different children based upon ideas about, for example, class, gender, SEND, even ethnicity or race. This continues to be a contested issue.

By looking for evidence of how social factors such as gender or social class are represented within social policies, we can see how policy has impacted on practice and how it has shaped childhood throughout recent history. This does not only apply to education policy but can also be extended to other legislation and policies such as those relating to safeguarding, age restrictions or parenting and family life. By considering policy we will be able to consider how policy shapes our ideas of children's independence, vulnerability and outcomes, and how these impact on how we treat children in society and how we parent our children. In turn, it is these sorts of insights that you will often be required to use or discuss within your assignments, and we will give advice and guidance on how to do so in each chapter.

It is also the case that we often need to consider the relationship between the State and families and how this impacts childhood. We are not going to provide you with a full discussion of the State in this book as we have done that in a previous book, so we strongly recommend that you read Creasy and Corby (2023) for further ideas about the State and how it applies to the ideas discussed here.

Childhood not children

Note that in our attempts to provide an understanding of contemporary childhood it is the broader idea of childhood that we are referring to. There is a danger sometimes that if we just consider children then we miss the broader context that shapes children's experiences. Childhood is important because childhood is the context within which children grow up and children have little or no control over the childhood that they will experience.

Childhood shapes how children are treated, what they can do and, in many ways, it can shape their futures. Importantly though the childhood that is experienced by children is not usually shaped by them. That is not to say that they have no influence over their own childhood, something that we will discuss later in relation to the concept of agency, but rather, that childhood is the cumulative outcome of what adults believe about childhood, and children. It is what adults think about children and childhood, and how they act, which creates systems and structures which children then experience.

Note

There are many ideas about children that influence the more general ways that society behaves towards them. Here are three ideas that we can use as a starting point:

- children can be categorised, for example, a child with special educational needs;
- we can create types of children, for example, naughty children;
- there are preferred choices regarding what we want children to be like, either as parents, professionals working with children or just members of society who come into contact with children.

These ideas, and others, may combine to shape children's experiences.

You may have heard some old sayings, or proverbs, such as 'children should be seen and not heard'; or 'give me a child until he is seven and I will give you the man'. These sayings carry with them an element of guidance relating to adult behaviour towards children and how we expect children to be raised. Some might find the prospect of children being shaped attractive if we want children to 'behave' and 'do well'. This reflects the possibility of social engineering. Social engineering is a term which refers to how the State introduces policies and/or services with a view to changing how people think and/or behave. It is usually presented as being undesirable on the grounds that it undermines free will or that it stifles our individual nature, yet in reality all social policies reflect ideas about desired outcomes. When it comes to children, we can identify a general theme which argues that if we can shape children then we can shape their future, and the future of our society. For now though, let us just consider how different issues influence childhood and, in turn, shapes children's lived experiences and what this means for their lives.

Student task

In Figure 1.1 we have placed the child at the centre and then identified six factors which shape childhood.

Introduction

Figure 1.1: Student task

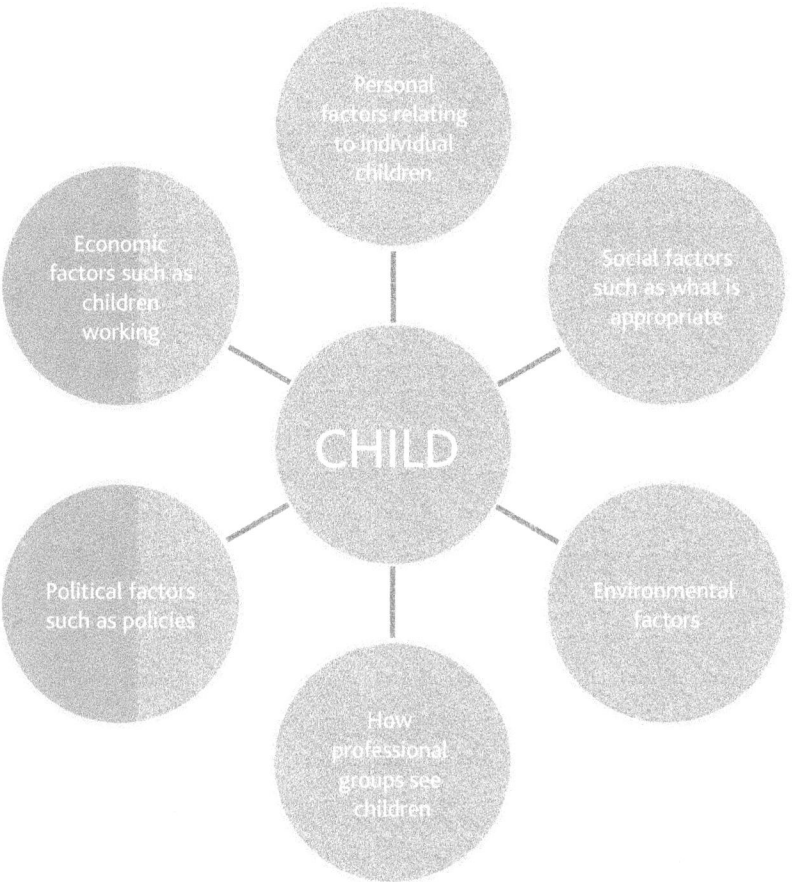

Your task is to consider each factor and what might fall under these headings.

For example, think about economic factors. In Victorian times it was normal for many children to work from an early age. In this way children contributed financially to the family. Today, we don't expect children to work but to be in education. This positions children and young people as an economic cost to their parents.

So, can you provide a similar discussion for the other factors? Some may be easier than others and some may overlap, but have a go.

In considering children working during the 19th century and comparing that to many children not leaving full-time education until they are 21 nowadays (three years after achieving adulthood), it can be seen that society changes. So, the factors that we have identified in the diagram are not fixed, they are dynamic, they change. As they change so they inevitably change childhood and the experiences of children.

When you encounter theories and ideas about children what is evident is that some theories, quite influential ones even, focus on the child as an individual. Others see children's development as being bound up within social relationships. As an example, consider the school leaving age (Woodin et al, 2013). As education policies relating to compulsory education change so the age at which children may end their education has also changed. Woodin et al point out that in England the Education Act 1918 raised the school leaving age to 14. In 1918, virtually all children left school and entered work at the age of 14. Now consider what this meant for their social relationships and the ways in which it shaped how 14-year-olds were viewed in terms of expectations and responsibilities. They would likely be working alongside older adults, have their own money and be experiencing the adult world in a way that children of that age do not today. The school leaving age then increased to 15 in 1947 and to 16 in 1972. It is now effectively 18 but very many 18-year-olds continue into higher education.

Our experience

We both had part-time jobs by the age of 14 and then full-time jobs at the age of 16.

None of our three children had full-time jobs before the age of 22, although they all had part-time jobs by the age of 16. What is your experience of working?

Think about how the experience of working shapes the young person's lived world; what they do, what they know and what they might learn about.

One aspect of this is that being compelled to stay in education until the age of 18 means to be subject to the power exercised by schools, and this can shape the lived world of children and young people. For example, in February 2023 there were a number of news stories about children organising and taking part in protests within schools against a number of things, one of which was school uniforms. In one case the skirts that girls wore were being measured to ensure that they complied with school policy (Burns, 2023). The wearing of school uniforms causes problems pretty much every year and we find arguments in favour of school uniforms to be very weak, but adults in many countries persist in enforcing what children can and cannot wear in school, often up to the age of 18.

The school that one of our children attended required sixth form students to wear uniforms. As such it was perfectly possible for a sixth form student to walk out of school and cross the road to the pub for an alcoholic drink as many of the students would have been 18 while at school. In a legal sense they would be an adult. This example demonstrates that sometimes children and young people may be located in confusing or contradictory social positions.

Social constructionism

Social constructionism is an idea that is important to the ways in which we understand childhood. We said earlier that childhood is a concept rather than something which is real and fixed. We are not saying that children are not real, we acknowledge and accept that there is a biological reality to being a child. However, the context of children's lives is social, and it is the social relationships and structures which children experience that are subject to change, and as these change so the lived world of any child is also changed. Therefore, childhood is not fixed, it changes, and therefore how children are treated and how they behave changes.

Note

Social constructionism is based on the idea that the world as we experience it is constructed within social actions alongside the language that is used to describe it. Even social phenomenon which appear to be natural or obvious, such as being competitive, inequality, gender differences and so on, are only real in the sense that it is social actions or language which make them real.

A consideration of social constructionism fits very well with the study of childhood and, as such, it is a concept that you should find very useful within assignments. To start though let us consider the opposite of social constructionism by asserting that there is a real world out there. This real world is the physical world of things. This is often referred to as the material world. It is a world in which we have, for example, laws of physics or biology. However, alongside this real world of biological and physical realities is another world, the social world. This is a world that is based upon ideas and relationships. The social world refers to the vast range of social and cultural organisations that exist and, importantly to the ways in which ideas are created, are shared and put into practice.

The material world is tangible. This means that we can touch it. There is something solid about it. We can also know about the material world by testing it. This tangible world though can be contrasted with things that are intangible. We cannot touch things that are intangible. This is the world of ideas. We hope that this makes sense because this distinction is important to sociology. The distinction rests upon the extent to which we can claim to treat the social world as if it was real in the same way that the material world is real. Can we investigate and know the social world in the same way that we can investigate and know the material world?

Note

The basic distinction within sociology rests on the philosophical difference between positivism and interpretivism.

Positivism asserts that we can know the social world whereas interpretivism asserts that we cannot know it, we can only ever hope to interpret it, to make sense of it.

This is something that we will come back to later, but for now keep in mind this idea about the material world and the social world being different because it is important to understanding the social construction of childhood.

The work of James and Prout (1997) is generally credited with establishing a social constructivist view of childhood within the UK. Giesinger (2017) provides a good, short summary which builds on the approach that is taken by social constructionism by identifying three key aspects to what it means to be a child:

- childhood is initially rooted within biology;
- childhood is the outcome of discourse;
- childhood conveys a social status.

So, at this point we want you to accept that as a concept childhood is socially constructed. We will discuss later how different societies construct childhood and how a range of things, such as gender, socio-economic group, ethnicity and other issues, impact on what childhood is. What these factors mean though is that individual children within any given society are likely to experience childhood differently.

Alongside this it is important to acknowledge that ideas about what childhood is should be seen as highly contested. In saying this we mean that there are many different ideas and theories about childhood. There are also some disagreements about it in our society, such as what rights children should have. We will raise a range of ideas about childhood to understand how that idea is constructed and why it is contested.

Note

Throughout the book we will consider various theories that go some way to helping us to understand the idea of childhood. Some students get a little anxious about the idea of theories so what we want you to do is to consider the idea that a theory is simply a tool for making sense of something.

Introduction

When we think about tools, we can see that particular tools are useful for particular jobs.

If we see theory as a tool, we can talk about how different types of theory apply to children and childhood in different ways. As such they make sense of children and childhood in different ways.

So, let's take this idea of theory as a tool a bit further by saying that the tool that you choose influences what you can do. It is also important to note that theories themselves exist within the context of different academic disciplines. The two most important disciplines in respect of what we are looking to do within this book are sociology and psychology. So, what we might say when we consider children and childhood is to what extent are these being looked at from a sociological perspective, and to what extent a psychological perspective?

Importantly, the perspective that you are looking from shapes what you see as the relevant issues. As such, psychologists are unlikely to be all that bothered about childhood. Psychologists tend to be more concerned with children themselves, especially in terms of how children develop and/or behave. Consider development. If you have studied child development previously, we are confident in saying that your studies would have been dominated by psychological theories relating to development. Most books titled 'Child Development' tend to be focused on psychology with very little, if any, space given to sociological ideas.

We said previously that sociologists were not too concerned with childhood until relatively recently. Sociologists were traditionally concerned with how children were socialised into a social group. Alongside this, psychologists have been more concerned with how children develop. One consequence of such approaches however means that any differences between children tend to be overlooked. Instead, theories about socialisation or development tend to homogenise children. To homogenise means to make the same, so children are seen as the same type depending on things like age, hence we get the theory of 'ages and stages' which we introduced earlier. There is a normative aspect to this in that some idea of what is normal socialisation or normal development is established and then children are viewed in respect of the extent to which they fit into this. As such, all children are expected to progress along an established path. For example, if you ever have a baby, you will often be told how the baby is developing in comparison to an average expectation of development.

This is not a book about child development. We will say some things about some classic approaches to child development which are rooted within the study of psychology, but that is to draw attention to the social and cultural contexts which relate to such studies and which shape those approaches. We are much more concerned with exploring the influence of social and cultural issues in relation to children and childhood. As such, an early attempt at providing an overview of the factors that contribute to a child's development, and which is very useful when considering children's lives and the nature of childhood at any given time, can be seen in the work of Bronfenbrenner (1979).

The value of Bronfenbrenner's socio-ecological approach

In seeking to understand contemporary childhood we are drawn into considerations of shared views about what childhood is and/or what it should be. At the same time, considering social and cultural issues sheds some light onto the realities of being a child by exploring the ways in which society and culture positions children.

One very useful and influential addition to the idea of considering children's position within society is offered by Urie Bronfenbrenner. Typically, you will see Bronfenbrenner's approach as being referred to as an ecological approach or, more accurately, as a socio-ecological approach. At first reading the idea that this is referred to as an ecological approach might seem odd, especially when we consider contemporary debates about ecological matters in terms of environmental politics. The trick is to focus on the idea that ecology is concerned with the environment in which animals, including humans, live. If we look at it that way, then we can start to see that what Bronfenbrenner is focusing on is the complex web of settings and relationships that influence the lived world of the child. The socio part of the socio-ecological label emphasises the social relationships that relate to the child's lived world.

Bronfenbrenner is covered in very many texts and his socio-ecological model is usually presented as a set of concentric circles where the child is located at the centre. Different labels are applied as the circles move out from the child at the centre. This starts with the micro level and moves through the exo level, to the macro level.

It is the micro level that can be seen as being the most obvious aspects of a young child's world, incorporating the child's family, care settings such as childminders, and schools. We should be careful to note however that these settings are not necessarily independent of each other. A change in one micro factor could have consequences for the child in another. We can also see how experiences within one micro factor may influence experiences within another. So, one notion relating to children reflects the idea that the relationship between the family and the school is important (Hughes et al, 1994; Whalley and Centre, 2007; Knowles and Holmstrom, 2013; Siraj and Mayo, 2014). Note that that not all families are supportive of the work that schools do; some do not engage with the school in the way that other parents do. As such, a child in a family that is not supportive of schools may find that this impacts upon their experience of school.

When we consider what might shape a child's life it is also important to recognise that factors outside of the child's immediate experiences play a part. This is where the exosystem comes in, exo referring to outside. This could be the role of neighbours in the child's community or ideas in the mass media, but maybe the most obvious issue here relates to the nature of parents' work. As children we recall how having parents who worked nightshifts or who both left for work before we got up for school shaped our experiences of life. Think about parents who are required to work weekends and how that may shape a child's opportunities, or parents who work long hours and therefore their children are looked after by others or have to look after themselves for periods of time.

Pause for reflection

Can you think about things in the exosphere that may have impacted upon your own childhood? Try to list a few ways in which aspects of your parents' or carers' lives had a knock-on effect on your own, such as how their work patterns may have had an impact on how or where you were able to play, or whether you had extended family or friends who lived nearby who you saw outside of school. Also consider any additional activities you did and the people that this brought you into contact with.

The macro system can be seen as a more abstract understanding of the society that a child lives in. When we say abstract, we mean that there is no real, material basis to something. It is a concern with ideas and beliefs rather than what we might call real things. We are back with tangible and intangible things here with abstract issues coming under the intangible category. The macro system includes more general things such as social values or religious practices. Think also about social policies that are in place and how these may act to provide support and opportunities, or not.

A final system, the chrono system, was added later and is often included when representing Bronfenbrenner's socio-ecological model. This is important for this book because it reflects changes over time. Chronos refers to time. So, as an example of this, consider that although all adults have been children, the childhood experienced by children who have grown up immersed within social media is very different to that childhood experienced by those of us who grew up before social media.

Note

Think about how social media creates an environment which may intensify experiences for children leading to negative feelings such as ridicule and shame, or which might facilitate bullying.

We, the authors, did some very silly and embarrassing things as children and young people but thankfully what we did was often only observed by one or two people who could not instantly share or distribute videos of our behaviour in the way that this can happen nowadays. We were able to make mistakes and move on, albeit with red faces for a while; many young people find moving on difficult now that so many things get filmed and shared.

Bronfenbrenner's socio-ecological model indicates the many influences upon a child's life. It helps demonstrate that childhood is shaped by so many factors; some of which are more immediate to the child, and some of which are more distant. Importantly though he emphasises the dynamic or changing nature of relationships between all aspects within his socio-ecological model.

This is relevant because when we consider the ages and stages approach to child development there is a tendency towards a relatively fixed understanding of development; at a particular age, a child should be doing specific things regardless of the other factors in the child's life. By acknowledging change, we can see how movement between ages and stages takes place within a context that is not fixed but will vary from child to child and vary over time. Bronfenbrenner also demonstrates that childhood is shaped by political ideas and by the policies which are in place in any given time. Maybe the key thing that Bronfenbrenner does though is to offer a theoretical model for understanding the lived world of the child that moves away from viewing the child in isolation, as is often the case in psychological theories, by considering children's positions within families, communities and society.

There is a practical side to this in that Bronfenbrenner was instrumental in developing the Head Start preschool programme in the 1960s in the US. Head Start drew upon evidence which indicated that poverty impacts upon children in negative ways, demonstrating that children from deprived backgrounds performed less well at school. The aim of Head Start was to counter the effects of poverty and improve life chances for children experiencing poverty. Head Start was deemed to be successful in its aims and a similar policy programme was introduced in the UK by the Labour government in 1997, Sure Start.

Although Sure Start was initially intended to overcome the disadvantage typically experienced in poorer communities it was developed as a universal service providing support for all families. Sure Start was successful (Anning and Ball, 2008; Lewis et al, 2011; Donetto and Maben, 2015; Hall et al, 2015), however, the change to a Conservative-led coalition government between 2010 and 2015 followed by Conservative governments saw Sure Start being effectively closed down due to reduced funding and changes in policy. The reasons behind why Conservative governments would close down a policy that appeared to be successful in helping all families is rooted within their political ideology which argues against State provision of public services (see Creasy and Corby, 2023). Politics is located within the exosystem of Bronfenbrenner's model. This is an example of how children's worlds are changed, and thus, childhood changes.

The political beliefs of a government will shape the lived experiences of the child's world. This is evident in the government approach introduced in 2010 referred to as austerity Britain (O'Hara and Thomas, 2014), and can be seen as an example of what Bronfenbrenner means when referring to the dynamic nature of relationships.

One further thing to consider in respect of Bronfenbrenner's socio-ecological model is that the micro system as presented suggests what we might call geographic contingency. In saying this we mean that the child's world involves those individuals and groups, such as family, peers and children's services workers, that the child comes into contact with. Remember that the socio-ecological model was proposed in 1979. However, technological developments in particular means that the child's world may now be lived to some extent online and this is very different to childhoods lived before the internet. Children and young people now often interact with individuals and groups who they will never meet face to face.

Children and agency

We have stated that our approach is sociological. We recognise that many students may come to the study of childhood without a background in sociology, so this section is intended to give a basic introduction to some relevant ideas about agency. This is because contemporary approaches towards the sociology of childhood tend to adopt the position whereby children are described as social actors who have agency.

Note

Sociology tends to look at the social world from one of two perspectives, focusing on agency or structure, often characterised as micro or macro.

The micro position is focused on individuals or small groups and their actions, or what they do. From the micro perspective society is the aggregate result of the actions of individuals. From this perspective we are considering what individuals can do or what 'agency' they have.

Structural sociology looks at large-scale structures such as class or gender and argues that large-scale, or macro, structures such as the economic system or gender shape individuals and what they can do. The structuralist perspective is much less concerned with individuals.

As a sociological concept, agency refers to our ability as individuals to act. It encapsulates the basic idea that we have free will. But if we think about this then we might recognise that our ability to act may be enhanced or restricted by our social position, for example whether we are male or female, rich or poor. As such it is not enough to state that agency is the capacity to act, we also need to consider what makes action possible. Manyukhina states that there has to be both a

> personal sense of agency and structural opportunities to exercise agency. A sense of agency concerns individuals' belief in their ability to act independently and exercise choice in the given contexts. However, merely having a sense of agency is not sufficient for the exercise of agency – actual opportunities need to be present for individuals to realise their agentic potential. Agency, then, is best defined as a *socially situated* capacity to act. (Manyukhina, 2022: 506, italics in original)

Sometimes it is necessary to decode what academics have written because at times the style of academic language is maybe a little different from the language that we employ in everyday use. Part of being a student is getting used to academic language and being able to make sense of what you are reading. So, when Manyukhina says that agency is best defined as a socially situated capacity to act, what they are saying is that there is a relationship between structure and agency. As such, the social position of any individual within any social structure either increases or decreases their ability or capacity to act. This demonstrates an interplay between the two positions. We do not act purely through our own agency, or just as structures dictate, but through an interplay of both structure and agency.

Pause for reflection

Think about the different social structures that you find yourself in. They may be the family, your workplace, organisations that you belong to and even society in general. Your position within a structure such as the workplace may make it easier or harder for you to act or contribute. Now consider how the position of children in families may shape what they can do depending on the resources the family have, the ideas or beliefs the family hold, the area in which the family live and other factors.

In sociology, class (socio-economic group), gender and/or ethnicity represent social structures. Now consider how your social characteristics such as class, gender or ethnicity as well as position or experience may mean that it is easier or harder for you to do what you might want to do, or to influence change.

The notion that agency is socially situated is relevant when it comes to children. This is because adults have traditionally seen children as not having the capacity to exercise agency. How adults see children limits the potential of children, who then may be aware of a personal sense of not being able to act of their own free will. Children are often bound by rules set by adults, and therefore their actions are limited to what they are allowed to do.

It may be useful at this point to draw attention to a key issue when it comes to children's agency. Children exist as a social group that, for a number of reasons, have legal restrictions placed upon them. But, when we discuss children's agency, we should recognise that sometimes the restrictions that apply to children are in place to protect them. In that sense any discussion of agency must be seen as a balancing act. We want children to be safe, however, we presume that they will only be safe if we, the adults, restrict them. As such, discussions of agency may involve a consideration of rights alongside the recognition that in certain areas children are denied rights, perhaps for good reason but based on what we believe children are capable of.

We write from the position that children should have rights, but we also recognise that this does not mean that children should have total freedom. We would also support individual rights but not where one person's individual rights are detrimental to the lives of others. As an example of this, in Creasy and Corby (2023), we note that the right to own slaves must mean that some individuals, slaves, have no rights. For us, that cannot be acceptable. That said, the position of children in relation to rights is summed up by Mayall (2000: 248) when she states that in all societies, as far as she is aware, 'childhood as a social status is defined within the generational order as inferior to adulthood. How children live their childhoods looks heavily structured by what adults want of childhood.' This demonstrates then that the rights of children are restricted when compared to the rights of adults based on a sense that in some way children are inferior.

When it comes to rights to agency, the place of the United Nations Convention of the Rights of the Child (UNCRC) cannot be overstated in respect of the extent to which children's agency is promoted. The UNCRC works to create a discourse of rights that children can engage with, though on a more specific level any child's agency relies on the cooperation of adults (Lundy, 2007). Such cooperation is not always forthcoming, and the UNCRC, though ratified by most nations in the world, has not been fully implemented.

If we turn our attention away from arguments and organisations concerned with the rights of children and on to children themselves, we can see that children are very aware of their lives and are aware of the context within which they live. We can say with some confidence that children take part in their own lives. For example, they are capable of responding to different issues, of making decisions and of selecting role models to copy as well as making choices about their own lives. That does not mean that how they do these things would correspond to what adults would want them to do but that is not the key issue here. The key issue is that children are aware of their lived world, they are not passive actors within rules set by adults. They are capable of thinking about themselves.

Children are also aware of the pressures that affect their lives and the issues that they face. In respect of articulating these pressures they may be restricted by the language that they have and the social role models which they have observed. So, when we say that children recognise that they have certain rights regarding these pressures it may be that some of these rights are limited due to such things as a lack of resources, a lack of experience or the way society accommodates for children's needs. For example, they know they have some decision-making rights over their free time, such as what to do or what not to do, and are aware of what parents and/or practitioners would encourage or even make them do.

In exercising agency children understand, and learn to participate in, their family through both observation and negotiation. Children can recognise that family is an enterprise in which they have an active role and from a young age they learn to perform this role. As such, children are aware that they are part of a family but also aware that they are involved in a parallel exercise; the project of their own life (Mayall, 2008). This means that they recognise some agency to act outside of, or differently, to the role set by the family. Mayall suggests a degree of ambiguity in that although we see children as being socialised by adults, and children accept this, it is also the case that even quite young children recognise that they have some part to play in this. In other words, children are able to recognise their own agency with respect to what they are expected to do and what they choose to do.

Pause for reflection

As an example of children's sense of agency think about parental authority. For Mayall (2008), children recognise and accept parental authority but they are also able to identify where this is weak.

Take a moment to think about how children may enter into some form of negotiation with parents over the exercising of power or authority. What strategies might children use and why?

Now think about when a parent makes 'threats' that they don't carry out. Children come to understand this and adapt their behaviour accordingly. Children negotiate, in both sophisticated and not so sophisticated ways, which means that children will argue or debate if they have the language or may throw tantrums if they do not.

Be aware also that children recognise that parents may not know things or be wrong. They can identify flaws in an adult's arguments, something that is likely to result in the adult response that you will surely have come across, because I said so!

Positionality

At this point we feel that it could be useful to say a bit more about the positions that we adopt within the book. This is because authors always have a reason for writing books and sometimes it is useful for readers to know where authors are coming from. You are most likely to come across the importance of positionality in relation to carrying out research. Understanding positionality contributes to the debates about methodology in that it points to the ways in which the position of researchers may make it easier or harder for them to carry out research and to generate valid data.

Similarly, there is a somewhat idealistic idea that is presented within many claims about carrying out research which suggests that researchers should be neutral when undertaking research, that they should be detached from what they are studying. This is unrealistic. At the very basic level researchers will make choices about what they study based upon their interests and concerns and these in turn will be influenced and shaped by the researchers' prior experiences.

So, when it comes to this book it is reasonable to state that we write from a socially liberal position and that we tend to adopt a critical perspective. When we say we write from a socially liberal position what we mean is that we are not consciously biased against individuals and groups who may possess or represent different characteristics to our own in terms of race, ethnicity, gender, sexuality, age or other features and so on. This is socially liberal because these are social characteristics, and to be liberal is to be accepting of difference and diversity.

Be careful though. It is easy to confuse social liberalism with the idea of neoliberalism. We may be socially liberal, but we are not supportive of neoliberalism. Our experiences in relation to studying and experiencing neoliberalism mean that we adopt a critical position when it comes to neoliberalism. We consider that neoliberalism has negative consequences for society and this book will often point to what we mean by this. Similarly, we are not supportive of neoconservatism. We will explain both neoliberalism and neoconservatism later. Neoconservatism exaggerates or reinforces social divisions in ways that we see as negative for individuals and/or groups who are deemed to be different. This idea can be seen in the concept of 'othering'. Othering involves the construction or exaggeration of difference in a way that constitutes some individuals or groups as others or being not like us. Positioning people as other usually involves positioning them negatively, and we reject this type of thinking.

Using this chapter within assignments

Early in the chapter we drew a distinction between the biological issues which can be seen in how children develop into adults physically, and the social, cultural and political issues which shape the context within which we understand children. It is this sense of understanding that gives shape to different childhoods.

One of the most enduring themes in relation to understanding children is the way in which they are seen in relation to their future. Children are seen in terms of becoming an adult and because of this they may be seen as in some way incomplete. However, it is also possible to see them as beings. We have adopted an approach that is centred on sociology, because sociology operates as an academic discipline which makes sense of the way that society, culture and politics acts to shape our lives, even in childhood. That said, it wasn't all that long ago that sociologists weren't too concerned with childhood, and this has allowed psychology to become the dominant way of understanding children. Because of this, ideas about child development are overwhelmingly ideas from a psychological perspective.

We are cautious about the role of psychology because it very often overlooks the fact that children do not develop within a vacuum, they develop within a context, and that context is childhood. Because of this it is how society understands childhood which shapes the experiences that children have. This demonstrates the value of social constructionism. Any assignment which requires you to discuss childhood really does require some discussion of the ways that childhood is socially constructed. Importantly though you should acknowledge that childhood is not something that is universally agreed upon, it is something that can be contested and it is something that changes.

A good way of making sense of how childhood is socially constructed is to look at it through the lens of Bronfenbrenner's socio-ecological model. This model provides a visual representation of the different social, cultural and political forces which can be seen to exert influence upon childhood, and on individual children. It also demonstrates that some of these influences may be more direct, or closer to the child, while other forces may be indirect, or more distanced from the child.

By identifying where children fit into a social structure we can start to see that their position may be more, or less, conducive to enabling them to exercise agency. In general children are socially weaker because of how adults shape the world, and this means that children find it harder to be heard or make their own choices. Sometimes this is because of legal restrictions that apply to children, sometimes it is because adults see their views or ideas as less valid. The consequence of this is that children invariably have fewer rights than adults, or their rights are ignored.

If we assume that you have an assignment to write which is focused upon the idea of discussing the nature of childhood, this chapter will provide a good basis. We started by establishing that childhood is social rather than natural and used that to explore why the biological reality of being a child is less important than considering society, culture and politics in respect of what childhood is. To illustrate this, you would find that Bronfenbrenner's socio-ecological model is useful, and this would also give you scope to focus upon certain aspects of the model as you see relevant.

We then jumped from the socio-ecological model to a discussion of agency as socially situated to talk about how children are often denied rights or rely on adults to secure their rights. As with many issues relating to childhood, the reality of children's biological bodies and their level of development can easily become the thing which makes it appear as though children's rights are in some way naturally reduced compared to adults. Similarly, we might consider that children are naturally different but that can close down an interrogation of how childhood is socially constructed. For us, the best evidence to support the argument that childhood is socially constructed is how it has changed over time and/or how it differs in different places. We provide evidence for this idea throughout this book.

In sum though, any assignment about childhood itself should cover all, or most, of the following points. Depending on the requirements of the assignment you would then focus on different issues:

- It is always important to recognise that childhood is shaped by social, cultural and political forces.
- The social world of childhood can be juxtaposed with the material world. So, where the social world is a world of ideas, the material world is rooted in things that we can touch.
- Children may be seen through the lens of becomings or beings.
- Children and young people may experience confusing or contradictory ideas about what it is to be a child or young person and how they should behave.

- Bronfenbrenner's socio-ecological model is good for visualising the range of influences upon a child's life.
- Agency is socially situated; social structures increase or decrease a child's capacity to act.
- Children generally have fewer rights than adults.

Further thoughts

Think about your own thoughts and ideas regarding children and childhood, including why you have chosen to study a course relating to childhood or to read this book. Try to pin down where you stand in terms of your interests about children and what ideas you hold or held before, such as whether you were more concerned with biological issues relating to development or social issues relating to childhood.

Consider what you have read here and what new ideas it presents, and what questions you may now have about childhood.

Further reading

Three readings that deal with the key issues covered within this chapter are as follows:

Giesinger (2017). This is a very good summary as to what constructionism means in relation to childhood.

James and Prout (1997). The book that is credited with underpinning what became known as the new sociology of childhood.

Shelton (2019). For a good account of Bronfenbrenner's work.

2

The persistence of attachment and seeing children as becomings

> **This chapter will help you to understand:**
> - Foucault's concept of discourse;
> - How Bowlby's theory of attachment promotes a particular view of family life;
> - Some of the consequences of seeing children as becomings or as beings.

Introduction

A key issue within this chapter is the fact that work with children and young people has been strongly influenced by a focus on child development from a psychological perspective. However, we will point to the social issues which have shaped the key psychological idea of attachment in particular and of developmentalism in general. We accept that there are some merits to attachment, but it is important to recognise that it adopts a very particular understanding of children and families, and that this can be problematic. Following from this the emergence of childhood studies reflects a critique of developmentalism that encourages some questioning of both understanding and practice (Woodhead, 2009).

As an approach, childhood studies incorporates a number of academic approaches other than psychology (Wells, 2018). One reason for the traditional dominance of psychology with regards to children is due to classical sociology seeing children as pre-social. This positions children outside of social concerns (Mayall, 2000) and effectively asserts that children are not suitable subjects for sociological study. As such, this turned the focus of sociologists away from children and childhood, so allowing for the dominance of psychological studies.

Walkerdine (2009) is an essential read for anyone who wants an extended account of how psychology has shaped practice with children, and for children themselves. She emphasises how a discourse of psychology has come to dominate an understanding of children. Alongside this though, pedagogy (teaching children) and psychology can be seen to combine and act in a way which constructs childhood as a process of becoming within a particular discourse of understanding children that is focused on their development (Wells, 2018). This broad discourse around development is what we can call developmentalism on the grounds that it funnels all ideas about children and childhood through the idea of development. At this point though the first task is to introduce the concept of discourse.

Making sense of discourse

It will be very difficult to complete a degree relating to childhood without encountering the concept of discourse. We may even say that discourse is one of the most important concepts that you will encounter within social science. It is usually attributed to the French social theorist Michel Foucault, however it is rooted in the work of both Saussure (Inglis and Thorpe, 2019) and Levi-Strauss (Jones and Bradbury, 2018).

The work of Saussure is focused on linguistics (the study of language), while Levi-Strauss was an anthropologist (anthropology being the study of culture). Both though were concerned with structures in society and with the role of language within structures. This seems to be going away from a concern with childhood but stick with us, it will be useful. Foucault develops ideas about language and structure by proposing that language creates structures of understanding.

Pause for reflection

To make sense of this think about the set of meanings that you associate with the word 'childhood'. Childhood represents a particular life stage that is associated with various ideas, such as being a time of innocence or a time when we need to learn. These ideas are just part of the discourse of childhood.

The idea of innocence suggests that children do not know or understand much about the world and should be protected from the problems of the world and everyday life. Few children really experience this innocence. Children are aware of their own world and what is going on and many are not protected but experience various challenges including abuse or neglect.

When we discuss children's lived lives, we often then speak about how children have their childhoods stolen. But is it really the case that they didn't have a childhood?

It is important to be aware then that language may lead to a way of understanding something, which in turn can lead to how we behave and respond to what we think about children and childhood. Think also how language and what we mean may change; childhood now is not what childhood might have been in the past. Some of this may result from a conscious decision to make changes. For example, consider how the law or policy changes, and how we then start to treat children differently because of those changes.

So, the key issue of discourse in so far as it is used by Foucault is that using a term such as childhood, with its shared ideas such as innocence, not only acts to change the meanings that are associated with children, it also acts to change behaviours. This is because the language that is used within any setting forms a key part of discourse. For Foucault, discourse operates as a system that 'regulates the meaning and practices which can and cannot be produced' (Smith, 1998: 254).

Note that Smith says regulate, not determine. Discourse does not determine how we act, it shapes, or influences, how we act. Bear in mind also, that discourse is not simply a focus on the content of communication, that is, the words spoken. Discourse when considered from a sociological sense draws on the idea proposed by Foucault to suggest that meanings are produced within language and forms of communication, and that this shapes the ways in which the social world comes to be organised and structured in a way that seems normal. In this way discourse is not just a concern with how the use of language acts to describe our social reality, discourse is the thing which creates that reality. This is important in studying childhood because it helps us to understand how childhood is created through what is said about children. Discourse shapes how we then act towards children and how children learn to act in the world.

What this also means is that knowledge of ourselves and of the world that we live in is never based only on individual experiences or understanding. As such we could claim that we can never have any individual agency in the sense of absolute free will. Who we consider ourselves to be, what we know of the world and how we think or talk about it is, from a Foucauldian perspective, always produced within discourse and the discourse already exists as a form of structure. Because of this it is important to recognise that discourses have power. As such, a discourse of childhood structures behaviour towards children and, in doing so, shapes the lived experiences for children.

Pause for reflection

One way of thinking about discourse is to see it as a script. A film or play script presents ideas about settings and characters as a framework or guide for actors. As such the script operates in the same way that discourse operates in terms of providing a framework within which we understand our lives and the society that we live in. We may have some options to say or do things slightly differently to the script, but this would be seen as a response to the script rather than being original or completely different.

Further, discourse is embedded within language, and the way in which language is used influences how we understand things. Importantly, the choice of language can shape our feelings in terms of something being positive or negative, acceptable or unacceptable.

If we accept that a discourse of innocence is now used in relation to childhood in a way that was not the case historically then we can appreciate that it is also not the case that there is only ever one discourse in relation to a subject. Although we may talk about discourse in general it is important to recognise that there are always competing discourses. Each discourse shapes the way in which we understand any particular subject through the meanings associated within the language that is used. This, in turn, creates a subject in a particular way.

In summarising discourse then it is important to be aware that discourse is embedded within language in terms of how language shapes meanings, but also how this fits in with a way of understanding the world, which means that we come to see some things as normal and natural with other things becoming unthinkable. For example, you might consider an example that we have covered in *Children, Family and the State* (Creasy and Corby, 2023), vulnerability. The understanding of all children as naturally vulnerable can be seen to downplay children's abilities. It is not that children are not vulnerable, rather that they come to be vulnerable within the language that we use about them and the way in which this causes us to understand and deal with them in a particular way that may differ from other societies.

So, there are some things that children did in the past, such as work, that we find unacceptable now due to a change in what we understand children and childhood to be. Consider how children have much less freedom in what they can do or where they can go when compared to children living in previous generations. This is influenced by the way in which a discourse of risk has become commonplace within society, and which has constructed an understanding of children as being constantly under threat or at risk (Creasy and Corby, 2019). At the same time though a discourse about parenting has shaped ideas about being a responsible parent or being a good parent. As these discourses combine, they increase the pressure on parents to restrict their children's freedom in response to commonly held beliefs about the risks to children alongside the idea that good parents will act to protect their children.

Developmentalism as discourse

As a further example of discourse think about the way that, within the UK, it is commonplace to focus on the age of children, especially when meeting children for the first time. This reflects the extent to which a discourse of developmentalism dominates Western thinking regarding childhood (Walkerdine, 2009; Woodhead, 2009). Because developmentalism positions children on a linear path through the stages of development it seems quite reasonable for us to enquire about a child's age. In this way age acts as a marker of social position for both adults and children (Watson, 2022). We have expectations of what children can do, what they should know or how they should behave based on their biological age. A focus on age though acts to divide children from each other and from adults, especially in terms of expectations. Importantly however, Woodhead demonstrates that this division by age is not so relevant in all cultures. It is only important within cultures where age and development are understood together.

Crucially, the discourse of development establishes what normal development is. Consequently, norms become established regarding development which rely upon the comparison of children (Watson, 2022). Such comparison then identifies children who do not develop in the ways that are expected; in turn such children may be seen as abnormal, or problematic. This justifies types of intervention. We could also say that the type of intervention that takes place will be a type of intervention that corresponds to the discourse that has established the problem in the first place. Additionally, we may also see children as problematic or different when they are more capable than we expect, or more knowledgeable perhaps.

In relation to how discourse shapes our understanding of the world and how this makes things appear natural, it is also important to recognise that at times this intersects with some real biological issues such as the fact that children do change as they grow older. Physicality does relate to abilities to some extent. As such, biology informs the way in which we understand children with change underpinning much of the way in which children are typically seen as becomings. In other words, children tend to be understood not in terms of what they are at the present moment, but, instead, in terms of what they will become. This reinforces the focus on investigating and theorising about children's development and a concern about whether they are heading towards what they should become.

The physical and cognitive changes that we can see with respect to children are central to this. We know that children develop so it makes sense to think about, and understand, how they develop. This is particularly the case when we think that children are not developing in ways that we would either expect or want.

Pause for reflection

If we start by stating the obvious, we can say that we know that children change, but as children grow and develop do they just shift from being mini-adults or adults-in-waiting to becoming proper adults?

Is it just about size? Or is it about what they can do or what they know?

How can we be confident that the child will become whatever we expect an adult to be?

When we consider it this way, we can see how it is problematic to define childhood and adulthood on ages and stages. Is it age, or completion of education, or starting work or being independent? What about becoming a parent?

What is evident then is that theories may adopt different positions and explain the process of development in different ways. For example, when it comes to development, some theories are focused on what we can call maturation whereas others are focused on learning. Theories focused on maturation tend towards biological and/or genetic explanations which rest on the idea that as we get older, we become more mature. These theories can be compared to theories of learning which focus on cognitive abilities increasing as we get older. Additionally, some theories focus on individuation, or how an individual behaves, while others are focused on enculturation, or how well we fit into our social group or culture.

One thing that you might recognise here then is that the differences between theories often rests upon the different concerns that academics have, things that we may not be concerned with in our everyday lives. However, theories do not exist in a vacuum. They do not just appear. They emerge out of concerns to explain what we see. Very often though they reflect certain assumptions about social life even though this may not be so obvious. For example, the psychological theory of attachment rests upon, and owes much, to social ideas.

How socially conservative ideas promoted a concern with attachment

We start by making the point that when children engage in behaviour that challenges our ideas about what we see as normal childhood behaviour, we often hear explanations that draw upon the nature of their parents' behaviour. It is not at all uncommon to hear people say 'I blame the parents' when faced with children's behaviour. On a simple level the claim that parents are responsible for the actions of children reflects ideas about socialisation and/or modelling.

We said previously that traditionally sociological concerns with children were often confined to concerns about socialisation. Many comments about children reflect the idea that children's behaviour will reflect parental behaviours and that this fits with ideas about socialisation. From this position then the key influence on children is their parents. However, such arguments are undermined when we acknowledge that children have very many role models in their lives and that socialisation is not something that only exists within or as part of the relationship between parents and children. Children do not always act in a way that their parents have modelled or promoted. A different explanation for children who are viewed as problematic or who have problems is the idea that problematic behaviour results from individual psychology. This is often associated with Bowlby's ideas regarding attachment.

Note

Bowlby's basic approach concerns attachment between parents, especially mothers, and their children. This is said to shape the type of person that the child becomes in later life.

Bowlby proposed that attachment reflects our earliest experiences with others and that from this, children construct an understanding of what to expect from other people, alongside an idea about their own level of what we can call 'lovability' or 'likeability'. He calls this understanding an internal working model (IWM).

Within attachment theory the IWM is positioned as an enduring psychological structure that influences each individual's behaviour throughout their life.

A concern with attachment is very well established with respect to understanding children, especially in terms of both working with or providing services to children. For example, attachment theory underpins the keyworker or named-worker approach within children's services, particularly in nurseries. It also reinforces ideas about the family being the best place for children and often positions a female caregiver as being central to a child's early life. The practice of social work students is often assessed through the lens of attachment theory and courts of law often draw upon attachment theory when coming to decisions about what is deemed to be in the best interests of a child (Garrett, 2022a). As such, Garrett argues that attachment theory has become accepted as 'common-sense'. Because of this it often goes unchallenged, in spite of criticisms (Garrett, 2022a; 2022b).

What is evident however, is that although attachment theory represents a psychological theory of mind, it is rooted in very specific social ideas which reflect particular cultural forms. Indeed, Bowlby pointed to the fact that attachment, and therefore the IWM, is shaped within a social setting. In the classic attachment theory approach, it is mothers who play the most important role in how the IWM develops. The social setting Bowlby foregrounded as being most beneficial for children was based on a child having a mother at home caring for them for most of the time for at least the first two years of life.

The importance of mothers arises because Bowlby argued that a positive mother–child relationship creates an IWM which establishes in the child's mind that *other people are nice, and I am lovable*. Conversely, a troubled mother–child relationship creates an IWM which tells the child that *other people are unkind, and I am not lovable*. For Bowlby the danger that is inherent when a positive relationship is not established is the development of an affectionless psychopath. The affectionless psychopath is said to have no moral or social concerns and little sense of guilt.

It is the focus on the mother, however, which lays the basis for early criticisms of Bowlby's work, as his ideas about the social ordering of roles and responsibilities with regards to childcare may now be viewed as sexist (Garrett, 2022a; 2022b). It is not hard to see that attachment theory as first proposed by Bowlby promotes a particular approach to parenting which positions mothers in the central role and sidelines fathers, or other caregivers such as grandparents, or nannies for example. In emphasising these roles though Bowlby is reinforcing a structure that was typical of UK family life when Bowlby was writing. Garrett notes that replacing mother with the terms parent or caregiver does not make Bowlby's work more acceptable. As well as having a very particular view of how society should be structured, Bowlby was also concerned that social structures should not be changed (Garrett, 2022b). So, suggesting anyone but a mother is a suitable caregiver does not fit with Bowlby's ideas.

A critical approach demonstrates how social values or ideas can become embedded within theories which in turn can influence how children are understood or positioned within society. Bowlby is not alone in presenting mothers as being the cause of characteristics or conditions that have been seen as problematic. The mother/child relationship is foregrounded in many theories that attempt to understand children and adults. Mothers have at various times also been seen as the cause of homosexuality and of autism (Courcy and des Rivières, 2017). There is an inherent conservatism in such deterministic arguments, and it means that women are under pressure not only to be mothers but to be a certain type of mother.

Bowlby's focus on relationships between mothers and children also ignores the fact that children may have early relationships with individuals other than their mothers. As such, later theorists added the aspect of multiple attachments to this concept. Accepting that a child can have multiple attachments provides the potential for more chances for children to experience positive relationships. However, if other relationships are also unsatisfactory, from the perspective of attachment theory the danger remains: the creation of an affectionless psychopath.

Mary Ainsworth is widely credited with developing Bowlby's ideas about attachment further by emphasising the quality of attachment (Ainsworth and Bell, 1970). Ainsworth is generally associated with the 'strange situation' test. This test involves assessing how children react to being placed in a strange or unfamiliar situation by Mum who then leaves them. Note that the strange situation was just one experiment that Ainsworth used to test her ideas about attachment. It is not something that is routinely applied to children.

Ainsworth proposed that a problematic IWM did not just result from mistreatment or physical neglect. The basic proposition of attachment theory following Ainsworth is that children would develop into one of three personality types and that these types were shaped by their relationship with their main care provider:

- Secure children, those who are said to feel that in a strange situation their mother was available and would come to their aid if necessary.
- Anxious Avoidant children, those who are faced with a strange situation and expect to cope alone, assuming that their mother was not available.
- Anxious Resistant children, those who are faced with a strange situation and who feel their mother would sometimes be available but were unable to predict when they might be left alone to cope.

Ainsworth's basic proposition is that the mother/child relationship facilitates how a child negotiates the world. This approach reinforces how Bronfenbrenner situates the relationship between the parent/carer and child and how it has an impact. It also illustrates how it is that children's lives, especially young children, are shaped by others, as well as drawing attention to the importance of how adults parent in terms of what it means for children (van Bakel and Hall, 2018).

In Ainsworth's theory, it is the unpredictability of a carer's behaviour that can be seen to be the problem, leading to the Anxious Resistant child having the most problems. This unreliability infers a lack of stability. Given that we often hear parents claiming that they would do anything for their children you might be thinking why it might be that some parents are unreliable. This draws attention to the complexity of parenting and how some people become parents when they are not ready to be parents or are ill equipped to be parents, such as those with addiction issues, or those who have to work and have inadequate support networks for childcare.

Attachment theory is generally accepted as explaining children's behaviour and as such further ideas relating to it have evolved. A fourth type of child, the

Disorganised child, has been proposed by Main and Solomon (1990). This refers to children who seem to have no usual, or organised, approach to such a situation. Van Bakel and Hall (2018) present this as the consequence of parenting which they refer to as distorted, or behaviour from caregivers that is unusual, and is said to be typically seen in children who have experienced physical and/or emotional abuse.

The strange situation is useful in demonstrating why we cannot see people as simple, or as always behaving in the same ways that fit neatly into categories. Psychological approaches often take the social and cultural context for granted and ignore how these contexts are more complex. By this we are referring to the ways that differences both within and between cultures can often be overlooked. It has been argued that cultural differences in terms of childcare undermine the claims of attachment theory (Sagi et al, 1991).

Study tip

The trap that students often fall into, and one that you should always be wary of, is in assuming that studies can be used to prove something.

We rarely prove anything within the social sciences. On the face of it that might be taken to illustrate the weakness of social science but what we want you to think about is the idea that seeking proof is not necessarily a valid endeavour with respect to social behaviours.

We are not seeking proof because people are not things. As such, when it comes to writing assignments always avoid saying that a study proves anything. It is always better to suggest that studies support ideas or theories.

Looking back on attachment, we may consider that it is important, but this does not mean that our experiences in relation to attachment determine who we are. Sometimes we want an explanation to be simple, but they rarely are. At a basic level attachment theory promotes the idea that the parental style experienced will create a particular type of person. In addition, experiencing maternal deprivation is said to make problems worse. From this we get the idea that this shapes who we are in adulthood, and that this will impact on our relationships with other adults and with our own children.

This is embedded in the idea that children who have been abused go on to be abusers or that children who experience adverse circumstances growing up will have problems in later life. It is another one of those ideas that are very seductive, they are attractive in their simplicity, but the relationship between childhood experiences and who we are as adults is not deterministic (Fergusson and Horwood, 2003). Early experiences do not necessarily lead to particular outcomes. Adverse childhood experiences may increase the risks for children of problems in later life, but they do not cause any particular type of problematic behaviour.

> **Pause for reflection**
>
> We can demonstrate that experiencing abuse or adverse childhood experiences does not necessarily result in children growing up to be abusive or to having ongoing problems by looking at adults who experienced such things as children.
>
> For example, if we say that children who are abused will be abusive as adults, why is it that most abusers are male?

In considering the idea of parenting and attachment we might also consider that there are always two individuals that are being considered; there is the caregiver, but there is also the care receiver. Children can, and do, have different types of temperament and this is obviously also important. A child's place or position on a placidity–irritability continuum has some impact on their carer's responses to them, and this can influence the experience of attachment.

With this in mind then maybe what we should also consider is that the child can influence parental style to some degree. The relationship between parent and child is both a social relationship, and it is one that is dynamic; it can and will change over time. Similarly, the relationship between the adult and the child does not take place in a vacuum. The adult–child relationship always takes place within a socio-political context. When we say a socio-political context, we are referring to the interplay between the social relationships that are relevant to any case and the political conditions at any given time. Linking back to Bronfenbrenner we can see that in every child's life there are a multitude of influences that will affect the child, and this may mitigate against poor parenting creating a different outcome.

Seeing children as becomings or beings

When considering psychological theories of development there is often a general view that children should be understood in terms of their progress towards adulthood. If we take that approach though it means that we might not see children as individuals in their own right, as beings; rather, we see them in relation to how far they have progressed towards becoming humans like us. This means that we see children as becomings. It also assumes that adults do not develop, that adulthood is an end in itself; this idea is something that can be contested. In this respect it is worth considering that in modern Western societies attaining full adulthood may be impeded by the high costs of leaving the parental home, and we may also consider that an adult is not the same at the age of 30 as they are at the age of 60, so caution is advised in seeing adulthood as some obvious end state.

That said, the discourse of children as becomings is very strong in Western culture. One reason for this is the focus on biological differences between adults and children, especially the biological changes that are evident during childhood.

Change is something which may be said to underpin an understanding of childhood as something that is transitory (Gillespie, 2013). Note though that change can be social as well as biological, as is evident in the emergence of tweenagers representing a stage between childhood and adolescence (De Leyn et al, 2022). This is cultural rather than natural; although 11-year-olds have always existed, they have not always been treated in the same way and have not always been called 'tweens'.

Seeing children as becomings is evident in a range of social practices from simple sayings to the types of scrutiny that children are subject to. Consider sayings about the need for children to be able to achieve their potential. This presents children as having some ideal capacity or ability that can be achieved by experiencing a certain set of social conditions or opportunities as they grow and develop. It also suggests the idea that what they can be in the future is predictable in early childhood. As such what is being presented here is an ideal version of the child as future adult, something which positions the child in the present as some type of work in progress.

This can be seen to an extent when certain professional groups adopt an ages and stages approach. In this way children are assessed on whether they have achieved various so-called milestones. As we said earlier though, the establishment and focus on achieving milestones in respect of any child's development reflects an approach which soon comes to act as a normative device (Fattore et al, 2007). This creates a culture where some children are seen as normal for their age, but also, where some children are then seen as not normal. Although we might initially consider this in terms of physical development we can also recognise how developmental psychology does much to reinforce the ways in children come to be viewed as becomings (Walkerdine, 2009).

In general it is fair to say that children have traditionally been seen from a deficit position; children are seen as lacking something and are positioned in terms of what they will be in the future rather than what they are now, or how they need to learn particular ways of behaving that align with a view of what is acceptable or not for a child. From this position it is reasonable to view children in terms of becomings. The move towards seeing children differently though emerged within sociology during the 1990s and soon became referred to as the new sociology of childhood (James and Prout, 1997; Qvortrup et al, 2009; Wyness, 2012). The key idea within the new sociology of childhood is the move away from seeing the child in terms of moving, or developing, towards adulthood, but instead seeing them in terms of being an individual and having value in themselves now, not just in terms of the future.

The new sociology of childhood positioned children as social actors. They are seen as active in their own lives, interacting with the world around them. This fits with the idea of how children are able to have a voice, the idea of the child's voice being an important part of contemporary policy and practice but something that is quite recent, as has been indicated. It also means that children have their own claim on rights, something that some adults find problematic. This new position can be summarised as the contrast between seeing children as becomings, or seeing them as beings (James and Prout, 1997; Wyness, 2012). It may be worth noting also that it seems odd to be referring to the new sociology of childhood when it is around

30 years old, so bear in mind that at the time it was quite a radical departure from what had gone before, but it has become a standard approach by now.

Note

Do not assume that before the development of the new sociology of childhood children were only and always seen as becomings but that afterwards there was a general acceptance of children as beings. This is not the case. It would be better to think that this new perspective created a tension between these two positions.

Children experience this tension. Although there is often pressure from some practitioners and institutions to treat children as beings, this is within a society that finds it difficult to move away from understanding children as becomings, as it can be hard not to see children in terms of what they might be or what they should be doing at a certain age.

Parents may also experience tension in relations with their children. They may say that they want their children to be innocent or to have a good childhood, but at the same time we can recognise that they will often think about their child's future and be focused on what they think their child will need for the future. So while parents might want their children to be happy and free from worry, they also want them to study hard or do well at school.

Remember also that we are not really concerned with individual children, we are concerned with childhood. Always bear in mind that the social, cultural and political context of childhood is shaped by ideas. Because of this we can say that there may be conflict or tensions between different institutions within society and that this influences how we provide for and deal with children. This may lead to inconsistencies. Our position within this book is to favour the idea that children should be seen as beings, but we recognise that the idea that children are becomings is embedded within many institutions and that many individuals will adopt this. This makes it difficult to move away from an understanding of children as becomings.

Seeing children as beings though means recognising the possibility of agency within the child that is associated with an understanding of children as having validity in their own right. When we see the child as a being they are much more easily understood as being worthy of having rights. This is important because historical studies of children illustrate how they were often seen as the property of their parents rather than as an individual with their own corresponding rights, and that other adults treated children in a way that ignored those rights.

Rights and the child's voice

We suggested earlier that developments such as the United Nations Convention on the Rights of the Child (UNCRC) (UNICEF, 1989) reinforce the idea that children are deserving of rights. However, very few parents or practitioners would use this to argue that children should have a right to self-determination in all matters. The UNCRC is not really saying this either. The value of the UNCRC is in establishing a baseline against which children's lives in different countries may be measured so as to assess how societies value children, but there are always challenges. Within the UK the ideas that are embedded within the UNCRC promoting the rights of children are often overshadowed by approaches which position children as becomings. The UNCRC has three themes: provision, protection and participation. However, some of these rights are more difficult to facilitate depending on socio-economic and cultural issues. Take play for example; play is important for children and we can say with some confidence that children enjoy playing, but consider how often a concern with learning means that the extent to which children are simply able to play becomes a matter of contention (Davey and Lundy, 2011).

So, starting to see children as beings has had a significant impact on the nature of childhood and, following from this, on children's lives. It is important to remember though that alongside this, an understanding of children as becomings continues to exert a great deal of power and influence over children's lives. This is particularly applicable in relation to the rights that children have (Cassidy, 2012).

However, one thing that has changed in recent years and which demonstrates the changing landscape of childhood is the idea of the child's voice. The idea of the child's voice is evidence of children being seen differently (Smith, 2010). The UNCRC has done much to promote the idea of the child's voice, establishing that children should be respected and listened to and that their views are valid (Lundy, 2007; Sudarsan et al, 2022). A concern with the child's voice then reinforces a move towards seeing children as beings and embeds children's rights within approaches to practice with children.

It would be very unusual to either study childhood or work with children in the UK in the 21st century and not encounter the idea of the child's voice. There is no doubt that contemporary ideas about children position the child's viewpoint as both valid and valuable. However, for a long time children were not listened to. In listening to the child's voice then we can see how adults can attempt to seek the viewpoint of children and understand a child's perspective. To do this we need to engage with the dichotomy of children as being or becoming and understand what this means to children.

Be aware though that although the child's voice is integral to contemporary practice, giving children a voice can be problematic because society (which includes parents and practitioners) is often aiming for a particular outcome for children which might not correspond with children's views at any given time. In part that is because adults tend to believe that they know things that children don't know.

This returns us to the reality of development in that children are likely to have less experience of many situations. Similarly, to give children a voice it is important to ensure they have the communication and language skills to articulate their viewpoint. Children may form a view about their life, but their life is generally shaped by adults. Any communication then between adults and children will be open to interpretation by the adult and may depend on the nature of the relationship between the child and the adult, including the power differences between them.

So, what is important in this chapter?

The aim of this chapter has been to establish the extent to which understanding contemporary childhood requires us to approach it by considering that childhood is social. We have previously said that the social study of childhood is relatively new, in that early sociological approaches were not so concerned with children. For early sociologists children were seen as pre-social and therefore the focus was on how children were socialised. The lack of interest displayed by sociologists facilitated the dominance of psychology in relation to children and a focus in particular that can be understood as a developmentalist approach. Developmentalism supports psychological approaches such as the ages and stages approach wherein children are seen to develop along expected lines that correspond to certain ages. This is an approach which foregrounds milestones.

It is also fair to say however that this ages and stages approach fits easily with what we see in terms of children developing. It makes sense when we think about the reality that children change and to some extent this aligns with age and/or size. In adopting this approach though we should recognise that we are placing the focus upon children rather than childhood, and as we have said before this means that as a consequence we disregard the ways in which childhood constitutes the context of development. An example of this is how the UK education system expects children to be able to read by age six, whereas some other cultures don't have this expectation of children. In developing assignments, it will always be useful to demonstrate an awareness of the distinction between children and childhood, especially in terms of establishing that childhood forms the context within which children experience their lives.

Traditionally the study of children has been much less concerned with childhood as a concept and much more concerned with how children have developed. This is a bit like the saying 'not seeing the wood for the trees'. Children are the trees; childhood is the woods that the trees make up. We focus on children and pay less attention to childhood. One reason for this is because of the way in which discourses can act to make things appear natural or normal. Because of this we do not routinely stop to think about things, or question why we think the way we do.

In raising the concept of developmentalism though we provided the scope to consider the concept of discourse. Discourse is so important when it comes to studying social sciences within contemporary society, and we cannot say it enough: make sure that you understand discourse. Discourse is a concept that you should be able to draw on in almost all assignments.

Discourse, as used within sociology, puts forward the argument that language operates as a social structure which makes the way in which society is organised and structured appear natural and obvious. It creates a framework within which we understand the world that we live in by constructing the meanings that we have about the world. This means that discourse has power. It has power in the way that it supports some forms of social organisation while negating or undermining other approaches to organising society. As an example, think about discourses regarding education which promote ideas about difference and which lead to different ways of organising education, creating different educational experiences for different children. This could be the establishment of different types of schools in the mid 20th century where entry was determined by the 11+ exam, or by the introduction of the Young Gifted & Talented scheme in the early 2000s. In each example, discourse about natural differences feeds into constructing real differences in terms of experiences.

Discourse was used to illustrate how certain ideas and beliefs seem to be embedded within society. The discourse relating to developmentalism was explored to illustrate this, as was a discourse around attachment. Attachment is strongly embedded within UK practice in relation to children, but it also provided us with an opportunity to demonstrate the extent to which psychological theories about individuals can be seen to be rooted in social experiences and beliefs. So, what we see in attachment theory is that Bowlby held a very traditional view of Western family life and that this socially conservative viewpoint became central to attachment in terms of the focus on motherhood and a mother's relationship with infants.

In considering discourse though it was stressed that discourse should be seen as plural. Although any particular discourse may be seen as dominant it is also important to recognise that discourses may be said to be competing. This contributes to the way in which society can change, because discourse is never fixed. This was illustrated in the way that there has been a move away from seeing children as becomings as per the discourse of developmentalism, and towards a discourse of children as beings. In turn, a discourse of children as beings is reinforced by a move towards accepting children as deserving of rights. This was seen as feeding into practice when we considered the child's voice.

In sum then you might take a number of aspects of this chapter and use them in a range of assignments depending on the task. When it comes to the key points of the chapter, we feel that the following stand out:

- Childhood is the context within which children develop.
- Discourse as associated with Foucault regulates the meanings that we hold about society.
- In regulating meanings, discourse makes some things valid or legitimate while also closing off alternatives.
- The psychological discourse of developmentalism has traditionally dominated how we understand and provide for children.
- Developmentalism underpins an ages and stages approach and has a normative effect.

- Attachment has become established as a common-sense approach to understanding children in spite of criticism.
- Attachment is not neutral, it reflects a socially conservative view of the family.
- Sociological approaches promote seeing the child as a being rather than a becoming.
- Seeing the child as a being supports children's rights and promotes the child's voice in practice

Further thoughts

When we try to make sense of why some people behave in certain ways it is not unusual to see that events from the past are presented as being the cause of their behaviour. Can you see how this is deterministic though? Experiencing problems as children will not inevitably lead to someone having a troubled adulthood. If this were the case it would mean it is near impossible to overcome challenges and difficulties in life, or that we could not live a different life to that of our parents or grandparents.

Also, consider that if Bowlby's attachment theory is based upon a particular type of family structure, what does this say about other family structures? This seems to condemn children who live in different circumstances to the nuclear family that Bowlby supported.

It is quite common to see children from a deficit perspective and to view them as moving towards an adulthood which will provide the basis for their capabilities to be realised. When we do this though we sometimes overlook just how capable children can be. Try to find out the ages at which musicians such as Kate Bush or Lady Gaga wrote some very successful songs, or see Schubak (2020). But also consider how learning and development does not stop at the age we become adults (18 years old, according to the UNCRC).

Further reading

Given how important attachment theory has become, Garrett (2022a; 2022b) is worth reading to understand what was influencing Bowlby.

Walkerdine (2009) provides three things: an account of changing ideas about children, a critique of developmentalism and an example of how discourse operates.

Woodhead (2009) provides a short account of how ideas relating to children and childhood have changed over time in a way that reflects discourse.

3

From working to playing

> **This chapter will help you to understand:**
> - what we mean by play;
> - how a concern with learning has shifted focus away from play;
> - how concerns with risk restrict how children can play.

Is childhood a new idea?

In calling this book *Understanding Contemporary Childhood* we are suggesting that childhood now is maybe different compared to what childhood was like in the past. In drawing attention to change we think that many people often overlook change. Childhood is another everyday term that is often just taken for granted. For many people, it is just what it says on the tin, it is childhood, there is little more to be said. With that in mind then we start this chapter by taking some time to consider what childhood is and focus on a significant element of what is considered to constitute childhood, play.

Student task

Spend five minutes jotting down ideas and/or issues that you associate with childhood. What is it that defines childhood?

Now, think about the things that you have listed. When we have worked with students on this task it is not unusual to see childhood being said to be a time of innocence or a time for play, so we want you to think about the way in which these ideas are rooted within the society that we live in. Innocence and/or play may not have been so obvious 200 or even 100 years ago. Childhood can, and has, changed over time.

Can you think about anything that might have changed regarding childhood over the last 100 years? It may help to talk to people you know who are of an older generation to you.

To address the idea that childhood has changed over time, think about the saying 'children should be seen and not heard', as introduced previously. This may have been said to you as a child. It is assumed that it was more often said or heard in Victorian times, but the saying is even older than Victorian times as it derives from a 15th century saying directed at young women. Now compare this somewhat old-fashioned notion that children should remain silent with the more recent idea that children should have a voice, as was discussed in Chapter 2. There is an implicit understanding within these two ideas which relates to the social position, and the value, of children in society. By stating that children should not be heard we are effectively denying a valid position for children within social settings.

In one sense we want to draw attention to the way in which both positions rest on the idea that children exist both in themselves and as a category within society. So, when McDowall-Clark (2020) asks 'has childhood always existed?', then this may sound like a rather strange question, but it may be valid to ask this question when we consider how childhood is a relatively modern phenomenon. Maybe the question to ask is whether or not children exist independently of childhood or do we only understand children within the context of childhood. This may feel like we are going round in circles, but it is worth considering again the difference between children, as small people, and childhood, the way in which those small people live, or are expected to live, in the world.

In saying that childhood is a relatively modern phenomenon we are reminded that ideas can and do change over time. This links to the issue of discourse again. How we understand childhood is rooted within a discourse which constructs a particular way of understanding it. Alongside the fact that our ideas about childhood have changed we can also point to the ways in which there is more academic interest in the concept of childhood. So, although we can be confidant in saying that children are real in respect of being at a particular stage in human development, we should see childhood as being a socially constructed concept. It may be the case that childhood seems very real, but we will use this chapter to demonstrate how it has been brought about through social actions and how social actions contribute to the ways in which it has changed. Importantly though this interest in childhood is relatively recent.

Student task

To start to understand the nature of childhood, take a few minutes to list some of the age restrictions that apply to children and young people. Based upon this, think about how policy and legislation act in ways which define childhood and shape childhood experiences, for example, how the age of consent acts to define what adults feel are appropriate relationships for young people and adults.

Now consider that our ideas about childhood are reinforced by what children are prevented from doing. Consequently, what children and young people are prevented from doing reflects and reinforces ideas about what is appropriate for children.

Once young people reach an age where they are permitted to do something it becomes harder to see them as children. However, different activities may be restricted at different ages, and this adds some confusion to the idea of when childhood ends.

It is not only academics who have shown a greater interest in children and childhood in recent decades; politicians, manufacturers, the media and parents have also focused on childhood in different ways and for different reasons. Parenting can be seen to have changed significantly over recent years, for example, consider how parents' involvement in their children's lives has increased over the last 20 or 30 years and how family life has changed.

In addition, policy and/or legislation may not only impose age restrictions preventing children from doing certain things, such as drinking alcohol, it may also act to compel certain behaviours, such as requiring children to be educated between set ages. We will say more about that later, but for now let us just take a moment or two to think about what comes first, and why, in respect of policy and legislation.

What we want you to think about is how we can identify a number of points in history where childhood comes into focus as a separate phase of life; for example, when children were stopped from working in industrial environments (such as in factories or coal mines in the 19th century), or when legislation has been introduced and implemented that places age restrictions on certain activities. When we consider the introduction of such changes then we can see how childhood takes on a new definition from that point onwards, and consequently how our ideas about childhood change.

It may be worth noting also that such changes are rarely welcomed by all. It is often the case that changes which restrict children from doing things may be resisted by some parts of society. Consider what restrictions on child labour may have meant to families on low incomes who were suddenly faced with the reality that their children had changed from being economic contributors to the family by bringing money in, to being an economic burden in that they required feeding and clothing but were no longer earning money themselves.

In contemporary UK society, children are rarely expected to contribute economically to the family. This is one way in which it can be seen that things change, because children were important contributors to the family in the past. However, this changed with the change in legislation and the way childhood was seen as a life stage where work was not appropriate. So, whereas at one time the concern may have been that children contribute to the family's finances, now the concern is that they are educated so that they can become independent adults and become economically active as adults. There again, do not make the mistake of thinking that all families are concerned with their children's education in respect of future employment. Within the UK, school absences have increased in the years following the COVID-19 pandemic, with anxiety often being cited as the reason for this (Adams and García, 2023; McDonald et al, 2023). This is not to say parents do not care about the future independence of their children, but it is not always an important consideration when parents are dealing with the needs of their children at the time.

So, let's consider some ideas which demonstrate how childhood has been understood and why it is important to recognise that childhood is socially constructed and the role of play in that construction

How Aries changed our understanding of childhood

We will start by saying that childhood changes for each generation. We can see how our own childhood differs from the childhoods of our parents or grandparents, and, if you are a parent, how your child's childhood differs from your own. Think about the games that children play, or the toys that they play with and how these have changed. With this in mind, you are unlikely to take any childhood/children's studies course and not encounter the work of Aries. Aries (1962) is significant in the historical understanding of childhood in that he was one of the first to present the idea that childhood is social. His basic argument can be summarised quite simply: in 'medieval society the idea of childhood did not exist' Aries (1962: 128).

For Aries, childhood emerges in the late Middle Ages. Before the 15th century there was little distinction made between adults and children. Prior to the Middle Ages the recording of age was limited and, in most cases, non-existent, so a concern about what age a child was, and what they should or could do, was not relevant. There was not such an emphasis on childhood as a life stage where certain things should happen or not. Aries suggests that for children, an early introduction to an adult world both of work and of sexual play was common. This was not to say that young children were not cared for or that they were commonly exploited as we would understand it today. It is simply to say that their role in the family and community was not defined as being much different to that of adults when compared to now.

One key factor in Aries' argument that childhood is a recent phenomenon is the concept of education within schools. Aries emphasises how the school rests upon distinctions being drawn between age groups and that this leads to schools becoming distinct institutions within society that are marked by forms of organisation which are both physical and ideological. By physical we mean that schools exist as a distinct building where education is provided for children relevant to age. By ideological we mean that schools are organised in line with ideas about children, education and discipline (Wyness, 2012).

Importantly, there is one key weakness in respect of how Aries carried out his research that is often raised. To further understand the criticism of Aries it is necessary to consider ontology, what we can know, and epistemology, how we can know it.

Note

The criticism of Aries based upon how he carried out his research demonstrates the importance of considering both ontology and epistemology. Ontology and epistemology are key concepts within social research. A simple definition of each is that ontology refers to what we can know, whereas epistemology refers to how we can know it.

You can probably recognise from research (or methods) modules that when it comes to methods of research, differences of opinion with respect to what we can know and how we can know it lead to different types of research methods being adopted.

So, is the criticism of Aries based on a weakness in his ontological position or his epistemological approach?

Although Aries' argument has been very influential, it rests upon the fact that Aries adopted an ontological perspective which asserted that we can know about childhood in a historical sense. However, although we might accept that we can know what childhood meant in a historical period, the problem that Aries faces is to demonstrate how we can know it, that is, what evidence is there for the ideas he asserts. For Aries, we can know about the history of childhood, or the historical position of children, by analysing and evaluating the evidence that he was able to access. The evidence that Aries relies on takes the form of works of art or written records of various sorts.

However, if we consider what life was like in the Middle Ages, we might guess that what was written about or painted was limited. It is reasonable to assume that only certain children would have been the subject of such evidence, not all children. The weakness then lies in terms of epistemology. The problem is that the evidence used by Aries is likely to over-represent the lives of wealthy children, while under-representing the lives of poor children. Even so, others have also adopted the same arguments when referring to how childhood is represented in paintings from the 15th and 16th centuries (Hanvey, 2019). So, we can accept that although this evidence does not tell us everything about childhood at that time, it gives us some ideas about what childhood was like for some children.

In one sense the view that childhood did not exist or was not recognised demonstrates that we have to be careful not to think that how things are now is how they have always been. So, although children may not always have been viewed in the way that children are viewed today, this does not mean that they were not regarded as children and that they did not experience a life period that could be described as childhood.

What we should take into account then is that changes in other aspects of life impact upon how we understand childhood. Gittins (2009) suggests that there are three things to focus on when approaching the history of childhood:

- changing material conditions;
- how psychological and sociological theories impact on child rearing and children's experience;
- the influence that governments have on childhood through legislation and policies.

So, in assessing the work of Aries it is fair to say that we cannot know exactly how childhood was really lived in medieval times, but what we can see is that there have been many changes in society since then. It is these points of change that are significant in understanding how childhood has evolved and why childhood is shaped as it is today. It is clear that childhood has emerged as a more defined life stage, and this is very probably the result of the changes that Gittins identifies, together with an increase in wealth in UK society. In families which became wealthier, children were no longer required to contribute to the household income and because of this the opportunity for them to be children, rather than workers, emerged.

Therefore, as socio-economic conditions improved in Western society in general, children's lives changed. That doesn't mean that it is a fast process of change or that it applies to all families at the same time. The development of childhood can be seen as having been led by the emerging middle classes as it is this group who would no longer have to rely on their children for an income. It is these wealthier, middle-class families then who were starting to present a view of children as important for the future (De Bellaigue, 2019; Cunningham, 2021). Consequently, as middle-class families started to see children in terms of the future, so education became more important.

However, for working-class families, those where children worked, a similar but slightly different process of change evolved. As children were excluded from the workplace due to concerns for their safety and health, schools evolved to contain children as much as to educate them, as once they were not occupied with work their freedom starts to be problematic.

Student task

Try to compare different areas of the world to see at what age children are expected to leave school. In thinking about how the school leaving age has increased over time, think about how this changes children and young people's lives.

What you will tend to see is that in the wealthier countries children are required to remain in school for longer. As such, childhood in wealthier countries can be said to exist as a protected period where children are not expected to earn an income; instead, they are required to be educated. This not only changes how childhood is lived, it also protects children from the adult world to some extent. In the UK this is officially 18 unless a young person aged 16 or 17 secures a job, but it is not unusual for education to continue up to the age of 21 for both males and females. This means childhood, dependency and/or the time for learning has extended over time. However, in some countries in the world today, education may not be available beyond primary school, if at all, and significantly the education of girls is severely restricted or banned. So, how we see children, what we believe them to be, will shape what we do to children and/or what we expect of them. So, what do we expect of children? Maybe this is a good time to go back and see what you wrote when you were asked what childhood is.

Childhood as a time of play

When we ask students how to define childhood, we often find that students refer to childhood as being a time for play. Play is central to understanding contemporary childhood. However, there is sometimes confusion about the definition of what play is. We need to consider this.

Pause for reflection

What do we mean by the term 'play'? Consider how we often talk about play as a way of 'learning', but is all play a process of learning? Consider also how play is not restricted to children.

Here's a good way of thinking about the qualitative difference between children and adults: think about the ways in which young children engage in pretend play, for example, acting out roles or pretending to be certain things or doing certain things.

Now answer this question: can adults engage in pretend play in the same way as children?

You probably answered no, adults cannot play in the same way that children can. There is something about being a child that makes play different. It doesn't seem contentious then to state that play is often viewed as integral to what it means to be a child; children play.

As a starting point in terms of considering play it may be useful to offer a simple distinction between those social activities that we may call play and those that we may call work. The relationship between play and work is very important when we try to make sense of what we mean by childhood (Wyness, 2012). The United Nations Convention on the Rights of the Child (UNICEF, 1989) acts to promote the rights of children to be able to play while also removing the responsibility to work from children. The position of children as not having to work is often underpinned by legal restrictions which apply to children with regards to what work they are permitted to do, and for how long.

In Western societies it is generally accepted then that children should not work, though it is important to acknowledge that many children do work. For example, some jobs such as newspaper deliveries were traditionally seen as children's work, though such jobs are not so common anymore. However, bear in mind that children are also employed in other types of work, such as acting across TV, film and theatre. There are also children who work in an unpaid capacity. Some children work as carers, such as when a parent has health needs or when they are required to care for younger siblings. These things are often ignored when we concern ourselves with children not working.

The focus on children's play and the comparison with children working is a useful frame through which to consider how notions of childhood have changed over time. If we consider historical evidence, it is obvious that attitudes towards children were very different in the past. Working-class children, even very young children, were expected to work in line with what was considered appropriate at the time (Humphries, 2010; Wilkes, 2011; Heywood, 2018). As such, the growth of campaigns against child labour and calls for legal restrictions have to be understood as being a reaction to what was at the time a very common practice (Gillis, 2009). It is also worth thinking about what might have driven some individuals to campaign against child labour.

We also have to be careful here not to see historical figures as having the same concerns that we may have. Although we might see such campaigns as a justified reaction against child labour in the context of our own ideas about childhood, that may not have been the case in the past. Concerns about child welfare were not the only concerns. Children could be seen as taking adults' work and, therefore, stopping them working could advantage adults (Hendrick, 2005).

Pause for reflection

If you were an adult male worker and it was perfectly legal to pay children less than you for carrying out the same work, might you support restrictions on child labour for reasons other than ideas about child welfare?

But, if your children are no longer able to go out to work, who will look after them?

It is also important here to reflect that across the world there are places where even very young children still work so as to support the family or themselves in ways that have been banned in the UK.

It is fair to say then that play and childhood are often seen as inseparable, especially in the West. The fact that play is so embedded within our notions of childhood though can be seen as one reason why play is often absent from other concerns about childhood. Because play is understood to be something of concern to children, and something that is seen as natural for children to take part in, it tends to be seen as both frivolous and unimportant and is rarely seen as a legitimate concern for policy makers (Voce, 2016). Furthermore, this contributes to the view that as we develop, we become more serious, and we play less. Consequently, play is for children and is not an important issue for policy makers.

In turn, ideas about play being frivolous may have contributed to recent developments in some Western societies which have seen the place of play in children's lives declining as a focus on learning and achievement are brought to the fore as being more worthy (Aras, 2016; Bodrova and Leong, 2019). This is something that we will return to later in the chapter. To begin with though it seems very useful to say a bit more about what play is.

> **Note**
>
> Play is one of those words or terms that is often accepted at face value. We say play as though no further consideration is required. However, as students you need to question things, to interrogate what we mean by the terms that we use.
>
> As such, it is important to recognise that the term play can be hard to define and that it can be understood in a number of ways and be seen to have a number of different purposes (Bateson and Martin, 2013; Howard and McInnes, 2013; Henricks, 2015; Powell and Smith, 2017).
>
> However, as a starting point we can use the ideas of Whitebread et al (2012: 10) who summarise five types of play that we will probably all recognise: physical play, play with objects, symbolic play, pretence/sociodramatic play and games with rules.
>
> Whitebread et al can be freely accessed online. It provides a very accessible introduction to play.

Alongside these five types of play we should also add that we are talking about children's play, and by definition this means that play should be what children want; play should be chosen and directed by children themselves.

You will often read that it is important for children to be able to engage in play of their own choosing, but this requires that children select what they do with their time. In reality, children are often limited by what adults allow or make available and therefore play is often restricted for children. However, it is also worth noting that children can be quite good at influencing or circumnavigating this. So, children will often demonstrate an ability to negotiate or engineer ways to spend time alone or with their peers or friends that allows them to choose what they do. Even small children will find ways to avoid the gaze, or supervision, of adults, with small spaces often being very attractive to children so that they are hidden from adults.

Avoiding the gaze of adults in a broader sense allows children opportunities to form their own cultures, especially as they get older. These child-led cultures can be difficult for adults to understand. These ways of avoiding the interference of adults are very important in children's development and learning. In shaping their friendship groups children take what they have learnt from adults and from interaction with adults but adapt it to fit their own ideas and test it out in their own time.

Corsaro (2015) does much to illustrate how children's play is underpinned by a central value of peer cultures which involves building friendships and doing things together. This is particularly important for children in childcare settings such as nurseries and kindergartens, where, unlike home, toys and equipment are communal. The communal nature of toys and equipment in childcare settings means that children must navigate and negotiate the use of toys and equipment in a way that may be very different to the home setting. Corsaro points out that sharing is central to such settings and is positioned as an important social behaviour. However, where children are seen to be acting in exclusive ways, such as when restricting access to other children, this should be understood not as anti-social, but about preserving or even protecting peer groups and the resources that they have gathered that are important to their group. It is not necessarily that different from how adults behave.

Play, Vygotsky and the role of scaffolding

Another concern regarding play is the role of play for learning and development. Play is often incorporated into developmental theories as having a number of roles. So, when reading about play you should expect to see it as being presented as a key part of children's development, as opposed to just being an activity that fills children's time. As such, it is often referred to in relation to the work by key theorists such as Piaget and Vygotsky.

Vygotsky is often presented as providing an understanding of play as important, if not vital, to children's development. Play in this regard is seen to afford children the opportunity to achieve something that is not possible in real life, in that through exercising their imagination children can learn and develop into social beings (Colliver and Veraksa, 2021). Note however that although we may see play as very broad in terms of what it can mean for children, Vygotsky adopted a narrow definition in which play is confined to socio-dramatic or make-believe play (Bodrova and Leong, 2015; 2019; Kingdon, 2020). At the same time, the play scenario that Vygotsky is concerned with is rule based to a large extent (Bodrova and Leong, 2019). Rules being those unwritten social rules that we abide by to fit into our society or social setting. What follows is that children are presented as using play in a way that corresponds to Vygotsky's concept of the Zone of Proximal Development.

Note

The Zone of Proximal Development (ZPD) is central to the work of Vygotsky. In sum, Vygotsky states that there are things that a child can do because of their level of development and things that a child cannot do because they are not sufficiently developed. However, in between these two positions are those things that a child can do with help or assistance. This is the ZPD.

Note that proximity refers to things which are close. The ZPD then is referring to the development that a child is close to but for which s/he is not there yet, hence the need for assistance.

Importantly though, the ZPD is dynamic, it is constantly moving. It's not accurate to suggest that the child moves through the ZPD, they don't. It is better to see the ZPD as moving with the child. The ZPD is like the carrot that is hung in front of a donkey, just out of reach so as to encourage it to keep on moving forward. A child moves within the ZPD as they continue to develop and learn.

Typically, the focus on assistance within the ZPD has meant that we understand development as taking place when an adult or more knowledgeable other provides a child with immediate help, such as in a teaching situation. We have explained this elsewhere by referring to Vygotsky's approach as seeing the child as being akin to an apprentice, learning from others (Creasy and Corby, 2023). This can be compared to Piaget's approach within which the child is seen as being like a little scientist but working on their own. However, when children play make-believe games as part of a group then the actions of the group may take the place of the more knowledgeable other by providing support within the group as a whole (Bodrova and Leong, 2015).

In terms of support the concept of scaffolding promotes a Vygotskyan view of child development. The concept of scaffolding was first put forward by Wood et al (1976: 90). Importantly, they also point to what can be seen as a key weakness of many psychological approaches, the fact that 'discussions of problem solving or skill acquisition are usually premised on the assumption that the learner is alone and unassisted.' Wood et al introduce the concept of scaffolding in referring to the context that is provided by more knowledgeable others such as adults or peers that help children to 'solve a problem, carry out a task or achieve a goal which would be beyond his unassisted efforts.' An important aspect of scaffolding in practice though is that there is a gradual withdrawal of support as the child's knowledge and confidence increase.

So, when we look at what happens in classrooms for example, we see that adults engaged in teaching children can be seen as being most effective when they create opportunities for children that correspond to a child's ZPD. For Schaffer (1996), effective teaching is where the adult transfers responsibility for a task or activity to the child. You may see this described as both internalisation or appropriation. This is concerned with how the child takes on the ability to do more, and so less support is needed. Now consider that the same principle can be applied to social settings such as playing with other children. In play we can say that children are learning something, albeit in an informal sense. Learning is not restricted to formal settings, and it may very well be restricted by formal settings!

Risk and play

Although we may often think of play as something that encapsulates the idea of freedom for children, this ignores the way that adult ideas about play have a number of consequences for how, or what, children play, which may restrict or control children. Play does not take place in a vacuum, it takes place within social and cultural contexts which shape it in a range of ways, such as the beliefs and concerns of parents and/or others in society. For example, Hughes (2010) points to the differences between what may be termed advanced or technological societies where children's games are more competitive, compared to other countries where children's games have a much greater focus on sharing and working together. Walk around any toy shop in the UK and note how many games, even for quite young children, emphasise actions which lead to one person winning. This focus on winning can be seen as fitting quite comfortably into Western ideas about individualism.

A concern with individualism has a long history within Western societies so it is not surprising that it has influenced ideas about play and/or games. A more recent concern within Western societies however has been with risk, and we can see that this has also come to have some real influence upon how children play.

In raising the idea of risk, be aware that it is immediate and/or obvious risks such as injury which dominate. We stress this focus on immediate injury to distinguish immediate harms from long term harms, such as the risks that may result from children being sedentary. In relation to health and safety in respect of children's play and risk, concerns with safety tend to overshadow concerns about health (Wheway, 2008). Because of concerns about immediate harms and/or injury (safety issues), adults often intervene to guide children's play in ways which reduce or restrict physical activity. This however ignores the potential for long-term consequences in respect of children's health that may arise if children become less active (health issues). That is not to say children's safety is not important, but rather that the focus on what children do or don't do can have unintended consequences.

Allowing children to play outside, unsupervised, is now seen to be fraught with risks. Although risks have always existed in outdoor unsupervised play there is now an expectation that parents should not take that risk nor allow their children to take risks. In restricting what children can do when they play though it is not only children's possible future health that is affected as they become less active, opportunities for growth and development are also restricted by removing risk. Risk is beneficial to both physical and emotional development. Children need challenges and risk can be seen as an essential part of challenge (Biesta, 2013; Harper, 2017). So, while we advocate for children being safe, such as where risk is obviously greater than their ability to negotiate a situation or activity, we should also be concerned that we are not restricting children's play negatively.

In this regard, it is worth considering where children play. Playgrounds are purposely planned spaces for children's play. Compare this to many other spaces where children may play such as on the street or in woods, or waterways and so on. However, although playgrounds are spaces which are provided to facilitate play for children they are not always utilised effectively. One issue is location. Children's playgrounds have to be accessible (Wheway, 2015). When access is less easy, playgrounds that may be considered very good may be under-used as children utilise other, less obvious public spaces because they are easier to get to. Additionally, planned playgrounds can sometimes be misused, for example by dog owners who do not clear up after their dogs, and this makes playgrounds unattractive or even dangerous. Here we can see how wider society, not parents, are ignoring the needs for children to have safe spaces in which to play.

In many countries children will have access to planned spaces for play within schools, though school playgrounds may be supervised or controlled. Although school playgrounds have previously existed as spaces within schools providing opportunities for free play, both during and after school time, in recent decades these opportunities have been reducing with playgrounds being locked outside of school hours and playtime being reduced within school hours (Pike and Kelly, 2014). In addition, the supervision of playgrounds by adults has the consequence of restricting how and what children play. For example, Marsh and Bishop (2014: 108) describe how one school within their studies employed 'play workers' who are tasked with ensuring that 'playtime ran as smoothly as possible'. But what might be meant by running smoothly? This suggests that play can be right or wrong. Such a goal may be at odds with what children want, the notion of free play and even with what play workers themselves think their job is.

By the end of the 1960s adult supervision of school playgrounds within the UK had become commonplace and this has seen children's play being increasingly restricted (Blatchford, 1989; Thomson, 2003). We have previously argued that the restriction on children's activities results in the impoverishment of school playtime, but it is also worth considering that this may be the only time some children get to play with other children outside their family. This is because opportunities for children to play freely, to use their imagination and to challenge themselves through play are reduced as supervision by adults increases (Creasy and Corby, 2019). Although it may appear to be a minor thing, consider how many schools now have painted hopscotch grids or other similar fixed play-guides in playgrounds (Marsh and Bishop, 2014). Although this seems innocuous or even helpful, in providing such guides schools direct children's play rather than providing an environment for play that is both flexible and adaptable, and led solely by children. Although such hopscotch grids may be provided for the right reasons, the ideals of play work may promote the provision of chalk for children to draw their own grids as a better approach (Brown, 2008).

We suggested earlier that one important factor in the increased supervision of children's play within school playgrounds is an adult preoccupation with risk, and a concern to prevent accidents. This is evident when safety is put forward as the reason for schools banning a range of games and pastimes. As a consequence, traditional games such as British Bulldog, conkers or versions of tag are now unlikely to be seen being played within British schools, and many types of climbing frames have been removed (Gill, 2007; Wheway, 2008; Schouten, 2015). Along with the demise of pea shooters and spud guns (do an internet search), that we remember from our time as children, school playgrounds are now dominated by concerns with safety so much that Hyndman and Telford (2015) have suggested that rather than seeing risk as having been eliminated, we could say that there is actually a surplus of safety.

Risk is not confined to health and safety though. Parents also exert some influence on schools, with schools being aware of expectations from parents that children are supervised at school in a way that avoids their child suffering any injury. There is often an additional expectation, however, that there will be no loss or damage to property. This contributes to school staff acting to create what they deem to be an acceptable degree of order during playtimes (Thomson, 2003). In addition, some schools have reduced the frequency or length of playtimes, impoverishing children's opportunities for play because of concerns surrounding bullying (Mulryan-Kyne, 2014).

So, contrary to the general acceptance that children benefit from free play, playtime within contemporary UK schools is becoming less free. Children's play is subject to being organised and play is often restricted in terms of what is permitted. Children in school playgrounds are not only subject to being observed by adults; they know that they are (Richards, 2012). They are also very aware of the rules and regulations that are in place when it comes to what they can do at playtimes (Thomson, 2007).

Play work

Another way of considering the extent to which play is seen as inextricably bound up with children and childhood is in the development of play work. In one sense the existence of play work supports two ideas. Firstly, that play is important for children and should be facilitated; secondly, that for a number of reasons, children may sometimes need support so as to be able to play and that this support requires guidance by adults, as opposed to just the provision of space or equipment. Play work within the UK is underpinned by eight principles. These principles are easily found in print (Brown, 2015; Russell et al, 2017) and online. See, for example, the Playwork Foundation:

1. All children and young people need to play. The impulse to play is innate. Play is a biological, psychological and social necessity, and is fundamental to the healthy development and wellbeing of individuals and communities.
2. Play is a process that is freely chosen, personally directed and intrinsically motivated. That is, children and young people determine and control the content and intent of their play, by following their own instincts, ideas and interests, in their own way for their own reasons.
3. The prime focus and essence of play work is to support and facilitate the play process, and this should inform the development of play policy, strategy, training and education.
4. For play workers, the play process takes precedence and play workers act as advocates for play when engaging with adult-led agendas.
5. The role of the play worker is to support all children and young people in the creation of a space in which they can play.

6 The play worker's response to children and young people playing is based on a sound, up-to-date knowledge of the play process and reflective practice.
7 Play workers recognise their own impact on the play space and also the impact of children and young people's play on the play worker.
8 Play workers choose an intervention style that enables children and young people to extend their play. All play worker intervention must balance risk with the developmental benefit and wellbeing of children.

(Playwork Foundation, 2005)

Ideas about play work can be traced back to the mid 1940s and to a concern that living within urban environments or landscapes both changes and restricts the opportunities for play when compared to children who live within the countryside (Brown, 2008; 2015). Brown draws on the ideas of Sorensen, a Danish architect, who advocated what he called 'junk playgrounds' so as to provide an environment for free play. Junk playgrounds are just spaces where children can play unsupervised in an environment that is not designed specifically for play by adults.

Pause for reflection

The idea of junk playgrounds reflects our childhood experiences. As children playing in the 1960s and 1970s we frequented parks where old trains or farm equipment were provided for play, old underground bomb shelters from the Second World War were explored, old buildings became children's meeting areas and a wood yard provided materials for making dens. Isolated haystacks also provided lots of scope for play.

Some of these 'junk' playgrounds present unsafe environments though and parents might not want their children exploring these areas. What were your experiences of junk-type playgrounds, whether officially provided or child-appropriated? How did you, or other children you know, appropriate space for child-led play? Is this something that children do in the UK now?

However, the freedoms that were enjoyed by children in the past were maybe not shared by children growing up in the 1990s and onwards (Brown, 2008). It is noticeable that the children of adults who themselves might have enjoyed unrestricted play often find their own lives very restricted. Why might parents who had freedom as children feel their own children should be more supervised?

It is interesting then, in light of this, that the job of the play worker is often to facilitate a freer environment for children. The principles of the play worker are not necessarily principles that are commonly enacted by parents and other carers for children generally. The job of providing freedom for children to play is subject to challenges, with play work in the UK in the early 2020s being subject to pressures resulting from austerity and the COVID-19 pandemic in particular (Newstead and King, 2021). This is alongside the social and parental concerns which restrict children's freedoms, and which often confines them to the home due to parental concerns regarding safety and how the media presents issues of children's safety.

In addition to these pressures though there is also the powerful discourse of children's learning. One important consequence of the idea that children need to develop and learn has led to a move away from play and towards an increased focus on learning. Sutton-Smith (2008) points to the developmental theories of Vygotsky and Piaget as underpinning the idea of children's need to develop under the guidance of adults, but we would also point to the competitive and utilitarian ideas contained within neoliberalism as fostering the idea that learning is of more importance than play.

When we say utilitarian, we mean that something has a defined purpose or that it operates as a means to an end. Within neoliberalism, education and learning are always positioned in terms of getting a job. Supporters of neoliberalism are unlikely to promote learning for its own sake, it is always promoted as being for a purpose. This aligns also to ideas of children as becomings, that is becoming adults who have learnt certain things relevant to being an economically active adult. Play does not fit with this idea.

So, whereas the psychological idea of development such as in the work of Piaget presents the idea that adulthood is the child's goal, neoliberalism adds a competitive aspect to this. The neoliberal idea of individuals existing within a competitive environment acts to intensify parental and societal concerns about learning and achievement. Given that UK governments since 1979 have been strongly influenced by neoliberal ideas it is not surprising that play has become squeezed out by concerns with learning, often manifest as the idea of school readiness (Yates, 2018).

Is it ever just play?

This chapter has continued to explore the idea that childhood is socially constructed with a particular focus on how childhood has changed. We drew upon the classic contribution to understanding childhood provided by Aries so as to develop the idea that childhood is something that is modern rather than something that has always existed. For Aries, childhood only starts to be recognised towards the end of the Middle Ages, during the 1400s.

A modern understanding of childhood then can be said to emerge as some families became wealthier and where concerns about children shifted in a way that means that they became less associated with work and more associated with both education and play. Play is argued to be central to childhood, but although organisations such as the United Nations have done much to establish a right to play, differentiating it from work in the process, play can be tricky to define and is often resisted by adults.

Given that play is not so easy to define and has multiple interpretations, you may find that the books and articles you read provide different definitions regarding play. In our experience, students tend not to like this. Students have usually experienced a school system, at least in the UK, which emphasises the idea of a right answer, so to say that it is hard to present a correct definition of play can be problematic. The definitions that you will encounter will generally be shaped by what the writer is aiming to do, and as a student you need to take some time to consider this. It may help to think that adults are expected to work, but work comes in many forms. In the same way, play comes in many forms.

We can see how play fits in with a Vygotskyan approach to learning and development whereby children learn with, and from, others while engaged in play. In this way we can see play as an important aspect of learning and development. Vygotsky though was not suggesting play as formal learning and his ideas contradict the move towards increasingly formalised learning for younger and younger children. An increased focus on learning tends to position play as frivolous compared to learning, but this ignores the fact that play is how and where learning happens for young children and is beneficial for their wellbeing.

If you are tasked with writing assignments about historical views regarding childhood you may find that these key points are very useful:

- Aries proposes the idea that childhood did not exist in the medieval period.
- Childhood is shaped by a number of social, issues including how legislation imposes age restrictions.
- For Aries, the social organisation of schools in particular gives meaning to childhood.
- Establishing a distinction between work and play is embedded within our ideas about childhood.
- It is not easy to define play.
- Play is important for children's learning and development.
- Social concerns, such as the concern about risk, shape children's experiences of play.

We also used Aries to introduce the concepts of ontology and epistemology as a way in which we can assess the value of what is being argued, and although you will often see these concepts being covered when addressing research methods, they are important when it comes to being critical and assessing what you read. So, the key criticism of Aries is that he relied on evidence provided in the form of paintings or in literature, but this would be focused on the wealthy. You can usefully ask questions of any study that you are reading by focusing on ontology, what we can know, and epistemology, how we can know it. So, when reading about a study relating to children and childhood, always think about what the author(s) are proposing can be known, and then think about their research method as this informs how it can be known.

This concern with ontology and epistemology should become part of your overall strategy as a student. You can even use it in respect of your own contribution to the classes that you attend and the assignments that you write. As students you are usually called upon to provide evidence for the claims that you make. Sometimes this is one of the tricky aspects of being a student and it contributes to the mistaken belief that as a student your ideas are not valid. We often hear students telling us that their ideas are not valid. That is wrong. Your ideas are valid but there is a qualification to this; they become valid when you have evidence.

You get evidence from the books and articles that you read as part of your studies, and some are better than others. One way to evidence the claim that ideas about childhood see childhood and play as entwined is to look at how the United Nations Convention on the Rights of the Child (UNICEF, 1989) establishes the rights of all children to be able to play, as was suggested earlier. It is in Article 31 if you want to read it, and is easily accessed online. We accessed it via the UNICEF website as per the reference.

The value in referencing the UNCRC lies in the fact that it is a set of principles that has been agreed at an international level setting out the rights that should apply to all children. So, as far as this book is concerned, this does at least two things. Firstly, it supports the idea that we can identify coherent views on what we mean by children and childhood; and secondly, it explicitly identifies play as important within children's lives. So, if the UNCRC is concerned to do this then it must mean that play is important. Of course, such a view is not necessarily shared by all.

A word of caution when it comes to using resources. It is sometimes easy to fall into the trap of assuming that if a word such as 'play' is present within an article title, it is going to be useful. Sometimes it is important to recognise that although classic theories of development may comment on play, they are not theories *of* play, (Lambert, 2000). Note the italics! Just because a theory refers to play in some respect that does not mean that it is a theory that is about play. Lambert also offers a more critical approach towards Vygotsky, arguing that Vygotsky could be quite dismissive of the nature of play in very young children and that he presented play in older children in a manner that means that play is present but not central.

So, when it comes to what you do as a student it is maybe more appropriate to focus on epistemology. If you are going to make claims, how can you demonstrate that your claims are valid? The answer is obviously that you have used appropriate resources. We will say more about this later in the book, but at this point we are simply going to say that some of the most useful resources will be provided for you in the form of reading lists.

Further thoughts

Do children exist independently of childhood, or do we only understand children within the context of childhood?

Early in the chapter you were asked to make some notes about what childhood is. Now you have read the chapter, would you want to make any changes to what you said initially? If the answer is yes, try to make sure that you can say why.

Should adults direct how children play? Try to present an argument for children being free to determine what and how they play, if only for some of their time.

Give some further thought to the idea that we understand children through the lens of childhood. Does this mean that if our ideas about childhood change, then our ideas about children change?

Think about your own school days and consider if any games or activities were restricted on the grounds of risk, or because of health and safety issues. Do you feel you had the opportunity to take risks as a child?

Further reading

Aries (1962) is the classic text presenting childhood as something that is modern and is well worth reading.

UNICEF (1989) and African Union (1990) are both useful reference sources. UNICEF represents the United Nations approach and African Union is specifically African.

Whitebread et al (2012) provides a good basis for appreciating the value of play, but follow this up by doing an internet search for both Play England and the Playing-out Movement.

Read the Play Commission (2025) reports on the state of play within the UK. The reference is to the interim report, the full report was due June 2025.

4
Thinking about how and why we educate

> **This chapter will help you to understand:**
> - recent developments which promote learning as more important than playing;
> - different approaches to how education is provided, focusing on idealism and utilitarianism;
> - how neoliberalism has influenced the organisation and aims of education;
> - ideas about how education can be provided and what it is for.

Play v learning

If we return to the idea that frames this book, how we can understand contemporary childhood, then it is possible to say that childhood is a site of tension or struggle. This tension or struggle is a consequence of the different notions that exist regarding childhood and what is seen to be the right way to treat children and what we want for our children.

Pause for reflection

When discussing child development, students will often refer to the need to provide opportunities for children so that they will develop. Would you go along with this idea; the idea that for children to develop, adults need to provide for them?

If you said yes, then we are going to be contentious and say that it is not necessary. We are not saying this is wrong, but think about development for a moment.

Assuming that children are provided with the basics, such as food, and are protected from life-threatening or harmful situations, children will develop. That's it, they will develop. Human beings have the ability to learn and develop in all sorts of situations and do not always need another person to actively provide the opportunity to develop.

They may not develop how we would want them to develop (but that is not to say that what we want is always the best for children); they may not develop as fully as could be possible (not all children develop as fully as possible when adults intervene), but they will develop.

So, when we say that we need to provide for children so that they will develop, what we really mean is that this is so they will develop in a way that we want them to. As such we generally mean that we are more concerned with children behaving in a way that we want them to and learning things that we want them to know. This is not always the best for the child or for the adult they become.

In relation to this our notions of childhood in terms of how we understand development and in terms of how we might provide for children are shaped and/or reinforced by the social policies and legislation that are put in place. But these policies do not just happen. It is not the case that there is a universally shared view of what is best for children. The key thing here is that the policies and legislation that we end up with are the result of political ideas and struggles. These struggles may lead to policies at a local level, such as a school banning certain hairstyles, or policy at a national level, such as establishing a national curriculum. The policies that are in place within any society have always come about because someone, or some group, has the power to put that policy in place, often with good intentions but also often with a concern for controlling social behaviour, particularly that of children.

For a comparison and discussion of politics and the policy process we recommend that you turn to Creasy and Corby (2023). In *Children, Family and the State* we explain how the neoliberal and neoconservative ideas put forward by the Conservative Party since the early 1980s contrast with the social-democratic approach taken by the Labour Party and how this leads to very different policies being put in place with regards to both children and to the families that they live in. The relevance here is that political ideas can shape childhoods. It is also important to state that this book was being written during a time of political change. During the summer of 2024, the neoliberal and neoconservative-influenced Conservative Party was replaced in government by the Labour Party. This book was completed before we could confidently account for what this would mean for the UK. It takes time for policies to change so it is important for you to recognise that the landscape of childhood which exists during the 2020s is likely to change as we move forward. The important thing to note is that whenever you are studying childhood, you consider the political and policy influence that is shaping childhood.

In terms of the policy landscape, for example, in the UK in the 21st century it is common to talk about Early Childhood Education (ECE) or Early Childhood Education and Care (ECEC). In both cases we want you to think about how a discourse of education is central to these terms. This represents a political move away from very young children being cared for, as in the past, towards being educated as well as cared for. We also want you to think about how there is a very strong discourse of learning that operates with regards to children and young people, so much so that children and young people are often referred to as learners. We accept that this may sound very reasonable, but think about what we said regarding discourse earlier. The way in which a focus on learning can be said to have become dominant throughout provision for children has led to some commentators referring to learnification (Biesta, 2010; 2013; Hughson, 2021; Bruzzone, 2023; Papastephanou and Drousioti, 2023). This refers to this shift from care to learning.

Pause for reflection

You may be a practitioner working in the early years sector, or you may be a student intending to work in the sector. With that in mind, we want you to take some time to consider your position regarding what we should provide for children within an early years setting. Should we provide opportunities and space for children to engage in free play, facilitated by adults but led by children, or, alternatively, should we be focusing on children's formal learning and getting them ready to progress to Key Stage 1 in school?

What is important to you when it comes to providing for the early years? What priorities do you think we should have for very young children?

Now think about early years settings. If you work in the early years sector, or you are a parent who needs early years services for a child, might it be that what is important for the organisation that provides the service is different to your values?

At this point let us say that we, the authors, do accept that education and learning are important for children, and that children enjoy learning. Our work within education means it would be strange if we said that we did not think that education and learning were important. However, what is of concern is another political issue, what children and young people learn, and how they will learn it.

What they will learn is generally referred to as the curriculum and you may be familiar with the national curriculum from your own time at school. Think for a moment how our understanding of children is embedded within the structure and organisation of the curriculum (Soler and Miller, 2003). By this we mean that the curriculum is designed to teach children specific things in a specific way because of beliefs about what children should know and how children learn. How they will learn raises a concern about how we organise education, and this is also political. Note that when we say that this is a political issue, we are using the term political in a broad sense to mean power. Always think that politics is about power, it is concerned with how groups of like-minded individuals impose their ideas or the extent to which the voices of some groups are heard whereas other groups are not heard.

Wood and Hedges (2016) offer a very good account of how struggles over ideas about what should be provided in respect of Early Childhood Education have changed over time. They demonstrate that an approach that was informed by developmental psychology and which generally left children alone to play has been replaced by an approach that is more controlling and is much more focused on achieving certain outcomes, especially the concern with school readiness. This is evident in the establishment of the Early Years Foundation Stage (DfE, 2023).

So, if we return to the point that we made at the start of this section we can see that ideas about how we might provide for children, particularly in the early years, can see free play-based, child-led settings at one end of a continuum moving to very structured, adult-led settings focused on learning and the achievement of identified outcomes at the other. This continuum can be characterised as a progressive or idealist position on the one hand, and an instrumentalist or vocationalist position on the other (Soler and Miller, 2003).

Note

A progressive position or idealism reflects child-centred approaches whereby children are understood to learn through play and where adults provide opportunities for children to play as they please. Goals, outcomes or targets are of little, if any, concern in this approach, with children seen as directing their own development at their own pace and where outcomes are fluid or more concerned with wellbeing.

Instrumentalism refers to an approach whereby provision, such as a nursery or school, is provided for a specific purpose with outcomes that are well defined.

Vocationalism follows from this with the provision being geared up to preparing children for work. Goals, outcomes and targets are central to instrumentalist approaches, with monitoring and testing being an essential part of the instrumentalist curriculum.

What this means is that a society may end up with a progressive model of Early Childhood Education, or an instrumentalist model or something at some point in the middle. This reflects how, within each society, supporters of each position get their ideas put into policy and legislation. In addition, ideas about children in each society shape the way that policy and legislation evolves. Ideas become real through the provision of services.

Student task

A good comparison as to how different approaches come to be established in practice can be seen by comparing the three different policy approaches in the UK, Italy and New Zealand: the UK's Early Years Foundation Stage, Italy's *Reggio Emilia* approach, and New Zealand's *Te Whāriki* (Moss et al, 2000; Soler and Miller, 2003; Wood and Hedges, 2016; Chicken, 2022).

Read up about each and try to identify how each reflects a different understanding of childhood.

It is not just policy that shapes how we teach. Sometimes research or scientific ideas become prominent and change how we see children and childhood. Currently, the dominance of ideas around developmentalism are being challenged by ideas emerging from the study of cognitive science (Powell, 2020). In turn these are being used to promote changes to how practitioners work with children. Powell also demonstrates the importance of being precise by noting that cognitive scientists are often critical of play as being in some way inefficient. However, in making this claim they generally mean free play, and a more independent learning experience, even though it would be very unusual to find proper free play in early years settings. Play in early years settings is very often based upon a scaffolded approach as discussed earlier. This reflects the idea that children are becomings, who have a specific purpose to develop in a particular way. As such, cognitive science falls into the more general utilitarian approach of seeing education as a process, something that we have criticised previously (Creasy, 2018).

It is also worth considering that the contrast between idealism and utilitarianism may result in pressure being experienced by practitioners within their everyday work. Although individual practitioners may express a preference for an idealist position, it is important to recognise that the demands made of service providers will influence the way that settings work. As such, targets and inspections act as forces which impact upon practitioners and often lead to what is referred to as performativity at work.

Performativity is another concept that is rooted within the work of Foucault. It encompasses the range of ways in which practitioners change their working behaviours so as to 'work to expectations' rather than working in a way that aligns to their values or their view of what is beneficial for children (Moyles, 2001; Chicken, 2022). This has resulted in what has been termed the schoolification of early years settings (Gunnarsdottir, 2014; Brogaard Clausen, 2015; Ring and O'Sullivan, 2018; Bradbury, 2019; Fisher, 2022).

Note

Schoolification is a term that has been coined to reflect changes within early years settings which involve a move towards a more formal approach of teaching children, reflecting what happens within schools, and in a way that facilitates measurement. It is strongly associated with neoliberal approaches towards achievement and accountability.

Concerns about how well children are doing in their compulsory education and formal examinations foregrounds failure and has led to policies that seek a solution to failures. The solution that has been sought by previous governments is a strong focus on getting children school-ready earlier and earlier.

School readiness is a contested term. It does not necessarily lead to improvements in educational outcomes at 16 years old.

So, when we said earlier that Early Childhood Education could be seen as a site of struggle and of tension, this sense of struggle and tension can be seen not only as a concern for individual settings but also for individual practitioners. For example, if a practitioner's own values are supportive of a focus on play but government policy emphasises learning and school readiness, how does a practitioner deal with this?

Think also, that in this way the idea that each child is unique becomes overshadowed by a need to ensure that all children within a setting achieve the targets that are laid down. This then brings us back to politics, in that the power of practitioners is often somewhat negligible with respect to resisting the policies that are introduced. Instead, it is the power of governments which leads to policies being introduced or revised. Crucially though, the interests and/or aims of government may not correspond to the interests and aims of practitioners (Basford, 2019). Similarly, parents have little power in relation to government policies or to how service providers operate.

Why do we educate children? Back to idealism or utilitarianism

At this point we have introduced the tensions that can be seen to be associated with developments in the early years sector, such as schoolification, and how this goes hand in hand with school readiness. We will say a little more about these ideas in this chapter as well as saying more about other concepts such as learnification and seeing contemporary education systems as though they were a process. It would be fair to state that compulsory education is the norm for children and young people around the world. As such, being required to be educated is a normal part of childhood, albeit with some differences relating to how this is provided, from what age or to what level. As we have indicated previously though, what education is provided and how it is provided is shaped by social and political forces.

In considering why and how we require children and young people to be educated reflects how we understand children, and this shapes provision. The most basic notion of all is that which is generally attributed to the philosopher John Locke (2000). This is usually referred to as *tabula rasa*, meaning empty slate. For Locke, children's minds at birth are empty and they require education in a broad sense to fill their minds. This includes establishing the type of knowledge that is required to enable children to function or operate within communities and society, but it also reflects moral understanding about good and evil, or right and wrong. Locke was not just thinking about academic knowledge, but about children learning about morals and social beliefs.

In one sense starting from the position of seeing children's minds as empty but requiring of filling is to adopt a position wherein education is seen as being focused on providing content rather than generating a child's interest. Taking this further involves not only considering what children should learn but also how they should learn it.

Note

It has been argued that education is so important that it must be seen as a right, as demonstrated in the UNCRC, but rights are never automatic and there have been times and societies when there has been no right to an education (Wrigley, 2009). At the time of writing, girls in Afghanistan have been prohibited from attending school. Be careful here though, when Wrigley says that at times there has been no right to an education, that does not mean that children and young people have not learnt anything. What is being referred to here is having access to formal education systems. We learn things informally all the time, as girls in Afghanistan will be doing.

As we have indicated earlier though, it is also the case that there are debates about both the value and the purposes of education. Alongside this we can also say that education has both an intrinsic and an extrinsic value. Intrinsic means within and extrinsic means without. So, the intrinsic value of education is the value or benefit to the person that is being educated. The extrinsic value is the value or benefit that society gets from having people who are educated.

Student task

Firstly, think about the idea that we also raised in Chapter 3, the idea that we can see education from two competing positions, idealism and utilitarianism.

Take a few minutes to consider what you think education should be for. Should education facilitate a child's development in a way that enables them to understand and participate in the world by providing them with critical understanding? If so, we should expect education to be challenging at times and to push individuals to do their best.

Or should education be focused on getting pupils and students simply to pass the courses they take and to be focused on providing them with an education to get a job? If so, we should teach to the test.

How you answer is likely to reflect your values. These are not right or wrong, but may be different from the authors.

To summarise, the idealist position considers that education has value in its own right and that it exists as a key element within the concept of personal development. The idealist position can be contrasted with a utilitarian approach towards education. From the utilitarian perspective, education exists to serve a purpose that is extrinsic, which means outside of each individual. The utilitarian approach is strongly linked with neoliberal ideas in that from the position of neoliberalism, education should be judged on the extent to which it contributes to the economy. This issue of contributing to the economy also reflects the idea of human capital theory. The basic premise of human capital theory is that individuals invest in their own education so as to maximise their income in later life (Hartog and Oosterbeek, 2007).

As an illustration though of how this is far from straightforward, consider the authors' own education. We both entered higher education as mature students and this education led to better-paid employment. So, we could be seen as supporting ideas of utilitarianism and our experience aligns to human capital theory. But it is not always so simple or straightforward. Income differences between a range of occupations demonstrates that human capital theory is not a strong argument. The benefits from education in respect of securing a higher income have been reducing over the past fifty years (Blacker, 2013). We also know that doing well at school, or not doing well, does not always correlate to the expected outcome of good jobs or unemployment. However, if the argument that the value of education in securing work, or better-paid employment as per the utilitarian approach, is no longer the case then we might argue that this just serves to reiterate the importance of education having value in its own right with respect to self-development, and that is just as valid.

Pause for reflection

Think about student fees in higher education for a moment and consider how these reflect the idea of intrinsic and extrinsic value.

A key argument put forward to support the introduction of student fees within the UK was about taxes. Why should taxes fund some young people getting a degree, which would mean that they would then be able to earn higher salaries in the future? As such, the person taking the degree will benefit so they should pay for their own higher education

The argument against student fees is that the economy needs highly educated workers, think about doctors, teachers, engineers; we all benefit from the fact that some people choose to study, and not charging fees means that anyone with the ability to study can do so.

Can you recognise the two positions, idealism and utilitarianism, here?

Some brief notes on neoliberalism and education

We said earlier that utilitarianism is strongly linked to neoliberalism and have mentioned neoliberalism a couple of times previously. It would be unusual to take a course on childhood and not encounter the argument that neoliberalism has had an impact upon children's lived experiences or that it has influenced the services that are provided for children and young people. Understanding neoliberalism is really important. Creasy and Corby (2023) provide a good account of neoliberalism but read some other books also; we like Roberts-Holmes and Moss (2021) for its focus on the early years sector. To summarise, neoliberalism is a political ideology which privileges private businesses operating within free markets. It is always critical of State-provided services. In respect of society, it promotes individualism, seeing inequalities as naturally occurring and rejecting arguments about social problems or inequalities that are said to be based on social categories such as class, gender or race.

However, although neoliberalism is strongly associated with utilitarian views on education, we have to be careful not to suggest that neoliberalism is the only driver behind the utilitarian view of education. Neoliberalism may promote the idea that education should be directed at securing work, but this approach clearly existed before neoliberalism.

For example, the tripartite system of education that was established by the Education Act 1944 reflected ideas about social class in the middle of the 20th century, and is clearly premised upon preparing children and young people for different kinds of work. This system provided different schools that aimed to prepare children for different types of work depending on their class as much as their abilities. Similarly, there are still many schools up and down the country which display carved stone signs for boys and girls. This rested on the notion that boys and girls required different types of education to prepare them for different roles as adults. Both these examples reflect utilitarian ideas. What can be said then, is that neoliberalism may promote a utilitarian approach, but neoliberalism is not the cause of it.

At the same time, we can see how neoliberalism also promotes two other ideas that are influential within the way that education has developed in recent decades. One is to impose free-market business practices onto public services. The second idea is that workers should be accountable.

At the heart of neoliberalism is the idea that businesses competing within free markets will always generate beneficial outcomes, though the problems resulting from the privatisation of services such as the water industry or railways within the UK demonstrate that this does not always work out well. The issue with respect to UK education is that the State has provided most education for a long time and it would be difficult for any government to privatise it.

The solution for neoliberal governments has been to create an education system that somehow reflects what happens within a free market by introducing some degree of competition and choice. For example, since 1988 parents have been encouraged to choose which school they want their children to go to based on exam results, among other things. This is sometimes referred to as a quasi-market (Le Grand and Bartlett, 1993; Bradley et al, 2000; Exley, 2014). The best way to understand the term 'quasi' is that it means resembling something, so education is provided similar to a business. So, a quasi-market in education is a way of understanding the education system as being like a free market in certain ways without actually being a free market. If education really operated in a free market, then parents would have to pay to send their children to school and college, and providers could charge whatever they liked. In addition, the product (education) would have to do what it claimed to do, or parents would ask for their money back!

Neoliberal reforms can be traced back to the Education Reform Act 1988. This changed education by introducing an element of competition between schools as a consequence of establishing the principle of choice, as mentioned earlier. The idea behind it is that parents will naturally want the best education for their children so will choose what appears to be the best performing school. However, for parents to be able to choose the school that is the best they need information. The information is generated by the introduction of standard assessment tests (SATs) alongside exams such as GCSEs and A-levels, which in turn provided for comparison such as in league tables. This reinforces the idea of competition. Crucially, it is important to say that not all children can attend the best school, there just isn't the capacity.

In colleges and universities, the Further and Higher Education Act 1992 marked the beginning of a more market-driven approach in post-16 education. This act removed sixth-form and further education colleges from Local Education Authority control and established them as independent businesses. The intention was that colleges and universities would compete for students and that this would drive up standards. In both colleges and universities things have changed, but not necessarily for the better (Creasy, 2018).

One consequence of these neoliberal reforms across education has been a much greater concern with student results as schools, colleges and universities have all sought to establish their value through demonstrating that they can ensure students pass exams and gain qualifications. The simplest way of establishing value is in terms of what pupils and students in each institution achieve, so it is not at all surprising that children and young people have become very aware of a growing pressure to succeed. This has certain consequences. One consequence is the increased stress that children and young people are subject to, another is that children and young people also become very focused upon the marks and grades that they receive alongside their parents. This is all premised on an idea that this will lead to a more successful and prosperous adulthood, which as we mentioned earlier is not necessarily the case.

From perfectionism to just being good enough

The development of a more competitive education system within the UK can be seen as generating two outcomes that are of interest to us here. Firstly, we would say it has contributed significantly to the rise in anxiety among children, in the context that anxiety is problematic for children rather than normal or acceptable; and secondly, this is argued to have led to a rise in perfectionism among children and their parents. We will say more about anxiety later in the book. In this section we will focus on perfectionism.

Having taught undergraduates for a long time one thing that seems to have increased significantly is our encounters with students who are very vocal in stating that they want a first. During our time as undergraduates in the 1980s and 90s, to be awarded a first was quite unusual; first-class marks were very hard to achieve and very few students graduated with first-class degrees. One aspect of this was pointed to earlier in that it could be that higher education, and society in general, was less competitive than it has come to be; we don't recall the same level of fixation on getting a first. It was recognised that to get a first was exceptional and only a small handful of students were exceptional.

We can draw upon discourse again here in the way that a widely accepted neoliberal discourse about competition does not just apply to the educational system, it also constructs a model of society for children and young people. Within this model, not being a high achiever is correlated with being restricted to a less successful life. One consequence of this discourse is that competition becomes normal for children. This creates individual pressures for children and young people regarding the educational results that they achieve.

On reflection, we think that this has led to a subtle change with respect to how education results or marks are seen. When we were students, getting a first-class mark for an assignment would have been seen as excellent, a real achievement; for very many of our students, not getting a first-class mark for an assignment is a personal failing that is difficult to overcome or rationalise. Sometimes it leads to defensive behaviours such as blaming the teaching, or it is seen as a mistake on the markers' part. This is where the idea of perfectionism becomes particularly relevant to education.

A simple reading of perfectionism is likely to see it being associated with doing one's best and being hardworking. In this way, perfectionism may be seen as a positive trait. From this perspective, perfectionism is certainly not something to be concerned about as being in any way problematic. A more accurate way of understanding perfectionism though is to see it as being multi-faceted and quite complex. As such, perfectionism can be nicely summed up as the combination of striving for high performance alongside high levels of self-criticism, together with a concern regarding being judged by others (Hayes and Turner, 2021; Handberg et al, 2022).

It is this striving for high performance alongside high levels of self-criticism which means that perfectionism can have a negative impact upon children and young people (Dickinson and Dickinson, 2015; Hayes and Turner, 2021). This can continue into adulthood. It is not necessarily that self-criticism will always lead to a sense of failure or of less worth, being self-critical can help us to improve. Problems arise in being unable to recognise or appreciate why we are receiving marks which are lower than we would want or why we are not able to do as well as we want to in some aspects of our education.

Note that we are considering perfectionism as being something that has resulted from an intensification of competition following from neoliberal policies changing educational experiences for children. However, Hayes and Turner (2021) suggest that competition and ideals in relation to what children need to achieve have led to changes in parental expectations and heightened concerns about their children's achievements. This is related to the development of helicopter parenting. The consequences of helicopter parenting have a major bearing on the development of perfectionism in children. This in turn may be seen as arising out of competition among parents.

Note

Helicopter parenting refers to a style of parenting where parents take a very active role in organising or managing the lives of their children. Helicopter parents are likely to intervene in their children's lives by making decisions for them and even contacting organisations such as universities and employers about their children with a view to achieving particular outcomes.

Although helicopter parenting is likely to have negative consequences for children (Creasy and Corby, 2019), it is important not to be deterministic, in that this form of intense parenting will not always create the same outcomes. Importantly, we should not see it as a characteristic of some parents, rather, helicopter parenting can be seen as a cultural phenomenon. Think back to the approach taken by Bronfenbrenner and recognise that this style of parenting does not take place within a vacuum. Helicopter parenting has emerged within a more general neoliberal discourse reinforcing the idea of a competitive world in which schools and other aspects of social life, such as fiction and dramas on TV or in the media, also promote the need for high achievement. When viewed alongside the ideas which have emerged in recent decades about being good parents it is possible to see helicopter parenting as having some sort of logic. Helicopter parents believe they are being good parents by being so heavily involved in their children's lives.

The focus on high achievement then creates a public discourse which will inevitably shape the child's lived world. In doing so it will influence ideas about how we should be and how we should live our lives. In this way we may start to see perfectionism as one aspect of a neoliberal world. Importantly, this is a world which promotes individual success as being a consequence of individual ability and explains social inequalities as the consequences of individual failings and/or poor choices. Any barrier to success, such as poverty or gender, is disregarded in this discourse.

In making the claim then that neoliberalism creates stressful environments for children and young people by intensifying competition and promoting high achievement as the only valid measure of success, we can return to a question that has been raised before; what sort of world would we want for our children, and is this it?

In considering a type of world that is more accommodating and/or more supportive of children, one response to a focus on perfection is a concern with being good enough. In drawing attention to being more accommodating we are mindful of two things. Firstly, that children may develop at different times, and secondly, that schools operate on the basis of a school year group comprising children born between 1 September and 31 August. There can be significant developmental differences between older and younger children who are grouped together in a school year group. This creates a situation where competition can strongly favour some children because they are significantly older than others, and therefore more capable. Six months can be very meaningful when it comes to young children. This can be seen as particularly important when we consider the early years and ideas such as school readiness; the idea that children should have reached a particular level of development before starting school.

The response to the increasing pressures that lead to perfectionism is the idea of being good enough (James and Oplatka, 2015). James and Oplatka offer a response to the claim that schools need to be constantly raising expectations and standards. On the face of it, raising standards and expectations seems quite reasonable, but raising standards is one of those seductive ideas which is difficult to argue against but is not as good an idea as it first seems.

The logical inference of constantly raising expectations and standards is that eventually a situation will be achieved wherein every school is perfect and every child is achieving the same high standard. The perfect school as described by James and Oplatka reflects a model of education as being a process, with the only goal being the achievement of qualifications; but qualifications as determined by the State that focus on particular types of knowledge and skills. They see this as both unachievable and undesirable. Instead, they draw upon the idea of good enough mothering to put forward the idea of the good enough school. The good enough school is not limited to the achievement of one particular outcome, which in the case of schools is the achievement of a particular educational award. Instead, as the child or pupil becomes more able the school backs off to provide space within which individual interests can develop, just as in the idea of good enough mothering, the mother (parent!) provides space for children to develop.

We think that this can be best understood as being a bit like the Zone of Proximal Development, as is found in Vygotsky's ideas about development, discussed earlier. In the space that is created by the parent/carer or the school pulling back, the child/pupil then has scope to become an individual and develop their own skills, abilities and interests.

Now let us repeat the question that we asked earlier regarding the type of world that we would want for our children. We often hear that all children should be valued. We agree, but we do not consider that all children are valued. But then again, neither are all adults, and the discourse of perfectionism actually works against this, especially at a subjective level. Remember that we said that perfectionism encompasses self-criticality, an ongoing process of self-reflection whereby we find fault with ourselves and constantly consider how we need to improve. A concern with critical self-reflection is now embedded in work for many people under the guise of reflective practice. Now consider the idea that the neoliberal approach to organising and providing education is one in which the chasing of perfectionism leaves workers such as teachers constantly feeling that they are just not good enough (Sturrock, 2022). If teachers are feeling that they are not good enough, how do we think children feel?

Kids need character

At this point it might be useful to have a brief discussion of how children deal with the situations that they are faced with, or how they approach the world, by offering a discussion of character. The phrase 'character building' has often been applied to experiences or situations that are in some way uncomfortable. In considering character though we will also consider families and resilience, before ending with how neoliberalism can be seen to have shaped more recent ideas relating to character. The family is relevant if we accept that it is the basic institution of human learning (Frydenberg, 2008), and neoliberalism is important when we consider that it has been of significant influence in terms of the culture in which families live.

The family is also important as being the place wherein culture is mediated, that is to say where culture is discussed and/or engaged with or rejected. This is where children learn to cope with the messages they receive from the world around them. As Frydenberg (2008: 107) states, 'The cultural context in which families are embedded determines how we learn to cope by determining what is perceived as effective coping.' For example, compare how different families may cope with stressful situations or even in respect of responding to upsets or happiness. This may differ from family to family and change over time and space.

Furedi (2001) and Guldberg (2009) draw attention to families where parents seek to do all they can to prevent children being upset alongside a more general approach towards eliminating all risks. Now consider what this does for children's development. Children need to experience some setbacks as part of their development. They have to experience setbacks and be able to put them in perspective, so while something might be distressing, in time we can recover or feel stronger and move on with life. As such, over-protective parents are not helping their children to develop if they avoid risks simply on the grounds that this may lead to upsets (Coleman and Hagell, 2007). If parents want their children to go on to live independent lives it is important that they experience some challenges and adversities when growing up so as to be able to do so.

Challenges may come from a range of experiences; for example, outdoor pursuits provide significant developmental opportunities, such as being away from home or doing something that is scary and risky, but mundane aspects of our lives can also throw up challenges (not being able to do an everyday task, for example, or being bored). The key point is that the parent who removes all disappointments from a child's life is impoverishing their child's experiences. How children experience the world is important, but as we have already suggested the place of children within society means that in general, children's experiences are shaped by others, by parents, teachers and other adults.

In terms of parenting, parents may hold ideas about how to raise children, but parenting is something that takes place within societies that hold cultural ideas. So, today, in the UK, and across much of the world, when we consider parenting it is usually accepted that children benefit from a warm, loving and supportive environment. We may also recognise that British attitudes towards children have changed significantly over time, with children playing much more central roles within families and being treated with more care.

Families who are unable to provide warmth and love are often castigated as uncaring, regardless of how they might provide in other ways for their children. In considering the relationship between parents and children then it is worth considering the parenting approaches that are often associated with the very wealthy, as this can often be seen to involve outsourcing their parenting to others. Texts about the boarding school system and the effects on children are not that common, but consider Duffell (2000). Duffell assesses how sending children as young as seven years old away from home into a very regimented and structured environment can have negative effects upon their social and emotional development, yet parents who send their children to boarding school often argue that it is for their benefit, and it is often portrayed in society as a desirable choice. The idea of character building is usually integral to this argument. This returns us to the idea that parents will have ideas about what they want their children to be like, and what they want them to achieve, even though sending children to boarding school can be seen to deviate from more generally accepted ideas about loving parents.

Previously we have argued that children are very often viewed as becomings rather than beings. From this perspective, children are seen as things to be worked on and developed with a view to producing a certain type of adult. This idea can be seen in the recent revival of the idea of character education. Character education has a long history (Arthur, 2019), but has come to the fore once again after a period when it seemed to have faded away. As such, character education within the 21st century 'has begun to encourage schools to promote virtues like perseverance, confidence, motivation, drive, neighbourliness, tolerance, honesty, and conscientiousness among children' (Kotzee, 2019: 436). It is maybe best understood as being an umbrella term for a type of education rather than something that is clear and unambiguous. As such, the traits seen as contributing to character education are numerous and contested. Some state very specific characteristics that should be taught to an individual and some ideas are much broader (McGrath et al, 2022).

Character education is yet another concept that can be criticised in regard to educating children. This is because it can lack focus or can be too focused on quite particular aspects of character because of an association with particular political ideologies. What can be seen then is that critics of character education do not always agree in terms of what is wrong with character education or may not always be focused on the same aspect of it (Peterson, 2020).

It has been argued that recent ideas about character education are underpinned by a neoliberal position, and that this can be juxtaposed with citizenship education (Hart, 2022). The idea of being juxtaposed represents a comparison of two opposing ideas or issues. As such, proponents of character education generally focus on the development or promotion of individual traits, whereas citizenship education emphasises social understanding or fitting into society. Hart's discussion of character education then illustrates how the neoliberal view of character education represents a very particular notion of childhood.

So, the neoliberal view of character education emphasises character traits such as working hard, being focused and applying oneself. This is within the context of a view of society which is intrinsically competitive. This reflects things that we have written about in *Children, Family and the State* (Creasy and Corby, 2023), such as explaining social inequalities as being the outcome of individual choices and the idea of motivation under the guise of 'wanting it'. The idea here is that if you are less successful in life it can be explained by the fact that you made poor choices and/or that you weren't motivated enough, you didn't want it enough. These are very weak ways of explaining social inequalities, suggesting that an individual can overcome obstacles laid down by the society in which they live, such as a lack of resources, easily. They also contribute to a victim blaming approach. A victim blaming approach explains someone's misfortune or deprivation by suggesting that they are at fault in some way rather than how social structures operate.

Note

Hart demonstrates that character education is not necessarily a neoliberal project. It is perfectly reasonable to develop character education approaches which have a strong social, community and moral basis. This approach is embedded within the Narnian Virtues project based within the University of Leeds. This project promotes character education through the lens of the Narnia books, such as *The Lion, the Witch, and the Wardrobe* written by C.S. Lewis.

There are numerous resources and video introductions to this approach online at https://narnianvirtues.leeds.ac.uk/. Similarly, consider the Jubilee Centre for Character and Virtues based at the University of Birmingham (online at https://www.jubileecentre.ac.uk/).

One thing that Hart does very well in his discussion of character education is in showing how concepts or issues can be influenced by a particular political perspective. Governments in the UK are able to do this by incorporating a particular version of it within regulatory bodies such as Ofsted.

The concept of character education can be used as an example of how ideas come to be seen as real. By this we mean that in one sense character education can appear as quite an abstract concept, something that is intangible, it only exists as an idea. However, it is made real when it is put into practice and/or when it comes to form part of a regulatory system. Bates (2019) demonstrates this by considering how three issues that are bound up with character education have come to form part of the approach taken by Ofsted: resilience, respect and responsibility. It became real when Ofsted started to require evidence of how a school is developing resilience, respect and responsibility. When a school knows it will be required to provide evidence it starts to change what teachers do, which changes the educational experience that pupils have. Once again though we have to ask just how resilience, respect and responsibility are being promoted, because as Bates argues, they tend to be defined in a very narrow way.

Is hard work enough? Introducing cruel optimism

If we return to neoliberalism for a moment we want you to think about the way in which neoliberalism places a lot of emphasis upon how individual hard work, and/or making the most of individual talents and abilities, is the route to future success. There are times however when the contemporary focus on neoliberalism may give the impression that neoliberalism suddenly introduced a range of new ideas when it was introduced to UK society by the first Thatcher government in 1979. That would be wrong. In fact, the prefix 'neo' in respect of neoliberalism indicates that this is a new version or a reworking of the sort of liberal ideas that had gone before. Neo, when used as a prefix, such as in neoliberalism or neofascism, always means a newer version.

So, although it is fair to say that the idea of hard work being the key to individual success is a key feature of neoliberalism, it would be wrong to say that it didn't exist before neoliberalism or that as an idea it is restricted to neoliberal thought. The idea of working hard so as to get on clearly predates neoliberalism. It is certainly something that children have heard for a very long time.

Once again though we might stop for a moment and think about how this idea, working hard to get on, is yet another seductive message. We do agree that there is a need to work hard, but we also have to recognise that this is not always sufficient in itself. Hard work does not always result in success. Think about previous types of society in which working hard was not sufficient in itself to get on. In some societies social structures have existed which meant that no matter how hard you worked you were never going to be successful or go all that far.

Student task

Put your historical heads on and think about the various ways in which previous societies were structured. Try to list the social structures which have been present in previous UK societies, or in other societies around the world, which meant that hard work was not enough. As a prompt, think about girls being forbidden to attend school in Afghanistan.

To do this think about social characteristics which may mean, or may have meant, that some types of people within society would always be held back or even discriminated against no matter how talented they were or how hard they worked.

In terms of how individual characteristics may have held people back, one example that springs to mind is the term 'the glass ceiling'. The glass ceiling is a term which reflects the barriers that women face to be successful. It is the idea that there is a ceiling that cannot be seen but which holds many women back from achieving as much as men do in the workplace. Consider also the ways in which some societies have restricted opportunities to people based upon skin colour. Similarly, you might consider restrictions based upon sexuality or disability. For example, within our lifetimes there are cases of male doctors being struck off the medical register during the 1960s and of the General Medical Council investigating doctors because of their sexuality as recently as the 1990s (Gregory, 2024). Sometimes, social structures may work against us. Even so, we still hear the message that we can overcome this if we work hard, which gives children hope to aspire to do great things.

This leads to the idea of cruel optimism. Cruel optimism has often been used in relation to those who work within education, such as teachers, but has some relevance to children themselves. So, when we talked about the neoliberal emphasis upon working hard to get on and be successful then this can be understood as reflecting optimism. We are encouraged to be optimistic that if we work hard, we will do well. Education systems clearly operate within a discourse of optimism. We have indicated already that we both entered higher education as mature students, and that we did so with the aim of improving our lives. As such it would be fair for readers to suggest that we were going along with the optimism that is often embedded within education. We accept this, even to the extent of saying that education should be optimistic, it can be life changing for some, sometimes.

But we also have to consider then where the cruel bit of cruel optimism fits in. The idea of cruel optimism was first put forward by Berlant (2011). It proposes that optimism is misplaced if society does not enable us to achieve what we desire while encouraging us to still desire it. It is a useful concept when we think about the ways in which neoliberalism has changed the social world.

Neoliberalism has done much to change the nature of working relationships in ways which have made workers weaker, which has then led to making them poorer. By making workers weaker, such as by reducing the power of trade unions, wages have been driven down for very many workers. At the same time the deregulation of work is a key part of neoliberal approaches to the economy. This has led to a major growth in insecure or precarious work; what is usually termed the gig economy. Think about this alongside the situation within the UK whereby young adults are increasingly finding it difficult to buy a house and have to rely on the private rental sector. In the UK the private rental sector differs from many other European countries by being very insecure.

So, children are being asked to work hard so as to get on in life, but the nature of jobs and the world of work is one wherein the rewards for hard work have diminished significantly (Blacker, 2013; 2019). As an example of this consider reports which have indicated that for adults born from the 1980s, so-called millennials, the thing that will constitute a major determinant of their economic position is not education, but instead will be inheritance (Bourquin et al, 2021; Gill, 2024). Note also that income from inheritance is neither worked for, nor taxed. As such, inheritance operates to reinforce existing social inequalities. The optimism presented in schools then is inevitably encountering the cruelty that can be said to be inherent within the neoliberal economy. The pressure to work hard is continually present as a form of individual self-improvement, which we may recognise in the term lifelong learning (Di Paolantonio, 2016), but at the same time the rewards of working have diminished.

The idea of cruel optimism can also be seen in ideas about parenting (Edwards et al, 2015) and the idea that parents need to actively engage with infants so as to ensure that children become sufficiently attached and to ensure that they achieve satisfactory neurological development. This does not seem too much to expect of parents. However, as Edwards et al (2015) argue, the pressure that is brought to bear on parents operates within a particularly neoliberal discourse in that the consequences of social class on children's future outcomes is ignored in favour of an individualist explanation which rests upon parental behaviours. Parents of children who do not do well at school are blamed for their children's poorer outcomes, rather than any other factors that affect children's education, such as lack of resources. The cruel optimism operating here reflects the more general ideas that were covered earlier regarding active parenting and learnification. The social inequalities that may be experienced by infants in their future is being presented as resting upon the behaviours of parents in the child's infancy.

Education: what is it good for?

To start to summarise this chapter it is important to state that there is no single way of viewing how or why we provide education, but it is the case that education is a normal part of childhood around the world. However, the way in which education is structured or organised, and the reasons that underpin this, reflect different ideas about what children need and how they learn. In turn this raises the issue of politics, because how we provide education, and indeed, what we provide, will always be the outcome of political struggles. This can be seen in the way that early years provision has become more concerned with learning and less concerned with providing care or opportunities to play.

Taking a step back then it can be seen that idealist views of what children need will promote free play and that this can be contrasted with utilitarian and vocationalist approaches in which provision for children is organised to provide a very structured approach, with particular outcomes being linked with children's futures. So, how children experience care or educational settings is never neutral, providers and practitioners are guided towards certain approaches, with certain outcomes in mind. In turn, this can create dissatisfaction for practitioners when their values are overshadowed by other values.

As we have previously stated, in the UK the provision of education has been subject to neoliberal reforms since the 1980s which have sought to impose a free-market type structure, often described as a business model, on to a State-provided service. It has done this through means such as giving schools more freedoms over who they enrol as pupils and creating competition through publishing exam results. Encouraging, and sometimes compelling, schools to leave local council control has been facilitated through promoting academy trusts. Again, academy trusts adopt business-type models to provide children's education.

What we have also tried to convey though is an understanding that the way in which education is provided and experienced has consequences for children and young people. We pointed to the rise in anxiety and discussed the idea of perfectionism to illustrate this. In considering perfectionism though we also introduced the idea that rather than being perfect, schools could be organised in such a way as to be termed good enough. The good enough school is one which provides more scope for children to develop individual interests, but it is an idea that requires a very different imagining of what schools should do.

If you are writing an assignment about educational issues and how education contributes to shaping contemporary childhood, covering some of the following points could be useful:

- How we provide education can be on a continuum with progressive or idealist ideas at one end and instrumentalist or vocationalist ideas at the other end.
- Neoliberalism has established quasi-markets within education and has done much to promote a process model of education which foregrounds outcomes.
- Performativity can be seen in how practitioners work in ways which reflect expectations.
- The move towards early years learning is often packaged as a concern with school readiness and is reflected in the terms learnification and schoolification.
- Educational experiences may combine with other experiences such as helicopter parenting to produce negative experiences such as perfectionism.

At the time of writing, neoliberalism has been very influential for over 45 years. Note that although neoliberalism has been presented as a key ideological influence upon education over recent decades, the election of a Labour government in 2024, together with some obvious failings in terms of neoliberalism, may result in a move away from neoliberal approaches. However, these approaches are very well embedded in our system of education, so to change them will take time. One key consequence of neoliberalism is that social inequalities have become wider, especially relating to income. As such we juxtaposed the idea that is often heard in schools about the need to work hard to get on with the fact that neoliberal policies have set out to make workers weaker and to reduce labour costs. This has seen a long-term decline in the value of wages as well as a rise in insecure work. Taken in this context, working hard is maybe not enough and this in itself can be seen to undermine the vocationalist arguments about education. Following from this it may be that in seeking to understand contemporary childhood we start to see that education has value for self-development and not just in terms of getting a job.

Further thoughts

If you work in an early years or an educational setting, do the aims of the setting always correspond with your values? If not, how do you reconcile this?

When you read about education or listen to discussions, can you recognise arguments reflecting either idealism or utilitarianism?

Think about the sort of education that you experienced. Can you see how the policies and practices that you experienced shaped your childhood and that your childhood would have been different if your experiences had been different? With this in mind you could explore ideas about alternatives to schooling.

Think about your own experiences of school. Consider if there is a fine line between encouragement to do better, which can be seen positively, and how this may have sometimes crossed into setting unachievable targets which can undermine self-esteem.

Further reading

Hart (2022) offers a good account of character education using Alasdair MacIntyre's ethics.

Biesta (2013) provides an excellent discussion of why we cannot treat education as a mechanical process. Similarly, Creasy (2018) provides a good account of how education across all levels has been changed.

Roberts-Holmes and Moss (2021) provide a good account of the relevance of neoliberalism to Early Childhood Education and Care.

5

How policy shapes the child's world

This chapter will help you to understand:
- some of the ways that children become the objects of policies;
- ways in which policy shapes the landscape of childhood;
- how concerns with policies can lead to children being overlooked.

Poor children in a rich country

We ended Chapter 4 by considering the way in which neoliberalism creates the conditions for cruel optimism in respect of how children are urged to work hard to get on in life, but where economic developments influenced by neoliberalism have made this harder to achieve. Consideration of social policy in relation to poverty and inequality will be provided in this chapter as it is relevant to understanding contemporary childhood, but for an extended discussion of inequalities and poverty in relation to life chances see Creasy and Corby (2023).

The history of social policy is rooted in attempts to alleviate poverty, and as such this chapter provides a brief discussion of the extent of poverty in relation to children, as well as some consideration as to how it is that in a country as rich as the UK almost 30 per cent of children live in poverty (JRF, 2024). In addition to considering poverty this chapter also considers some more general ways in which childhood is shaped by approaches to policy, with a particular focus on the way that contemporary approaches to policy lead to children often being viewed as data points.

Note

Poverty is generally understood from one of two positions: absolute or relative.

The premise of absolute poverty is that an individual or family does not have an income that is sufficient to cover basic needs such as housing, food and energy.

Relative poverty refers to having an income that is low relative to what is normal within any given society. This means that an individual or family is unable to live the sort of life that is expected within any given society.

The distinction between these two types of poverty is important because it means that it is possible to claim that there is no poverty within society by referring to absolute poverty while knowing that there are individuals and families who experience relative poverty. The welfare system within the UK does a lot to ensure that absolute poverty is prevented, but the widespread development of food banks across the UK during the 21st century indicates that it does still exist. Food banks could be presented as empirical evidence that some families are experiencing absolute poverty (Lambie-Mumford and Green, 2017; O'Hara, 2020; Williams and May, 2022). That does not mean that such evidence would always be acknowledged.

The issue of poverty within the UK is something that is contentious, with right-wing politicians in particular often suggesting that poverty is not a social problem. In making this claim it is typical to point to material possessions as evidence that people are not poor. With this in mind though it is worth noting that since the late 1980s it has become much easier to obtain what is often called credit. When we say credit, we are referring to the range of financial loans or facilities such as are provided by credit cards, bank loans, store provided loans and 'buy now, pay later' credit such as Klarna type schemes or facilities. Credit is important because of two consequences:

- many individuals are responsible for servicing and repaying significant amounts of debt;
- credit means that poverty can be hidden or obscured.

Credit means that poverty can be hidden because it can make it harder to identify the poor compared to how it was before the 1980s. It could also be said that it is now easier to give the impression of having a higher income than is the case. This is because it is now possible to access goods much more easily. The point is that we see the material things that others have, we do not see the debt that they are responsible for. In this way, poverty can be obscured or hidden.

One aspect of poverty that is particularly relevant is the way that politicians and the media often refer to child poverty. When thinking about poverty though note that as children are rarely permitted to work within the UK, they will rarely have an income and therefore we would expect that all children will be poor. Of course, we don't adopt this position when discussing child poverty, even though that is what the term child poverty suggests. Instead what we mean is that some children live in households that are deemed to be in poverty.

In this way, the financial position of children within UK society reflects the financial position of the adults that they live with. With this in mind, and noting that relative poverty is being referred to, both the Child Poverty Action Group (CPAG, 2023) and the Joseph Rowntree Foundation (JRF, 2024) note that 4.2 million children were living in poverty in the UK in 2021–22. This figure equates to 29 per cent of children. This means that in a classroom of 30 children, nine will be living in poverty. These figures come from UK government statistics, but be aware that there is always a choice being made regarding where to draw the poverty line. So, Organisation for Economic Co-operation and Development (OECD) figures draw the poverty line at 50 per cent of the median income and this presents the UK as having 11.9 per cent of children in poverty (Dyvik, 2023). The median is the mid-point figure. Median income is the income whereby there are as many employees being paid more than that figure as there are being paid below that figure. This way of determining poverty sets a lower standard of living as being not in poverty.

You might think that these are high numbers, especially as the UK is one of the richest countries in the world. However, poverty is not simply related to the overall wealth of a country. The issue to consider when it comes to children and childhood is inequality. Some poorer countries may have fewer children living in poverty, but this is because the UK is a very unequal country. So, poverty is not necessarily a feature of the overall wealth of any given country; poverty is best understood in terms of how wealth is distributed within a country. Dyvik (2023) provides a useful comparison of a large number of countries, with Finland being the OECD country with the fewest proportion of children experiencing poverty at 2.9 per cent. Finland is recognised as much more of an equal society.

Poverty is important. It is generally accepted that living in poverty is detrimental to a child's life, as well as to their future prospects in a number of ways, such as their health, their education and their more general opportunities among other things. It is not surprising then to find that some political parties have made claims that they will end, or reduce, child poverty. However, by this, they mean they need to end adult poverty as well, as children rely on adults. The way in which governments seek to alleviate or eradicate poverty is always through policy measures, and as policies change so the numbers experiencing poverty will change.

The Labour governments under Blair and Brown from 1997 did much to alleviate the effects of child poverty and to reduce it. A concern to end child poverty can be seen in the introduction by Gordon Brown's Labour government of the Child Poverty Act 2010. This act also introduces us to how it is that children may often be seen as data, in that one consequence of the Child Poverty Act was that all local authorities were required to report on the numbers of children experiencing poverty within that authority. They were also required to outline how the authority was working to reduce it and how they were providing for children who experienced it.

Child poverty did fall for a time as policies to reduce it started to have an effect, but cuts and restrictions, introduced initially by the Conservative-led coalition in 2010 and by subsequent Conservative governments since then, have seen child poverty rising. A change in social policies, such as in the provision of child and family services, moved the focus away from both children's lived experiences and from the issue of child poverty.

The Child Poverty Act is a useful example to consider how different political parties view society and can be used to shed some light on what they see as important. In the same year that the Labour government introduced the Child Poverty Act they were replaced by a coalition government led by the Conservatives, under David Cameron. A coalition government is a government that is formed by two or more political parties. It is unusual in the UK. Unsurprisingly, the change of government led to a changed approach to dealing with the issue of child poverty, as is illustrated by the requirements of the Welfare Reform and Work Act 2016.

Note

The Welfare Reform and Work Act was introduced by the Conservative government in 2016. It had two consequences in relation to child poverty:

- it scrapped legal targets relating to the reduction of child poverty;
- local authorities no longer had to establish poverty reduction strategies.

What is also important in the Welfare Reform and Work Act, however, is the way in which the discourse surrounding child poverty is changed as a consequence of retrospectively renaming the Child Poverty Act 2010 the Life Chances Act 2010.

In doing this the Conservative-led coalition government removed child poverty as a matter for political discussion.

There is a subtle shift of focus to be found within the Welfare Reform and Work Act 2016which reflects neoliberal ideas. For neoliberals, inequality can be seen as something that is essentially positive and natural, and where poverty is seen as just a fact of life. The neoliberal-influenced Conservative government that introduced this act shifted the focus from a concern with what poverty means for children and their childhood, and towards a concern with those children who might be at risk of experiencing poverty in respect of how they can escape poverty in the future, if they wish to (Calder, 2018; Dickerson and Popli, 2018). This reflects neoliberalism because the focus is, ostensibly, on supporting children to escape the poverty of their childhoods once they reach adulthood rather than reducing or even eradicating poverty.

In respect of poverty and inequalities within the UK, the Welfare Reform and Work Act shows how things can change over time. Concerns about poverty and inequality are always subject to change. It is important to recognise though that changes, especially policy changes, do not just happen. In respect of inequalities, governments have a big part to play in respect of how they make choices as part of their political decisions. Neoliberal policies were first introduced by Margaret Thatcher's governments from 1979. For Thatcher, Britain was becoming more equal, and this was not good (Dorey, 2015). To illustrate the problem that Thatcher was pointing to in terms of how Britain had become more equal, Dorey notes that 100 years ago, in the 1920s, the richest 5 per cent of the British population owned over 80 per cent of the total wealth of the country. However, this had fallen to a little under 52 per cent by 1973. At the same time, the poorest 80 per cent in the country saw their share of wealth rise from 6.4 per cent of the total in the late 1920s to 18.5 per cent of the total in 1970. The UK was becoming more equal.

> **Pause for reflection**
>
> What do these statistics mean in real life? If we round up or down a little, we can start to make sense of them.
>
> Imagine a seminar group of 20 students, each of whom requires a laptop. In the 1920s, one student possesses 16 laptops. They are the richest 5 per cent (5 per cent = 1 in 20). Because of increasing equality, by the 1970s this student now owns only ten laptops.
>
> In the same seminar group in the 1920s, 16 students had to share one laptop. They are the poorest 80 per cent (80 per cent of 20 = 16). By 1970 those 16 students had improved their position so much that they now had four laptops between them.
>
> For neoliberals such as Thatcher this growth in equality was not desirable. Consequently, since 1979 policies have been introduced which have had the effect of making society more unequal.

There have been a number of policy changes since 1979 which have reversed the moves towards more equality, and which have made the UK more unequal. The Joseph Rowntree Foundation illustrate how inequality has changed under different governments and with different prime ministers (JRF, 2024). One important approach has been to reduce the power of workers through weakening the power of trade unions. Trade unions have traditionally been able to improve working conditions, establish fair pay rates and secure paid annual leave. Without union support it is harder for workers to maintain the value of existing wages or to improve conditions. This can be evidenced in the way that the real value of wages have stagnated or fallen over recent decades. As indicated previously, for those children who aspire to, and work hard towards, gaining qualifications, the jobs they secure will not necessarily make them better off in the way that might be expected.

Another change that governments can make, and which impacts upon inequality, is to change the taxation system. As such, in the early days of Thatcher's government taxes were reduced for the richest people in the country while being raised for those that were poorer (Cronin and Radtke, 1987). This is one way in which hard-working students find they are not as well off as they expected to be. Alongside this the value of welfare payments or how they are paid has been changed so that people on low salaries, or who have disabilities, are less well supported by the State. Since 1979, individuals and families who have been supported through the benefits system have seen the value of benefits reduced or have had access to benefits restricted. The Conservative-led coalition government and subsequent Conservative governments from 2010 to 2024 also followed a neoliberal approach which involved significantly reducing funding for public services alongside reducing or cutting the benefits system. This approach was generally referred to as austerity (O'Hara and Thomas, 2014).

Neoliberalism always adopts a critical approach towards State benefits. Part of this criticism is the associated idea that being on benefits will inevitably mean being poor, and being poor is seen to be the fault of the individual. This affects children in the way that their parents are less supported through child-related benefits or other forms of support. Following this, a somewhat consistent theme in the last decade or two has been the idea of making work pay, irrespective of whether it is the Conservatives or Labour in power. From this perspective it is generally argued that individuals are responsible for working hard so as not to be in poverty and for their children not to be in poverty.

Importantly however, since 2011–12 the majority of people experiencing poverty have been in working families (MacInnes et al, 2013; Hick and Lanau, 2018; McBride et al, 2018). By 2023 over 70 per cent of children experiencing poverty were living in working families rather than in families relying solely on benefits (NCB, 2023). Low wages are the major factor for this, in spite of there being a national minimum wage (Hirsch, 2018). This minimum wage acts as a base line for wages, but it can be argued that it is not sufficiently high enough. This has seen moves towards what is called a 'living' wage; a wage that is set on the basis of what it may cost to provide the basics for living.

However, to focus on the value of the minimum wage is to overlook other factors that have an impact upon family finances. A more recent development relating to work and which contributes to in-work families experiencing poverty is the increase in precarious and insecure work, as characterised by zero hours contracts such as is typical of the gig economy (Gerrard, 2017; Gross et al, 2018; Choonara, 2019; MacDonald and Giazitzoglu, 2019). This should be seen alongside cases where workers have been required to be self-employed, as self-employment means that workers are denied benefits such as employment-related sick pay or pensions. Parents may have to choose this type of work to fit it around childcare and school times, which appears to be positive, but the precariousness of this work means these families are likely to experience poverty.

In seeking to understand contemporary childhood, then, it is important to take into account the way in which government policies may improve the situation for children and young people or make it worse, even when policies are not directly related to what children do or what is provided for children. As a consequence of changes introduced by the Conservative-led governments since 2010 the situation for poorer children and families was investigated by the United Nations in 2018. The UN report noted that,

> After years of progress, child poverty has been rising since 2011–2012, almost entirely in working families. The Equality and Human Rights

Commission forecasts that 1.5 million more children will fall into poverty between 2010 and 2021–2022, bringing the child poverty rate to a shocking 41 per cent. One in 10 girls in the United Kingdom has been unable to afford menstrual products, and many have missed school because of their period. Changes to benefits, and sanctions against parents, have unintended consequences on children and are driving the increase in child poverty. The Child Poverty Action Group found that Child Benefit will have lost 23 per cent of its real value between 2010 and 2020, due to sub-inflationary uprating and the current freeze. And low-paid jobs and stagnant wages have a direct effect on children, with families where two adults earn the minimum wage still falling 11 per cent short of the adequate income needed to raise a child. (Alston, 2019: 16)

Some ideas about policy and practice

Although we started by saying that the history of social policy was initially driven by concerns about poverty, it is important to note that policy is not restricted to poverty. Although poverty is very important in relation to children's lives, policy can also influence a much broader set of circumstances which shape the lived experience of children. For example, we said earlier that legislation which establishes age restrictions shapes what children can do and that this impacts upon the ideas that we have about what children should and should not do and how childhood is defined. So, the range of social policies that are in place at any given time can all shape childhood and our understanding of it because policies impact upon families, the environment in which children live and the services that are provided to families and children

You may recall that we previously used the school leaving age to demonstrate this because it distinguishes between those who are required to be in education, and therefore dependent upon others, and those who are able to be independent through working. The key point to start with then is that legislation and policy are influenced by the ideas that we hold about children and childhood, but once they are in place, they reinforce these ideas and become accepted as normal or the right thing, even as natural. Consider if a government suggested lowering the school leaving age to 14, say, because young people were required in the workplace. There is no natural reason why this could not happen, but it is unlikely to be seen as a good thing.

Note

You will often come across the idea of policy, sometimes referred to as social policy, in your studies. We have tended to refer to policy alongside legislation. It may be useful to have a basic definition for each, and of practice.

Legislation refers to laws that are in place. Legislation is introduced to compel some types of behaviour, such as being required to attend school. Not complying with legislation may result in penalties being imposed.

Policy refers to the formal approach to doing things, such as providing services. So, social policies refer to the government's approach to providing a range of social services. Similarly, organisations such as a local authority or a school, for example, may have their own policies about how they do things. Government policy may lead to legislation and organisational policy may follow from legislation.

Practice refers to how workers go about their duties or tasks. You may encounter the term 'in line with best practice'. This means that we expect workers to replicate ways of doing things that are generally agreed to be the best in terms of achieving particular aims.

As a simple summary, we could say that legislation will often establish what has to be done, policy formalises what will be done and practice refers to how it is done.

We could reasonably ask though why it is that governments take an interest in something. Why might a government want to introduce legislation or policy aimed at children? It used to be the case that parents decided what children could do or would do, and though parents still have some power in this regard, children have become the concern of governments for various reasons. Sometimes a concern with children is because of an initial concern with something else. So, if a government is concerned with the economic performance of the country – for example, the country may want to increase work relating to engineering – it might argue that a more educated workforce will provide economic benefits, and because of this it will seek to provide education for children and young people, in this example by encouraging children to study STEM subjects. Children are the workers of the future, and the country needs children to become the right sort of workers.

It is also worth noting that sometimes the links between concerns and policy are not so obvious. A government's approach towards providing services to improve children's health may appear to be rooted within a concern for children in themselves, but could be understood as being rooted within concerns about something else. This is evident in the case of national defence and military policies in the past. During the Boer War at the start of the 20th century, and, to an extent, the First and Second World Wars, the illness and disability that resulted from poverty was highlighted as resulting in large numbers of people being unfit for armed service (Billingham et al, 1996; Glasper, 2011; Hanvey, 2019). As a result the government became concerned with children's circumstances. This underpinned the development of contemporary services which are provided for children.

Concerns about poverty and public health around the late 19th century were often focused on the unsanitary living conditions endured by the urban poor. In turn, this can be seen to have led to the development of the role of lady sanitary worker, a public role which developed to become the health visitor, a role that is very influential to this day. The intentions of the government at the time can be seen in how the health visitor role began with an ambition to change parenting practices with a view to improving children's health (Billingham et al, 1996; Peckover, 2013). When we try to make sense of why this policy approach was developed, though, we can see that it is likely to be less a concern for children and more a concern that the country had healthy workers and soldiers. There have been significant points in history when governments were made aware of the needs of children or how childhood was lived because of some obvious deficit or problem displayed by adults. This has contributed to the growing concern about childhood, as mentioned earlier.

When considering the examples given here, it is clear that a government's concern with something does not necessarily mean that the legislation or policy that follows will be obvious. Although a need may be identified, in this case improving children's and thus adults' health, how to meet that need is going to be subject to a range of issues which often rest upon how the government of the day views society and therefore what provision they see as appropriate. This is also affected by how views change, about what society needs, what is effective and what research tells us, as these will influence policy.

So, childcare practice has changed over time, often as a consequence of new ways of understanding children. These changes may result from research that takes a particular theoretical view of children, for example about how play is beneficial for children, but they may also represent wider social changes regarding children and what is seen as being beneficial for them. As social ideas change, often influenced by economic and cultural change, such as the current ideas about school readiness, this feeds into legislation and policy and changes how we treat children.

In a broad sense, then, legislation and policy not only rest upon the particular notions of childhood that exist at the time, they also come to shape childhood in a number of ways and what we come to expect, or see as normal. As such, notions of what a child should and should not be doing in terms of work, education, play or leisure time, or at what age a child should or should not be taking part in certain activities, as well as how parents should be caring for their children, all come to be embedded within policy and legislation.

That is not to say that legislation sets down absolutes for childhood. The nature of childhood may still be contested, laws may change or be broken and children or parents may resist, reject or ignore what they are advised to do. An example of this is attitudes to education. At the time of writing there is a growing concern that parents are becoming less concerned about their children regularly attending school, with some being happy to sanction absence. In respect of taking a critical approach though we can see that sometimes policy and practice becomes distorted in a way that is less beneficial for children. This idea is central to the next section where we consider how recent governments have emphasised a need for service providers to meet targets and how this takes place alongside governments seeking to demonstrate their achievements. What this has led to is a shift of focus away from seeing children as individuals and a move towards a focus on data.

Children as data

In this section we focus upon the idea that social policies are managed and monitored by organisations, regulatory bodies and governments, and that this shapes a different notion of childhood. By this we mean that policies are not simply put in place, they are monitored to see what effect they are having. This generates the need for information about the success or otherwise of the policy and this information can be best understood as data. Note that sometimes data are referred to by the term metrics. To be accurate, metrics refers to the approach which uses data. We will stick to the term data. Following from this we can say that policies aimed at children often consider children in respect of their future, which means seeing children as becomings, but with a focus not on what they may become per se, but rather, on the progress that they have made along the way (Archard, 2015).

In one sense it seems normal to want to know things about a child's progress. For example, in health terms we may want to know that an infant is developing in ways that are expected, even before birth (Lupton and Williamson, 2017). This could be because any significant deviation may indicate that medical intervention could be needed. At school, we may want to know how well a child is doing in terms of their education, as this could indicate the need for additional support.

It is hard to say that these things are not at all reasonable things to monitor, and data provide the evidence for that. However, the manner in which data are generated and used with respect to children can be seen as moving away from the idea of the child as being unique, something that is often presented in policy or documentation relating to children such as the early years foundation stage (EYFS). Moving away from seeing each child as unique can happen when social institutions adopt a data-driven approach and turn their focus towards the data rather than the child. This is becoming a central feature of education systems (Thoutenhoofd, 2018).

However, there are social implications which result from shifting the focus from what children do, or are, onto data (Roberts-Holmes, 2015; Roberts-Holmes and Bradbury, 2016a, 2016b; Stevenson, 2017). Underpinning this shift of focus is the idea of outcomes. Data-driven approaches to providing education within the UK during the early 21st century are often associated with a concern about outcomes, where outcomes are specifically about passing tests or gaining qualifications. This has had an impact upon what schools do and how they do it.

Evidence of a concern with outcomes within the UK education system can be identified in claims regarding potential and/or added value. This is where children are identified as having potential to achieve educationally or not, and the school then can evidence that children have achieved their potential, or even better, achieved more than their potential (added value). One reason for this is that education has come to be dominated by an approach in which it is seen as a process (Creasy, 2018). Achievement underpins the process. This represents the outcome especially where achievement is demonstrated in qualifications. This makes sense if we accept that any process will inevitably have an outcome, but it is a different model of education compared to seeing education in relation to self-development and/or personal growth as per the discussions in Chapter 4.

Following from this, situations can be identified where children are subject to actions which constitute them as data points, rather than as unique individuals who may have other skills or attributes. As children come to be identified or represented as data, it is possible to see how this often serves to justify actions being taken towards the child, such as being separated into school bands which reflect ability as indicated by previous educational achievements (Neumann, 2021). In turn, such actions contribute to the development of a sense of capability or position relative to other children. School bands, or sets, may influence not only what children think of themselves (whether they are clever or not) but how teachers determine the ability of the child, regardless of other factors, such as late development.

A concern with data is central to recent developments in respect of computing and data analysis that has led to the introduction of so-called learning analytics (Clow, 2013). This implies the analysis of learning and suggests that collecting and using data is essential to optimising teaching. However, although learning analytics systems may generate significant amounts of data about pupils and students they often lack a clear understanding of what learning is (Wilson et al, 2017). Data may indicate information about activities and results, but such systems are unlikely in themselves to offer useful guidance to children and young people. Instead, learning analytics rest upon certain assumptions being made about the nature of teaching and assessment (Knight and Buckingham Shum, 2017), which look back at the educational process. This is often in a superficial way and simply reinforces a focus on data. Importantly though, learning analytics contribute to an individualised understanding of education which undermines or negates the reality that most educational experiences are social in nature (Brooks and Timms, 2024). Learning is not a simple and smooth process that is done step by step, and it does not follow a specific course dependent on what has already happened.

What developments such as learning analytics really do then is act to foreground data, rather than learning, and the experience of individual children. As such, they should be understood alongside the growth of apps associated with devices such as smartphones and smartwatches that generate data for the individual. This has made data a key aspect of many children's lives and created childhoods that are constantly being measured and assessed. In turn this contributes to the normalising of self-tracking (Lupton, 2016). Self-tracking will be seen to be pertinent when we consider the concept of governmentality later, so keep this idea in mind. In turn, as the development and use of technologies that make it easier to generate data become more accessible, the subsequent growth of data generation impacts upon the way that we see children. This comes to act as another factor in the way that childhood has changed when compared to previous generations. It also reinforces the idea that what a child might be in the future is determined at an early stage in their life.

Pause for reflection

Thinking about self-tracking, have you ever found that data about you influences how you have approached education? Have teachers ever provided you with data regarding your performance and outlined what an improvement in performance may mean for your outcomes?

Do you possess a device such as a smartwatch that you use to provide data about your everyday life, and then find that you are constantly seeking to meet goals?

Is the data a distraction or does it help? If so, how does data help in forming your ideas about yourself and your own abilities?

Competition and datafication

It is fair to say then that data now plays a very significant role in all our lives (Beer, 2016; Lupton, 2016) to the extent that it is reasonable to talk about the datafication of society (Beer, 2016). We may also consider that data intensify the competition that has often been implicit in education. In assessing why datafication has grown in the way it has it is worth revisiting the political context. As has been established, UK politics has been strongly influenced by neoliberalism for over 45 years now and this has seen governments increasingly seek to replicate business models and/or practices in all areas of social life. This reinforces the view of children's education as a process with an emphasis on outcomes, as was suggested earlier.

Importantly, in a system of datafication, it is the data, not the child, that take precedence. It is data that dominate how we relate to and provide for children. So, on a simple level, data may be presented as being a tool to support individual children but in practice the focus on the child is lost. Within a data-driven environment and where children's education comes to be viewed as a process it is easy for an organisation to lose sight of children. Instead, in this process, the only real thing of importance is the producing of results (Roberts-Holmes and Bradbury, 2016a; 2016b). An example of this is when a school or college focuses upon getting pupils or students from an expected grade 3 GCSE up to grade 4. As grade 4 is deemed to be a standard pass it benefits a school or college to get as many candidates as possible up to this standard because educational institutions are often understood in terms of how they perform compared to others.

It is not difficult to see how it is that within an education system that promotes competition, the achievements of children acts as a de facto measure of the quality of a school, college or university! Consider for example the way in which grammar schools in England are held up as being superior to other schools because of the results that are achieved by their pupils. This should not be surprising when they operate an admissions system which only admits children who were performing better than others at age 11. Similarly, consider how some universities within England are talked about as good universities. When we scrutinise what it is that makes these good universities, or why grammar schools are presented as good schools, we find that in both cases they are highly selective in terms of which pupils or students they admit.

> **Pause for reflection**
>
> Think of it in terms of football teams. If Sheffield Wednesday were able to buy the world's best players, it is reasonable to assume that they would be the best performing team in England because their players were better than players at other clubs. Unfortunately, they do not have the finances to do this, so currently they aren't England's top team, though some of us live in hope.
>
> Universities do not buy students, but they can limit student entry to those students who performed the best in A levels, just as grammar schools restrict entry to those children who perform better at age 11. We should not be surprised then that selective practices by educational institutions appear to produce the best results.

In thinking about the attention that is often given to children's academic performance, we can see the basis of an understanding of how it is that children start to be categorised, with some children being seen positively, and others less so. Categories are numerous within education. They act upon children in a way that shapes how children understand themselves. For example, a 21st century form of categorisation is evident in the Young Gifted & Talented scheme that was introduced to UK schools in 2002. The idea behind the Young Gifted & Talented programme was that it would benefit the most able (Stewart, 2006; Koshy et al, 2012) within a general context of promoting social mobility among pupils from poorer backgrounds (Casey and Koshy, 2013).

There was also an intention to change the behaviour or attitudes of some teachers so as to counter concerns that some teachers had low expectations of children due to their background, or the place in which the school operated (Radnor et al, 2007). Note that the term 'gifted and talented' is no longer encouraged and has faded away. Instead the preferred term when referring to higher achieving pupils is the most able. Data are argued to be necessary to identify the most able.

> **Pause for reflection**
>
> Some children may have been looked upon more favourably by being deemed to be gifted and talented, but there is inevitably a flip side to this. Consider for one moment that in the

discourse of gifted and talented, some children may subsequently end up being viewed as not only less able but not having any gifts or talents.

Might some schools consider these children as undesirable if the expectation is that these children are less likely to do well within the education system and be less likely to generate positive data? In this case schools that can 'select', such as grammar schools, are likely to not offer these children a place.

With that in mind we might question what the consequences of datafication are for those children with SEND, behavioural or emotional challenges or for the child whose educational success may be held back because of their home life. Are all these children lacking in talent?

It is fair to say at this point that we hold reservations about the growth of data, or metrics, within a range of children's services, including education. In the most basic sense this is because metrics often see children being viewed in a manner that removes the child from any consideration of the context, especially where the context ends up being understood as predictive. Bear in mind that the idea of what we know about children (data) being used by teachers to predict performance is nothing new. It was summed up in a classic study by Rist (2000) in 1970, showing how in one school children's family backgrounds were used to band children. The 2000 reprint is useful in including Rist's comments regarding how race and class may each be drawn upon to make predictions. The generation and analysis of data using computer systems simply moves this forward.

How the idea of governmentality makes sense of contemporary childhood

One thing that should be recognised is that children are best understood as being both socially situated and socially constituted. Now that sounds a little deep and meaningful so we need to be clear what we mean by this, which should also indicate why it is relevant and important. When we say socially situated, we are saying that children exist within particular social structures (as exemplified by Bronfenbrenner). So, on one level we can recognise children as pupils within a school, or even as learners as they have recently come to be called. At another level however we can also understand children by their place and performance within the structure that is the school. A key point here is that we are not referring to any one particular school. School exists as a recognisable social structure within our society, but other factors shape how children perform in the school and the experience they have.

There is a useful point to recognise here in that even when they do not attend school, as increasing numbers of children seem to, children are still understood in terms of their relationship to school. Those that don't attend school are still school children, but they are non-attenders. As such, the label 'non-attender' demonstrates that the social institution of the school exerts a very significant pressure in terms of how we understand children and their social role within society.

The ways in which children are situated within school can be seen then both in terms of the schools that they attend, as was indicated earlier, and in other ways which reflect how schools organise children. This reflects internal policies and although these may be similar, schools can have different approaches that reflect their values, focus and situation within their community. The key thing here is that children are organised in ways that go beyond issues concerning education.

We commented earlier on how schools organise pupils into academic bands, but Pike (2008) assesses how schools often organise children in ways which reflect the source of meals to be eaten on the school premises. So, in many schools, children are separated on the grounds that some eat a lunchtime meal provided by the school whereas others bring their own packed lunch. Some children will have their lunch provided free of charge. In this way school lunches, or dinners, come to construct meanings which go beyond the mere eating of food. This is because policy contributes to a particular understanding of each child.

Our experience

When Creasy was at secondary school, children would buy school dinner tickets from the teacher during Monday morning registration. However, those children, such as himself, who received free school dinners were required to queue up at the school office during Monday morning break to be given dinner tickets.

These dinner tickets were all stamped on the reverse with the term 'free'. Now think about how being in receipt of free school dinners has meaning in contemporary society and how it might operate as a marker of need that shapes how the school staff see and treat the child, but also how the child understands their own identity.

What purpose is served by stamping 'free' on a school dinner ticket?

So, if we are saying that children are socially situated in terms of where they fit within society, we now want you to think about how it is that our understanding of children is constituted; how it is made and shaped, within the range of socially organised provisions that we make for them. In this way, the child does not exist as a natural being, they cannot, because children are constantly being shaped in ways which create a particular type of child, and this depends on the social world in which they live.

Smith (2014) argues that governments are concerned with how children are constituted, how they come to be a particular type of child. One reason for this, as has been said, is a concern with the child's later role and contribution to society as an adult. Ideally then governments desire children, and later adults, who can be said to be self-regulating, or self-governing, and can function in the society in which they live without encountering or, importantly, causing problems. Following from this, and in making sense of how the child is constituted within society it is useful to draw upon Foucault's concept of governmentality (Sonu and Benson, 2016).

Note

Foucault provides a number of theoretical approaches that are useful for making sense of childhood. Governmentality is one of them.

Governmentality refers to the way that we accept and internalise systems that are set up, such as Ofsted inspections, and see them as natural or normal. The concept of governmentality can be used to analyse aspects of social life and to explain how power is exercised over a specified population, where individuals internalise the aims of those bodies that have power, usually without question (Dean, 2010; Smith, 2012; Sonu and Benson, 2016).

This links to the term bio/power in Foucault's work in that it is concerned with power over the biological. By this Foucault means that the population accepts the rules set by those in power as if it is the natural way one would go about living their lives.

Foucault develops the concept from the starting point of how governments think about and seek to exert some power and control over the population. Governmentality helps us to analyse the influence of the varying discourses which act upon us, allowing us to identify ways of behaving that are shaped by policy and legislation. However, governmentality is not referring simply to the actions of the government. Instead, governmentality is exercised by a range of social authorities or institutions, churches, schools and even businesses, which employ different forms of technology with the aim of achieving particular results. These results rely on a form of self-policing (Bennett, 2003; Miller and Rose, 2007; Elliott, 2009; Powell, 2014).

It is important to understand technology, as referred to here, in a broad sense in relation to this concept. Technology when used within Foucault's approach is not confined to machines. It can also be seen as bureaucratic or administrative processes that encourage compliance with policy, laws and other rules. This applies to adults but to children as well who, from an early age, begin to understand what they are expected to do, how they are expected to behave and what they may expect to become as adults.

In this way a rational and planned approach to governing populations is embedded within the discourses that are shaped by authoritative bodies such as professional groups and this comes to regulate how populations conduct themselves. Importantly though, when populations internalise these discourses then the need to exercise actual physical power is rare (Smith, 2012). It can be argued that no one forces us to go along with policies. A good example of this is school uniform, for which there is no law or national policy which states that school children must wear uniform. Schools which require pupils to wear a uniform however will have ways of ensuring compliance and many adults accept arguments which promote uniforms without any evidence of their value. Note that when we refer to populations in this context it may simply be the population of a school or a workplace, children or adults.

As an example of this think about how what is deemed to be valid learning is established by institutions that are directed by the government through policies such as the national curriculum. It is then necessary to ensure that teachers in schools teach to this definition of valid learning rather than getting distracted by pupils' interests or in terms of other interesting issues. To keep teachers focused, pressure is brought to bear on them in an indirect manner by considering pupils' results within the public testing or examination system together with management strategies such as performance reviews.

Alongside this testing system, regulatory bodies such as Ofsted have oversight into what teachers and schools do. Teachers are not free to do just anything. The pressure to achieve results alongside pressures regarding how to achieve results sees teachers internalising the general direction of the system. Pupils find themselves being characterised in terms of the expected grades that they will receive, with school staff often directing attention on those pupils who are just below an acceptable grade band in order to push them higher so that the data are 'better'. Teachers fall into line with the systems through internalising the discourse of what is understood as successful outcomes, or what the ideal pupil looks like.

Of course, pupils and students fall into line also, often with the encouragement of their parents. Think about your own assignment tasks. Over the previous 20 to 30 years almost all universities fell in line with a move towards seeing education as an outcomes-based process. This created a system whereby what was important was the result rather than the experience of learning (Creasy, 2018). This can be evidenced in the adoption of a learning outcomes approach to assessment where learning outcomes relating to assignments were presented to students as part of the assignment brief. Students would then be advised to write to the learning outcomes because not meeting the learning outcomes would be grounds for failing. The problem is that regardless of what you have learnt or what you know, only the information relating to the learning outcomes becomes relevant.

In this case the system of learning outcomes represents the technology that exerts power. Of course, it may be the case that you are not given learning outcomes; some universities are, thankfully, moving away from this approach as it is problematic (Creasy, 2018). However, when we have argued that learning outcomes are a tool for planning teaching rather than assessing student achievements, we have encountered resistance from teaching staff who have internalised this approach and who ask how assessment can be undertaken without learning outcomes. Governmentality!

To bring the discussion back to children, think about the numerous ways in which power is exercised by different authorities or institutions, by professionals and practitioners, in ways which shape what it means to be a child within any given society. Consider the ways in which parents are drawn into discourses regarding what it means to be a good parent. Again, one example is the emergence of a focus on learning or development. Have a look at children's toys and note just how many list the learning or developmental benefits of toys compared to how many toys are marketed as simply being fun. Another example is the way that homework logs can be seen as a technology by which the aims of the school enter the home. Parents may then experience pressure to engage with learning or homework logs to the extent that some schools insist that parents sign homework logs when no homework has been set. This reflects a system in which homework operates to promote self-regulation of not only the child/pupil but the parents (Ramdass and Zimmerman, 2011).

This idea of self-regulation can be seen as the key outcome with respect to governmentality. Simply put, it is the way in which society requires us to behave that means we don't create problems for others. Governmentality encompasses a wide range of forces which act upon populations and where individuals develop their sense of self. So, through the actions of these forms of power being exercised on children, children come to understand who they are.

Does policy matter?

In our teaching about children and childhood, students often raise questions relating to what policy is and why it matters. It matters because the range of policies that are in place at any given time will act to shape our experiences; often though we are unaware of what is shaped by policy or whether we must go along with it. In this chapter we have taken a broad approach to policy with the aim of illustrating what it is that influences policy and also how policy can not only impact upon how children come to be seen, but importantly how children start to see themselves. The relevance for the typical reader is that assignments will often ask you to write about the sorts of things which shape childhood. Policy is one of those things. With that in mind, maybe the best way for you to understand policy is to start with the idea that policy operates as a sort of framework which shapes three things:

- how practitioners and parents treat and deal with children;
- what is required of children;
- what is restricted in relation to children.

The relevance for your assignments is that these three points combine in different ways to shape how children experience their childhoods. Note also though that the policy landscape is dynamic. It may change as social ideas about children and childhood change. In turn, social ideas about children and childhood are influenced by political ideas. So, this chapter took a fairly straightforward idea at first by considering poverty. This is because policies come about when there is a feeling that something should be done about some aspect of society because it is a problem, not for the individual particularly, but for society. At a national level, poverty is often considered to be an issue that should be tackled. This is particularly the case when poverty is presented as 'child poverty'.

As many studies demonstrate that experiencing poverty in childhood is detrimental for children there are often calls to address this and to lift children out of poverty. It is at this point though that political ideologies and perspectives come into play, and this is something that you have to come to terms with. Political parties, and supporters of those political parties, hold particular views about how society is and how it should be and therefore how poverty should be addressed. Because of this they approach policy making in different ways.

For example, we drew a distinction between absolute poverty and relative poverty. This distinction is important because when you read arguments stating that there is no poverty within the UK this tends to be referring to absolute poverty; in other words, that everyone has a basic standard of living and that we can all afford the basics. This is disputed, but where individuals or families are said not to have the basics then an explanation usually refers to the idea that this is because of some personal failing in respect of budgeting or behaviours of the parents. So, as a student, when you read arguments which make a claim about something such as poverty it is important for you to identify which position the speaker or writer is adopting.

In general, then, it is hard to state that there is no poverty within the UK, but how we each understand what this means has to be seen as reflecting our political philosophy. It is generally agreed that poverty can be a negative factor within children's lives, yet around one third of children within the UK experience poverty. This is striking because the UK is one of the richest countries in the world, which demonstrates that the wealth of any country is of less significance than how wealth is distributed. The key thing following from this is that addressing poverty is a political concern.

In considering poverty our aim was to explore how we might view social issues. However, once policies are put into place to address social issues then we can also recognise that policy can influence practice in a way that changes how we see individuals. So, when policies that relate to children are established it can be seen that this may change the way that we see children. This may even result in children becoming overlooked or even blamed for their circumstances. For example, children who do not do well in school may be seen as lazy or badly behaved. One aspect of this that we have tried to get across within this chapter is the way in which individuals or organisations that are involved in policy making can be so concerned with the policy itself that sometimes children are overlooked. This is evident within the idea that children have become subject to a process of datafication. We are not claiming that individuals or organisations set out to see children as data. Instead, it is important to consider that data are a tool by which policies can be assessed and judged and that a focus on data comes about when there are pressures to demonstrate the value of a policy, such as how pupil premium is measured.

When it comes to assignments you may not be asked to produce anything that ties in specifically to the examples that we have used, so we want you to take these examples as illustrating how policy can impact upon our lives in general. As a general approach, then, think about the following points as reflecting the basics of policy and how policy shapes lives:

- Legislation establishes what has to be done, policy formalises what will be done and practice refers to how it is done.
- Policies are shaped by social and political ideas.
- Datafication refers to how data about what children do seems to take precedence over the children themselves.
- Organisations such as schools may enact local policies which shape the child's lived experiences.
- Children are socially situated and constituted within the landscape of policies that are in place.
- Governmentality reflects the internalisation of the power that is exercised over individuals by governments or organisations. It is evident in how practitioners work towards regulatory structures.

Further thoughts

Consider the growth in the number of food banks across the UK since the early 2000s. Is this a positive social response in supporting the poor, or is the need for food banks evidence that both the welfare system and the jobs market is failing? Why might people who have jobs still need to use food banks?

With respect to child poverty, consider the benefits of policies that focus on the child, such as pupil premium or free school meals, and those that focus on the family, such as a living wage or other monetary benefits that might lift the whole family out of poverty. Which would you favour, and why?

Think about the way children are recorded as 'data' in school. If you work in an early years setting or a school, think about the extent that data are used and shared in your institution. How does this shape the childhood experience of school for the pupils?

Further reading

Dorey (2015) is good for illustrating the ideas behind the neoliberal policies that have been introduced since 1980. Follow this with Albertson and Stepney (2020) and Larner (2000).

O'Hara (2020) provides a good account of what contemporary poverty means and the discourses around it.

For any assignments which involve some consideration of social issues such as inequality, the Joseph Rowntree Foundation website will be a useful resource. We suggest having a look at this and reading one or two articles about child poverty. There is a section on child poverty at https://www.jrf.org.uk/child-poverty.

Roberts-Holmes and Bradbury (2016a; 2016b) provide an insight into how datafication impacts upon early years settings and apply this to the concept of governmentality. In doing so they demonstrate how theory such as neoliberalism and Foucault have a place in understanding contemporary childhood.

6

The landscape of childhood, or knowing and telling the truth

This chapter will help you to understand:
- some of the ways in which children understand their world;
- some of the ways in which we might come to know how children understand their world;
- the relevance of modernity and post-modernity in relation to truth/s and post-truth;
- issues related to culture wars and being woke.

The changing habitat of the common, or garden, child

If we want to make sense of contemporary childhood, it is worth thinking about what children's lives are like. In Chapter 3 we asked you to make notes regarding your ideas about childhood. If you did this then it may be useful to have another look at what you wrote. We have undertaken this exercise lots of times with students and one thing that crops up a lot is the idea that not only is childhood a time for play, but that a key part of playing reflects the idea that childhood is a time of freedom. That may be so to an extent, but we want to suggest that the landscape of childhood has changed and that older people such as us – we were children during the 1960s and 1970s – had more freedom. Importantly though we need to ask, freedom from what, or to do what?

Pause for reflection

Just for a few minutes we want you to be David Attenborough or Chris Packham or anyone else you can think of who looks at wildlife in the natural environment. If you were wanting to observe children and young people, where would you look for them? Where do they roam, where do they congregate? Where do we find them without adults?

Make a list of these places.

Now make a list of the age you were when you went places on your own or with friends, such as to the local shop, a park or playground, to a youth club, to the nearest town, to sports events, to see a band and so on. We mean that you made your own way there, not that parents transported you.

We are confident that if we were to make such a list our list would show that we did things on our own at a younger age and that in regard to going places we were self-reliant at a younger age. Self-reliance is something we will consider later.

Having freedom, something which we consider children do have, is an important discussion point in terms of understanding contemporary childhood. By freedom we tend to mean not having worries or responsibilities, but also being able to do what we want, rather than work or do chores, as adults have to do. However, we made the claim earlier that children have less freedom now than in the past. To make more sense of the claim that children have less freedom now than they once did, think about the place of children within the contemporary landscape. If we go back 50 years or more, we would expect to see children playing out with others on the street, at playing fields or recreation grounds, in woods, in town centres. Where would we see them now? Consider the extent to which children are free to travel or roam unsupervised and play in these spaces. In saying this, we see travelling as being on a journey to a destination and we see roaming as just being out and about. There is evidence to indicate that roaming in particular has significantly reduced over the last 75 years for children, and particularly so in the last 20 years.

Think about walking to school. Did you walk to your primary school? A report from Manchester (Dobson, 2015) suggests that in the north west of England half the number of children walk to primary school when compared to their parents. Similarly, in 1971, 80 per cent of seven and eight-year-olds travelled to school without an adult. By 2006 this had dropped to only 12 per cent, and that was of seven to ten-year-olds. Almost every 11-year-old walked to school alone in the 1970s, but by 2018 only 55 per cent did so (Grunfled, 2018). By 2013 in the UK only 25 per cent of primary school pupils travelled home alone as opposed to 86 per cent in 1971 and compared to 76 per cent in Germany today (Elkin, 2013). What is very clear is that children no longer walk to school in large numbers, many are accompanied, or driven. Note though that some decisions may be taken away from parents, such as when schools set rules about children being allowed to walk home alone and/or require parents to collect children from primary school.

Our experience

As children we each walked to primary school unsupervised, and it would have been very unusual had we or our friends been accompanied by parents. But now think about what the experience of walking to school unsupervised was like for many children. For us it wasn't far; Creasy had the longest walk at a mere half a mile, though at 8 years old it felt longer. He would often do this twice a day, returning home for lunch. However, that half-mile walk

> provided opportunities to be with friends as well as to encounter some people who may not be so friendly. There was space to make plans, negotiate disputes and to have a laugh. Corby recalls going to the park on the way home from school or calling in at friends' houses.

This time and space to be away from adults has been lost by many children. It is no longer a normal part of life in many Western societies (Loebach and Gilliland, 2016). Walking to school is one example but in general in contemporary society children have become restricted in what they can do or where they can go unsupervised. This is often on the grounds that this is to protect them (Jenkins, 2006; Malone, 2007; Guldberg, 2009). Keeping children safe through supervising them is a major concern of contemporary parents and not something that parents in the past would have routinely had to consider. However, in seeking to protect children through increasing supervision and restricting their freedoms, opportunities for developing life skills and resilience are being lost and children may be less able to operate in society effectively because of it. Rather than having freedom, children are restricted and supervised for most of their time. This is in part due to the pressure on parents to keep their children safe from potential harms that exist in our society, including harms that society accepts, such as high levels of traffic.

One reason for a growing concern with our children having freedom may be because the way in which parents relate to their children has seen them become much more of an emotional investment (Gillis, 2009; Simpson, 2014). Gillis returns us to an idea that was raised earlier in the book which illustrated how children could once have been understood to have been an economic investment; children would help the maintenance and survival of the family by working. However, what we noted earlier was that the introduction of legislation which has removed children from the workplace, alongside the introduction of compulsory education, has changed the social position of children within the household. This change took place during a period in which childhood mortality has fallen. As children have been increasingly prevented from working for longer periods and as they became healthier and more likely to live longer, so they have become transformed from economic investments to emotional investments. Children now contribute much more to our emotional life or lifestyle.

Surveillance, supervision and the home

Alongside the changes that have taken place in respect of children, there have also been significant changes in terms of how we understand what it means to be a good parent. In contemporary Western societies the good parent knows where their child is at all times. Parents would be deemed irresponsible if they didn't know where their child was. One consequence of the contemporary concern with knowing where children are is that it has led to the development of apps which use

GPS to inform parents of their child's location (Simpson, 2014; Hasinoff, 2017; Mavoa et al, 2023). Alternatively, this could be understood as the development of apps which enable parents to maintain surveillance of their children.

Given the increase in the surveillance or monitoring of children it is inevitable that some have considered what the consequences are for children's development. Simpson (2014: 273) is explicit in stating that there is 'a tension between the need to protect children from harm and the rights of the children to develop their autonomy'. This links back to what was said earlier regarding the need for children to have space to grow. It is important for children to have unsupervised time, as part of their development, and to do things on their own without an adult monitoring them. What is maybe obvious though is that many children, middle-class children in particular, often have no free time to do this. Their lives are crammed with organised activities and when they have free time, parents are unlikely to let them out of the house to play.

Pause for reflection

One way in which the contemporary Western world differs from previous periods in history is that over time the practice of digital monitoring has become normal (Mavoa et al, 2023).

With this in mind we want to invoke a 'Handmaid's tale' scenario (if you have not read *The Handmaid's Tale* by Margaret Atwood, we urge you to do so; a next best option would be to watch the TV series).

Now, you may be comfortable with parents keeping their children under surveillance and tracking their movements, but what do you think about husbands or partners tracking the movements of wives or partners?

This is another example of how children can be seen to constitute a particular subgroup within society; a subgroup that is often subject to elements of control that would be strongly resisted by adults, albeit often under the guise of keeping children safe. It should be said though that knowing where a child is at any given time is not synonymous with ensuring their safety. A more extreme version of exerting control over where children are free to roam unsupervised though is the growth in the numbers of children who are not able to roam anywhere. For many children, free time is spent almost entirely at home.

Fifty years ago, a child might have been sent to their bedroom as a punishment, but would that work now? The idea is that confining a child to their bedroom, or simply to the home, is a form of punishment. We wonder if this has the same implications now given that that being confined to the home is a normal state of affairs for many children. This means that the degree of punishment that results from being confined to the home has lessened, or even disappeared. Something that was once seen as a punishment is now normal for many children.

> **Pause for reflection**
>
> Imagine you are being sent to your bedroom by your parents.
>
> Now think about your bedroom as a child. What was it like? Was it shared with other siblings? Did you share a bed even? Now think about technology. Did you have a TV or a computer in your bedroom? Does a modern smartphone make a TV and/or computer superfluous?
>
> If you had been confined to your bedroom, would you have been cut off from friends? Was it a punishment and would it be now?

Leverett (2011) raises the idea of pre-teen children becoming domesticated as their opportunities to spend time with others away from the home is being subject to regulation and surveillance. Importantly, he argues that this domestication changes the social position of children and reinforces ideas about both their vulnerability and dependency. We have previously written about childhood being tamed; it is not so different from domestication. This domestication or taming can be seen as problematic because by confining children to the home we reduce the opportunities that children have to forge their own identities, free from supervision. We also limit the opportunity for children to be self-reliant. Self-reliance is simply being able to do things for oneself and as an adult there are many things we need to do for ourselves if we wish to have a good life and be successful, particularly in work or running our own homes.

Space and childhood

The issue of children's space is interesting to consider in terms of understanding contemporary childhood. What space children have access to is likely to shape their childhood experiences and opportunities. Although confining children to the home may seem a natural and reasonable approach to parenting and/or caring for children, this shapes what childhood is and what children can do. Gillespie (2013: 69) discusses how in the 19th century, working-class or poorer families might share a house with other families, particularly if they lived in a city. Under these circumstances it is understandable that parents would want their children out of the way, and that children would want to leave the home for periods.

Gillespie uses evidence of 19th century living conditions to show why it was that adults may not have wanted children in the house as well as illustrating why children may not have wanted to be there. Further, in the mid 20th century many houses lacked central heating and had just one television. This had an influence upon how families would use space. It is not hard to imagine that families would spend more time together as a consequence, sitting together in one heated room watching the shared TV. Following from this, Gillis (2009) argues that changes in terms of space have influenced contemporary ideas about childhood. Families now might have more space, with many Western children having their own room and entertainment.

This can also be considered in a more sociological way by drawing a distinction between a house and a household. We can see the house as a physical space that may be more or less comfortable, but we can also think about the household as a social unit. The household in contemporary society is associated with the nuclear family (parents and children). Although the term 'nuclear family' is contested, as it does not reflect the many ways a family is constituted, it does reflect that in Western societies most households are just one or two generations living together. In some countries, and in the UK in the past, many households may have included multiple generations and more than one family. Furthermore, a household could be made up of servants, apprentices and lodgers, in addition to family members. Childhoods would be lived in a very different environment to what they experience today. Consider how children would learn to negotiate relationships with different adults, working out who they could trust and who they could not trust, in such a household.

Gillis also points to the way in which the space of the pre-industrial household incorporated a different understanding of time. The idea of linear time, of time moving forward, was not always as significant as it is within the 21st century. Birthdays were not celebrated in the way that they are now, and if we cast our mind back to the ideas put forward by Aries in Chapter 3, then we can recognise that children were not seen in developmental terms in the same way. For Gillis the development of industrialisation reinforced the separation of production from the household and introduced the idea of home and workplace as separate. This also influences our ideas about children and childhood.

As society changes then it is possible to see how children come under scrutiny when social changes disrupt ideas relating to space, place and development. So, children start to be seen as problematic as a consequence of changes in space and place, such as when they are restricted from workplaces. As children were removed from the workplace, they became displaced. In this way children became a problem when they appeared to be occupying a place which in some way offends a sense of order. One reason schools evolved in the way they did was to contain children who were excluded from working and now had nothing to do.

Being on the streets has become more problematic for contemporary children. Childhood is not something that we expect to be spent in this way. We can identify contemporary ways of controlling how children occupy space such as Educational Welfare patrols in town centres and/or dispersal orders. Similarly, Public Spaces Protection Orders (PSPOs) provide open-ended powers which enable council officials to ban particular activities in public spaces, such as ball games. Childhood is no longer something that we expect to be lived in public spaces.

The argument that children should not be in public spaces for their own safety or for the convenience of others works quite well when we can identify between the private sphere of the home and the public sphere of commercial, industrial and/or social spaces, but what about if these boundaries become less certain, less distinct? Indeed, for contemporary childhood the boundaries between the home and the outside world have become permeable. Previously, we asked if a parent would be punishing a child if they were sent to their bedroom. We asked this on the basis that for many children, their bedroom is likely to be their own space with access to computers and the internet. Consider how alongside a sense within contemporary society that space beyond the home poses a risk to children, the space within the home can also pose a risk, especially in relation to the problems that the internet and social media can present to children (BBC, 2017).

The impact of concerns about risk within society have contributed significantly to restrictions being imposed onto children's lives, with the aim of keeping them safe. However, the parents who restrict children's access to physical spaces beyond the home, ostensibly on the grounds of risk, may put children at other risks because of technologies which create virtual spaces. This emphasises why it is important to consider the ways in which childhood is accompanied by particular ways of understanding space, especially in terms of how children access space and what we see as appropriate spaces. In doing so what we see is that children's spaces are very often designed and monitored by adults for children. Making sense of childhood requires us to understand what space children have access to, why and how children use that space and what it might mean for their development of self-reliance. Once again, we see that there is nothing natural about childhood, it is something that is socially constructed.

If we think about the housing issues that we pointed to earlier then we might consider that housing conditions can be understood as material conditions in that they are real; this can be compared to abstract and/or intangible issues, like our ideas of safety. When we consider how parents may now restrict children going out it is often because of ideas about risk and threat, so the key issue here is not something that is necessarily material but rather something that is intangible. As such the next section takes a bit of a detour to consider how ideas have changed over time and how this may have consequences for what children can know about the world and their own place in it.

Modernity, post-modernity and the matter of truth

When we refer to the landscape of childhood, on one level we are drawing attention to the material, or physical, conditions that make up the child's world, for example, compare an inner-city urban environment with a rural village. But instead of taking landscape literally, consider instead that the landscape could also be understood as reflecting ideas, values and beliefs in any society, so not just where children live, but how they may live and the experiences they have. This is probably not a new idea by this point, and you should already understand that these things shape childhood. However, it is important because ideas, values and beliefs also shape the environment in which a child lives. Importantly though, ideas, values and beliefs can change.

This section might seem to be moving away from our central concern with childhood but stick with us, it is useful. We begin by introducing the historical development of ideas that is referred to as the Enlightenment. It is useful when we try and make sense of the world that children live in because how childhood evolves is dependent on what has gone before and this includes how ideas change. The Enlightenment is important in that it marks the origins of modernity. Modernity can be understood on a basic level as the urban, technological and industrial world typified by the mid 20th century in Western societies.

The Enlightenment happened during the 17th and 18th centuries. It refers to a time in Western Europe when philosophical ideas about the world changed. There are several issues relating to the Enlightenment that are interesting, but we want to draw attention to one key issue; the idea that there are certain aspects of the world that we live in that we can know to be true, and, importantly, that we can demonstrate as true.

The development of science is a key aspect of the Enlightenment and is central to the idea that we can assert and demonstrate truths about the world. Importantly, science rests on empirical methods, empiricism being concerned with what can be seen. Science should be understood then as a distinct practice which aims to distinguish the truth so as to make sense of the world (Aronowitz, 1988). As such, the rational approach of scientific method shapes a particular understanding of the world. This is important for childhood in that our understanding of children and the evolving period of life known as childhood is influenced by what was found out through scientific research, and continues to be so today.

Now, you will most probably have come across these ideas when considering methodology, especially the philosophical concepts of ontology and epistemology.

Note

In Chapter 3 we stated that although ontology and epistemology may sound complicated we can understand each in a simple sense as follows:

- ontology refers to what we can know;
- epistemology refers to how we can know it.

Ontology and epistemology are central to how we carry out research and they can be seen to underpin the development of science during the Enlightenment.

From a scientific perspective we can know the world by adopting the scientific method, often called the hypothetico-deductive method. This means that we have evidence that proves an idea we hold. The fact that we are asserting that we can know about things raises the idea that such things can be said to be true.

So, although our aims within this book may not be to provide a discussion of scientific research methods, we are concerned with how the principles of science have shaped general understandings about what we know about the world and what we know about children and childhood. It is science which has made the modern technological world possible. It has done this by establishing a type of knowledge of the world that we can have confidence in. It does this by focusing on, and privileging, truth.

To bring this back to childhood, think about what we said earlier regarding how children are regularly measured and/or tested as they develop and how this determines what we know about them and, in turn, often comes to define them. We can see this in education, where testing and examinations are used in a way which comes to act as a representation of some inherent truth about each child. Truth is very important within the landscape of childhood, as we will explore further later.

Given that the development of science promoted a focus on truth it is also worth commenting on how developments in social science towards the end of the 20th century have changed how we understand the idea of truth and what this means for understanding contemporary society. In one sense we do not expect anyone on a childhood studies course to have signed up to study social theory, but having some knowledge of it can be very useful when it comes to making sense of the books and journal articles that you may come across, so persevere.

Previously we introduced the idea that there are different approaches within sociology. The classical social theories, such as the structuralist approaches of Marxism or functionalism, and feminism even, have often been referred to as grand narratives. What is meant by this is that they claim to establish a truth about society in a way that makes sense of all aspects of social life. Grand means large or broad, and a narrative is an account. Therefore, a grand narrative means a large, or broad-based, account that explains how society works. It can be seen then how these narratives are general and do not explain all individual experiences.

However, it is obvious that the landscape of society changed throughout the 20th century; social class has changed, for example, and society became more culturally diverse. Work changed and, as mentioned, who worked where also changed, with children being removed from the workplace. The sociology of grand narratives was founded before the 20th century, so it is not surprising that sociologists started to question the basis of older theories, these grand narratives. This is usually referred to as the post-modern turn. All this means is that some social scientists started to turn away from the classical theories of society on the grounds that they didn't seem to apply so well with how society actually was anymore. Society had changed and some new theoretical approaches were required to make sense of society.

The grand narratives which underpin structural theories seemed to fit better in terms of explaining the industrialised societies of the early and mid 20th century. These were periods when social class was more obvious and rigid and where gender roles seemed clear cut. Similarly, structural theories never really seemed to accommodate the multiculturalism that had developed by the end of the 20th century and when we start to add in a greater recognition of difference, sexuality and disability for example, the idea that there was one truth about society, or one way of being, seemed quite weak.

So, what we want you to consider is that where the grand narratives of classical social theory present the idea of a truth about society (singular), post-modern theories represent a plural approach in that they present the idea that there are truths (multiple truths) rather than a single truth (Lyotard, 1984; Bauman, 1997; Detmer, 2003). Crucially, in post-modern theory there is no unambiguous claim to truth. Truth can only be understood as relative to context. This means that we must accept the possibility of competing truths. So, for childhood studies, research attempts to uncover the many 'truths' about what it is to be a child and how childhood is shaped.

Note that you may also come across the term post-structuralist theory. Post-structuralism provides the basis for post-modern ideas (Inglis and Thorpe, 2019). Foucault is often associated with post-structuralism, especially in the way that his ideas about discourse suggest that reality is shaped by the meanings that are produced within discourse, as we mentioned earlier.

This will become clearer and more relevant when we consider the debates about transgender issues and the arguments that focus on whether or not an individual who transitions from male to female really is female, or vice versa. Where does the truth of their identity lie? Within modernity, the claim to a singular truth underpins a very different approach towards understanding society compared to a post-modern position. In the past, the notion of transitioning would be unthinkable in the way that we understand it now. Post-modernity rejects fixed identities in favour of self-identifying within a world that accommodates diversity. Plurality is the key issue within post-modernity, not singularity. However, plurality is challenging as in some cases we want a fixed answer to something. What we are saying here is that to understand childhood, there are no fixed answers or 'right' answers.

There is another aspect that reflects the debate referred to here regarding transitioning though, an issue that applies to all children. Try to imagine being a child in the early to mid 20th century, a time when social characteristics such as social class, gender and ethnicity were much more influential in how lives were shaped.

The world in the early to mid 20th century was more rigid about identity and what it meant for you and your life, but that rigidity provided a degree of security in terms of your future role and identity. We could even go so far as to say that children in the industrialised modern world of the 20th century had a good idea as to what their future would be. For some people this could be understood as something that was experienced positively, a sort of certainty about knowing who they were and where they fitted into the world and what they could or should be doing.

In the post-industrial society of today, where diversity and equality are more firmly established in terms of equal opportunities, children have no real fixed future in a way that could have been said of some previous generations. This means that as children grow up, they have to create their identity in a way that their grandparents didn't. The post-modern society that children are growing up in may provide more opportunities for children (consider how at school you were likely told you could be anything you wanted to be!), but the lack of stability also provides significant pressures for contemporary childhood. In comparing this difference, we could say that the challenge for previous generations was in terms of breaking free from ideas about class, gender or ethnic stereotypes, which some people did or attempted to do. The challenge for children now is in establishing an identity in a world that is much more individualised and, in many ways, much more competitive. This shapes childhood as a time for considering who we are and what we want to be.

What can children know in a post-truth world?

So, in considering the Enlightenment we have seen that the idea of the scientific method has influenced how we can know the world and how this influences childhood. The scientific method, often referred to as the hypothetico-deductive method, operates at the level of epistemology in that it is concerned with how we can know something. In science we develop a hypothesis, something that we expect to happen, and then we test it and deduce from our results. Science is strong because of this focus on testing and on providing results that we can see: empirical evidence. What we know is different to what we believe. This is important in your academic writing, as you need to be clear about what evidence supports what we think we know about childhood.

The distinction between what we know and what we believe is important. We can understand this by comparing science with religion. Scientific knowledge differs from religious knowledge. The teachings of religion draw on scripture and emphasise faith, or belief. We are generally told what we should believe by clergy, the officials within any religion. These officials interpret scripture (the written guides for a religion) for the population and in doing so give shape to how we should live our lives. This is not at all surprising given that not all that long ago most people would have been illiterate and so unable to read. You might consider also that for many people key religious texts such as the Bible or the Koran can only be read if they have been translated from the languages that they were originally written in and that the process of translation always involves the translator making decisions about the words to use and what they think the original writer meant.

Note

We can characterise the distinction between science and religion as follows: what we know compared to what we believe.

In this way science and religion provide us with different knowledges. To say knowledges in this way seems a bit clunky, but it reflects the post-modern turn in that we are suggesting that there is more than one way of understanding or having knowledge.

> The distinction between what we know and what we believe is important for you as students in that what you write for assignments has to be established as valid by using reliable sources which are referenced. Assignments will be weaker if they are made up of things that you believe but for which you cannot provide evidence. Similarly, it is never a good idea to write 'I believe...' in an assignment.

Now consider how children come to know their world. Their experiences are obviously very important, but if we think about children then what they know about the world is strongly influenced by adults. We can see this most obviously in terms of the education that children receive, particularly the school curriculum. Children are exposed to information in their education alongside what adults tell them about the world.

So, in thinking about the nature of the information and messages that children are exposed to, it is useful to consider where information comes from. If we were to consider sources of information that children were exposed to 50 years ago, it was much more limited than is the case now. This will be discussed more fully in Chapter 7 when looking at the media. The growth of the internet means that children are very likely to encounter ideas and arguments from sources that are unregulated and unaccountable, some of which are particularly untrustworthy. What children know or what they are told shapes their childhood in that it shapes their understanding of their world and who they are.

However, it would be wrong to suggest that untrustworthy sources are only encountered online. We argued earlier that post-modernism led to a shift away from the idea of a single truth and towards the idea of competition between different truths. Even so, there is still some level of integrity with regards to how each truth is arrived at. As such, we may still claim that truth has some value. The key point that we want to emphasise here is that there is a difference in terms of using different methods and therefore arriving at different truths, when compared to making claims that are patently false or, at the very least, have no basis in any form of evidence.

To illustrate this, consider that what we know about society is different if we adopt a structuralist approach towards sociology than if we adopt an action-based approach. A structuralist approach would suggest that childhood is shaped by society and that children have little or no ability to shape childhood. An action-based approach would argue that childhood is formed within the interactions between children and adults. The approaches are concerned with explaining somewhat different things and use different methods of research to investigate the social world. This is one reason why social science is often criticised by individuals who are engaged in what is often called hard science. Hard science tends to be seen as the gold standard because of its commitment to testing by use of the hypothetico-deductive method and being able to present visible evidence. Because of this, traditionally, scientific knowledge was seen as stronger, or more trustworthy.

The hypothetico-deductive method is rarely appropriate when it comes to social matters though. People and society are not the same as physical materials. Social matters are rarely proven to have a single truth that is visibly evident. Life, and childhood, is more complicated than that.

In recent years, however, there has been a growing trend to deny the strength of science and to cast doubt on what science tells us; indeed, to cast doubt on what we know in general (Chinn et al, 2021; Ferrari et al, 2023). Linked to this is the way that some companies engage in activities which lead to social or ecological harms, for example, oil companies and tobacco companies have been shown to be engaged in the production of manufactured doubt by misrepresenting evidence (Michaels, 2008; Slater, 2014; Bramoullé and Orset, 2018; Goldberg and Vandenberg, 2021). This creates distrust in what sciences tells us, though to be fair sometimes creating distrust is the goal.

Note

Manufactured doubt falls under a broader approach which has been referred to as agnotology. Think of how being agnostic means to be doubtful or uncertain.

Slater (2014) draws attention to the way in which the manufacturing of doubt is part of a political and cultural struggle to create ignorance. From this perspective ignorance is not just an absence of knowledge, ignorance represents a state where we cannot know. As such, a state of public ignorance, not knowing, should be seen as the state which enables certain activities to continue even when they are against our interests.

A good example of this is the climate crisis, something that will be significant for today's children. The creation of ignorance by casting doubt on the scientific evidence means companies, politicians and world leaders can avoid addressing this problem.

Alongside this, contemporary politics has seen a growing trend to present messages which are both simple and which appeal to emotions rather than rationality. For some politicians around the world, it is evident that the relationship between truth and values no longer seems important. A concern with being truthful is being overlooked in the pursuit of political aims and ambitions. This can be seen when politicians simply lie or when they just make things up (Judge, 2022). The development of fact-checking in relation to politicians is something which responds to concerns that politicians are not always accurate or truthful; something they were always expected to be in the past.

In one sense to claim that truth is being ignored or purposively overlooked seems absurd, why would individuals in responsible positions ignore the truth? However, this has happened; some of the claims that were presented as part of the Brexit/Leave campaign in the UK, together with the presidential campaigns undertaken since 2016 in the US, have been demonstrated as being patently untrue

(McIntyre, 2018). When Donald Trump was inaugurated (officially established in position) as president in 2017, a member of Trump's staff was challenged about a false claim regarding the size of the audience. They responded to the interviewer by referring to alternative facts (Peregrine, 2017). The term 'alternative facts' was widely taken to mean that empirical evidence could be ignored. Remember that empirical evidence is evidence that we can see. In this example, the public were being asked to ignore empirical evidence and accept something that wasn't true. When politicians make statements that are not true, they are in part asking people to make decisions based upon emotions rather than to draw on what is factual.

Why this is important in respect of understanding contemporary childhood is that these examples illustrate the idea put forward by some commentators that we are now living in a society that can be defined as post-truth (Ellerton, 2016; Jaser, 2016; Sismondo, 2017). To be clear, post-truth does not refer to competing truths arrived at by different methods of research or competing ideas. Post-truth reflects the fact that within contemporary society claims are being made that are simply not true. When dealing with children, the term we use when we are trying to teach them to tell the truth is lies. Children are now growing up in a world where some adults who hold responsible positions tell lies with the intention of misleading us.

In relation to this, though, it is also worth considering something that can be considered as 'false balance' (Coen, 2016). The idea of false balance can be identified in how social and political issues are reported. It refers to the practice whereby news providers such as the BBC give space to commentators representing both sides of an argument in a manner which appears to suggest that their coverage is balanced, and therefore fair.

However, when we consider issues such as the climate crisis or Brexit, for example, it is important to recognise that giving a voice to a minority opinion, or an argument which is not evidenced in any way, can mislead the public into thinking that things are uncertain when they are not. For example, if the majority of medical researchers state that smoking is harmful to health, but a very small number of researchers say that this is not always the case, a news programme which gives space for both sides of the argument can create a sense of false balance. The result is that an unsubstantiated idea is presented in a way that makes it look like it may be valid. This can have far-reaching consequences.

So, to bring this back to children and childhood, it is worth considering that children are living within a world where truth is presented to them as being very important, but where adults often say and do things which undermine this.

Being woke in the culture wars

The idea that we are living in a post-truth world seems profoundly disturbing to us as academics. While we accept that there is a need for ideas to be questioned, it appears that we have reached a time wherein ideas are being promoted and accepted that have no truth or evidence to support them. This has implications for education as well as for society in general. We recognise that education is not as clear cut as it might seem and that there are significant debates and tensions with respect to what gets taught as well as how it is taught, but that said, the world of education has a number of checks and balances which go a long way to supporting the overall integrity of education.

A concern with the integrity of education is important with regards to values relating to what we know about the world. As such, when a Conservative government minister stated that 'people in this country have had enough of experts' (Coen, 2016), then we inevitably concluded that this was intended to undermine the value and integrity of both education and evidence. The claim was made to encourage people to ignore experts who were pointing out that the UK would be economically worse off by withdrawing from the EU. The government minister was asking people to vote for something that would be detrimental to the lives of millions of people in the UK and in relation to children's futures.

The relevance of the Brexit vote within the UK in relation to childhood is that it can be seen as an example of what has come to be known as the culture wars (Koch, 2017). 'Culture wars' is a term that has been coined to describe how the different ideas or values that people hold are being presented as being in conflict, rather than just different ways of thinking about the world. For example, if you choose to be vegetarian because you don't want to eat animals for whatever reason, this is often presented as a challenge to people who do want to eat meat, rather than a legitimate personal choice.

One aspect of the culture wars is the growing use of the term 'woke' as an insult or to dismiss an opinion. So, a vegetarian is not accepted as having made an informed choice about their own life, but instead is characterised as woke, and denigrated for their decision. This impacts upon children as they are growing up in a world where their choices about what they want to do, what they want to be, may be influenced by culture wars.

Note

Being woke is associated with being socially liberal and accepting of diversity. To be woke is to be concerned for equality, diversity and/or social justice. Social justice basically means that individuals should not be discriminated against on the grounds of some characteristic such as gender, ethnicity or sexuality. Being woke generally means being supportive of society being more equal, looking favourably on movements which promote social justice or recognising historical injustices such as profiting from slavery.

Supporters of right-wing politics tend to see being woke as a threat to traditional society. They are generally critical of the idea of being woke, presenting being woke in negative terms.

The idea of culture wars is not fixed and is quite broad. Among other issues it encompasses criticism of environmental concerns, attacks on transgender issues and criticism of movements and/or campaigns such as Me Too or Black Lives Matter. It has come to prominence as part of a general resurgence of right-wing politics which includes increased support for fascist politics within Europe in recent decades. It can be seen in what are sometimes called the alt-right movements. In the UK the Conservative Party, Reform and the right-wing media have promoted anti-woke ideas and made use of culture war themes.

One approach towards understanding what it means to be woke is to consider that wokeness disrupts or challenges the everyday, taken-for-granted ideas that we have about the world (Cammaerts, 2022). This disruption builds on post-modern ideas about adopting a critical stance and looking at something from different perspectives. In adopting a critical position, Cammaerts draws attention to the idea of hegemonic ideas and values. Hegemony is a term that is closely associated with the Italian social theorist Gramsci. In a simple sense hegemony means that there are ways of understanding the world that we just never question. We take them for granted as being perfectly normal. It is a way of understanding the world that is beyond questioning. Woke ideas, ideas that are informed and academic, disrupt hegemony by asking us to think critically and to consider that existing social structures may disadvantage some groups while advantaging others.

Note

Criticism of so-called wokeness reflects right-wing politics. However, right-wing politics has two aspects: neoliberalism (a concern with economics) and neoconservatism (a concern with social life or culture). These two aspects do not always fit together easily as they are concerned with different issues. See Creasy and Corby (2023) for an explanation of how these ideologies are relevant to childhood.

Many commentators focus on neoliberalism and overlook the role of neoconservative ideas in shaping legislation and policy. Neoconservatism underpins the culture wars. It promotes traditional values and beliefs, albeit specific values and beliefs in a very limited way. It is socially conservative and resists change.

In the UK the Conservative Party encompasses both neoliberalism and neoconservatism.

So, culture wars are a manifestation of neoconservative politics. One example of how neoconservative politics affects children can be seen in respect of teaching in the 1980s, in particular the policy introduced by the Conservative government under Margaret Thatcher known as Clause 28. Clause 28 restricted what teachers were permitted to say with regards to homosexuality and forbade teachers to discuss homosexual families on the grounds that these were 'pretend families'. Clause 28 was later repealed by a Labour government. In the US, the Republican governor of Florida has recently echoed Clause 28 in forbidding 'classroom instruction by school personnel or third parties on sexual orientation or gender identity' with respect to teaching five to nine year olds, meaning that children are not allowed to discuss these subjects or be given information in school about them. There are also restrictions on these issues for older children, but the guidelines are rather vague (Hadland, 2022: 584). These restrictions are usually referred to as the 'Don't Say Gay' laws.

With respect to both these policies, Clause 28 and Don't Say Gay laws, each provides us with an opportunity to consider how legislation may impact upon the everyday lives of children and young people. A good way to do this is to consider the idea of 'verstehen'. Verstehen is a German word that was promoted as a sociological tool by the sociologist Max Weber. You could make good use of this word in your future lives, at work or in relationships. It means empathetic understanding. Basically, what Weber is saying is that there are times when we need to put ourselves in someone else's shoes. So, if you are a child or young person who lives in a same-sex household, or who is gay, how do you feel if your personal position is not to be spoken about or if your family is deemed to be a pretend family? Consider how such an approach promotes social exclusion rather than social inclusion, and then ask what sort of a world would you want children to be brought up in, one that is exclusive or one that is inclusive?

Looking back on the landscape of childhood

When it comes to studying childhood, this chapter provided you with an introduction to some broader themes in terms of the relationship between society and childhood and the issue of studying childhood. As such we feel that you will be able to use it to develop a critical understanding of childhood by focusing upon how the lived experiences that children have are shaped by social forces such as culture wars. We feel that it provides examples of how ideas which may be seen as theoretical, or those that are abstract, can provide a frame within which childhood is viewed.

We have said previously that it is important to develop a critical understanding of childhood. We know from experience that students are often called upon to be critical within their assessed work. We also know that it can be hard at times to move away from the simple view of criticality that involves presenting one author as saying X and then writing that on the other hand another author says Y. Although it is useful to know what different authors say, this is not really being critical. Being critical means interrogating what you read, or the evidence that you have. In interrogating it you can identify weaknesses or inconsistencies and demonstrate how this matters to childhood.

In a very basic sense, though, criticality can be developed by looking at some social phenomenon, such as childhood, and coming at it from different angles so as to make sense of it. As such, we raised the idea that children in contemporary society have fewer freedoms to roam beyond the home, unsupervised, than in previous generations. To make sense of this it is necessary to start to consider the broader changes that have taken place within society.

So, when we suggested that changing ideas about what it means to be a good parent have led to parents restricting their children's free time beyond the home, or subjecting them to surveillance, we can suggest that there is a direct relationship between parenting and childhood which may create a paradox. Parents who become increasingly involved in their children's everyday lives as per social ideas about good parenting may paradoxically reduce their children's opportunities in terms of social development in a way that can be harmful. Children need space to develop, but in many families that space is reducing.

Considering historical developments is useful. We used Gillespie (2013) to illustrate how living conditions, the actual space that is available, may make it more or less likely that children are encouraged to spend time outside of the home. We also drew on Gillis (2009), who emphasised that changes in space can bring about a new understanding of childhood. This allows us to think about how the physical space or geography can affect childhood. This is what we mean when we refer to the landscape of childhood.

As such it is reasonable to argue that children are expected to be found within some social spaces but are not expected in others. We used space as a way into considering abstract, or intangible, ideas. Previous chapters raised the issue of discourse and of ideology. Both rest on ideas. What this chapter did was to demonstrate that ideas that are generally seen as unquestionable (hegemonic) can undergo significant change. The period in Western history referred to as the Enlightenment is the basis of what we call modernity, and is particularly important when it comes to what can be established as true.

What is particularly relevant for contemporary childhood is the move away from modernity towards post-modernity, because this changes how we understand the foundations of society and it is in the foundations of society that childhood is shaped. A further development is the idea that society has now become a post-truth society. Within the post-truth society, emotions and feelings take precedence over truth. So, in writing about the landscape of childhood, or what we might see as the general conditions under which childhood is lived, the following points may be useful to draw on in assignments:

- Children in contemporary UK society have less unsupervised time and fewer freedoms outside of the home than previous generations.
- Supervision and/or surveillance has become embedded in children's lives.
- Where modernity rests upon the idea of truth, post-modernity accommodates the idea that there are truths (many ideas that are simultaneously true).
- Identity within post-modern society is more flexible, more able to be constructed when compared to modernity.
- Modern technology facilitates the promotion of ideas which have little standing in terms of truth (or evidence that they are true) and some individuals and/or organisations act to manufacture doubt.
- Children are now growing up in a post-truth era.

Further thoughts

Children are much more restricted in terms of what they can do or where they can go without supervision when compared to previous generations. What might the consequences be for childhood if this trend continues and what problems might it result in?

Technology has facilitated the development of portals whereby parents can observe children at nursery or access information in real time about what their children are doing in school, such as if they have broken the rules. In one sense this intensifies parenting and places additional pressure on parents, but does it also make surveillance normal and has it become acceptable? How does this sort of technology intersect with ideas about snowplough parents and helicopter parents? Is there evidence that this is a better way for the family to operate?

How might a post-truth world affect childhood? And how might children be affected when they live in a society where some ideas are seen as woke?

Further reading

Gillespie (2013) provides an interesting account of how children's lives have changed by considering space.

Two short articles that relate to the idea of post-truth which are worth reading are Coen (2016) and Peregrine (2017). Peregrine discusses alternative facts and Cohen considers media bias, demonstrating why giving minority views a voice is not necessarily balanced, introducing the idea of false balance.

7

Living in a world of media

> **This chapter will help you to understand:**
> - the ways in which the media shapes our understanding of childhood;
> - how children interact with different forms of media;
> - issues and concerns relating to children's online worlds.

Has the media changed childhood?

This chapter will explore the idea that how we understand childhood is influenced by the media, including the ways in which children engage and interact with the media. As a starting point it is important to note that the umbrella term 'the media' incorporates a wide range of types and technologies. Because of this we will start by considering what we might call the old world of media before comparing this to the contemporary world of social media.

In the 1960s the Canadian philosopher Marshall McLuhan stated that 'the medium is the message' (reprinted in McLuhan, 2013: 12). The key idea of McLuhan's work is that how we communicate shapes how our society develops because it shapes how we understand what is said. It is not simply that different forms of media mean that messages can be communicated more quickly or over greater distances, it is that different forms of media transform the messages themselves. This idea will be seen to be very useful when we consider how the media has changed, but we start by thinking about what Smith (2010) means when he suggests that the media impacts on how we see childhood in two ways:

- firstly, in terms of stories and items that are about children;
- secondly, in the way that the media may be for children.

The first way reflects how children and/or childhood is represented within the media. How the media present childhood to us shapes a more general social understanding of what childhood is or should be. This is typified in stories from the early 20th century, such as the idyllic, and somewhat adult-free, childhood that is portrayed in Enid Blyton's *Famous Five* stories or in Arthur Ransome's *Swallows and Amazons*. The media also includes ideas about things which are portrayed as being some type of threat to children or childhood. The second way relates to how media organisations target children as users or consumers of the media. From this perspective the focus is on how the use or consumption of the media has the potential to shape childhood. As we move through this chapter keep in mind what Smith has said about childhood and what McLuhan has said about how the media has the potential to shape society. These ideas enable us to have a more critical understanding of the topic.

The media often reinforces the idea of children as becomings in foregrounding aspirations and concerns in childhood (Buckingham, 2009). By focusing on aspirations we get the idea that childhood can be understood as holding potential for the future, and by considering concerns we come to consider that children may be seen as being at risk of harm, therefore the potential for what they may become could also be at risk.

Pause for reflection

Before we go any further it may be useful to consider what we mean when we refer to the media; what comes to mind? What do you think is the media?

Jot down what you consider the media to be and then have a think about which aspects or forms of the media are more, or less, accessible to children.

Hopefully, you will have listed a number of different types of media and in doing so you should be able to recognise how things have changed over time. All forms of communication that surround us and present ideas that we hear or see, whether we are choosing to or not, constitute the media. Postman (1994) draws attention to how changing forms of media have implications for both children and childhood. He claims that the introduction of electronic media led to the death of childhood. Electronic media is often seen as a threat to children. Because of this it is not hard to see McLuhan's claim within what Postman is saying about a new media having reshaped this aspect of society. However, we need to recognise that as children are part of wider society, any change in society will affect children.

In making this claim, though, Postman was really referring to television; he was writing before the widespread adoption of electronic media such as video games and before the establishment of the online opportunities created by the introduction of the internet. He bases this claim on the idea that television rests upon visual imagery. The key aspect of Postman's argument is that prior to the advent of television the media was accessed by having the ability to read. Of course, we may suggest that Postman is ignoring the introduction of aural media such as radio and recordings, but his basic point is relevant. Children's limitations with respect to literacy means that the media which existed before the development of televisual media was much less accessible to children and therefore what children had access to was easier to control.

If we had been writing this 40 years ago or more, it is very likely that we would have seen the media in a much more limited way than compared to today. Going back to the mid 1980s, the media was really limited to newspapers, radio and television. Computer games were only just starting to play a part in people's lives. Sometimes newspapers, radio and television were just referred to as the mass media. This is because of the way that they had significant reach in terms of their audiences. Newspaper, radio and television were very important in most people's lives within Western societies, and they were seen as being very influential.

What is crucial, however, when it comes to the mass media, is that the messages carried by the mass media are transmitted one-way. In each of these examples editorial and production teams craft the message and provide it to the audience. The mass media didn't just report the news, they made the news; they decided what would be reported and how it would be reported. This can be seen as controlling who has a voice in the media, and who does not. Contrast the situation as it was in the 1980s in terms of the media with what it is now. For example, consider how the types of technology that children have access to now has given rise to a whole range of issues which may, or may not, be seen as problematic. It also means that there is more information and different voices.

How the media reinforces the idea of innocence

When we introduced discourse, we said that it is discourse which shapes the understanding of what is normal and even what should be normal. We also said that there may be a range of discourses operating at any given time. This is important when we consider how media now gives access to so many different ideas, and discourses. However, although we will demonstrate that there are some contradictions within the media when it comes to children and childhood, it is reasonable to say that a discourse of childhood innocence is very common indeed.

One way in which the media influences society is that the images of childhood which are presented within the media have the effect of suggesting what childhood should be. Holland (2004) describes these common images as desired images. They fit in with narratives that we are comfortable with, or indeed, what we want to see in relation to childhood.

However, Holland provides a wide-ranging account of the way in which images of children provide quite contradictory ideas about both children and childhood. So, where the imagery of childhood innocence may be identified as an enduring theme, a more recent development in terms of imagery may suggest the loss of innocence or even the idea of children as a threat. Although this is not new, it has become of greater concern in recent years. As such, contradictory images of children do not undermine the possibility of being able to understand childhood, but it is important to try to consider the context of these images and recognise that childhood is complex and varied. By this we mean that we should consider what the image is being used for as well as considering any text that may accompany the image and then attempt to put this in perspective regarding children's lives. Images do not just happen. Images are produced for a purpose. That may be paintings, photographs or video. In each case images hide things as well as reveal them.

Understanding images is a complex process. The images of children that we encounter, and the sense of emotions that they evoke, are part of the processes and relationships that take place between the image, the producers and the reader/consumer. Readers of images need to try and understand what it is that the producer is trying to say or do. Importantly, though, there is always more to the story than meets the eye when it comes to imagery, and other interpretations are possible.

Student task

To develop a further understanding of how images of children within the media can be used to present a particular discourse regarding childhood, look for five or six images of children or childhood within the media (TV, social media, books, the internet and so on) and see if you can present them in terms of common ideas about childhood, such children being at risk, representing potential, being cute and so on. Think about the imagery of children that is used within a range of stories about children and/or childhood.

Be aware that these stories do not exist in a vacuum. These stories are not inevitable or self-evident. So, with that in mind, consider these three questions:

- How does the story shape our understanding of childhood?
- What agenda might exist for portraying children in this way?
- Do you think this is how all children are, all of the time?

Consider how stories about children are limited in the news and how those stories that exist might fit into particular categories such as risk, exceptionalism, tragedy.

How social media has shaped a new generation gap

In some ways what we have covered so far in this chapter is likely to have been seen by our expected readership as being a bit old fashioned in that up to now we have focused on traditional media such as newspapers and television. Many children today will not experience newspapers nor access TV in the way that was usual 30 to 40 years ago. In doing this we are looking backwards, and we have yet to consider what has been a very significant change in terms of the media. That is the growth of social media alongside concerns about screen time. This is one aspect of social life that really does demonstrate how childhoods have changed.

Concerns about screen time are not all that new. During the 1970s and 1980s there were often concerns raised about the amount of time that children would spend watching television, with dire warnings about the harm that television could do to children. This reflects what Postman (1994) was suggesting about television being responsible for the death of childhood. Sometimes the concerns were about the content of television but compared to online content this was very different. The concern was that children could access adult TV programmes, but these were very different compared to online content.

Crucially, however, when we compare traditional forms of media such as newspapers, radio and television with social media, one key issue stands out, the potential for participation. Old forms of media, such as newspapers, radio and television, reflect a model of producer-generated content. Reporters and journalists generate items or stories which are selected and shaped by editors before presentation to consumers. There are also degrees of regulation that are applicable; there are limits as to what can be said in these old forms of media so as to support integrity and reinforce trust. Social media is very different in that anyone can produce and share content. This brings into being what has been called a participatory culture (Jenkins et al, 2009). This reflects what McLuhan was saying about the message being the medium and how the media shapes society. Think about how social behaviour has changed because of social media.

When Jenkins et al talk about a participatory culture they are drawing attention to how technologies are used. This is relevant to children and childhood and may be used as one way of arguing that childhood in the 2020s differs from childhood as it was experienced during the 20th century. The technology that underpins social media provides the potential for actual interactivity. Children have more access to media and can select more easily what they want to view. They can also engage with media in a way that was not possible in the past. Children can communicate with others or present their own view.

Note

Jenkins et al (2009) refer to interactivity as being the property of technology. By this they mean that different technologies allow for different levels of interactivity and that the nature of interactivity is shaped and bounded by the limits of technology. TV allows for limited interactivity whereas social media presents high levels of interactivity.

The extent of participation with the media then becomes a characteristic of the culture in relation to technology. Social media provides scope for participation in a way that newspapers or television do not.

What we have now then is a situation where children are able to use social media technologies to create and share content in a way that has not been possible for previous generations. This enables children and young people to generate wholly original content or to mix, synthesise and subvert existing content. The key point is that the technology that is available provides the ability to engage with the media in a way that is very different to how previous generations have been able to use the media. This ability to engage with media is both positive and negative for children but is generally presented as problematic. However, Smith (2010) draws from research into children's use of media to suggest that although children are presented as irresponsible and immature and should be protected from the media, they are more often competent in their use of media, avoiding what is not appropriate for them by utilising a form of 'hyper-responsibility' in selecting what they look at and what they engage with.

A further note regarding the participatory aspect of social media is also appropriate. Children and adolescents have often been criticised, or concerns have been raised, with respect to how engagement with recorded music or screens encourages solitary activities, for example, television or game playing (Lemish, 2015). However, Turkle (2012) draws attention to how video games can provide a focal point for children and following from this we can recognise how social media provides opportunities for young people to stay in touch even when separated by significant distances. Social media implies social engagement.

Lemish adds to how we can understand children's media activity by referring to incoming and outgoing content. In this distinction, incoming content is that which is created by other users and which children simply consume in one way or another. Outgoing content then is content that the child has created in some way and has made available for others.

Pause for reflection

Think of children's experiences being filmed as a relatively new social phenomenon.

Lemish describes three positions that can be identified in relation to the level of activity: content, contact and conduct.

1. Content activity describes the child as the recipient of content.
2. Contact activity is where the child takes part with others in some form.
3. Conduct activity is where the child takes a much more active role.

These ideas can be seen in relation to children filming and being filmed.

Consider how children from being babies are photographed and filmed by parents and others on a daily basis. This normalises the process of being the subject of images in a way that was more limited in the past. Does this alter how children behave?

The growth of home movies that was facilitated by the introduction of affordable video cameras was the beginning of contemporary social behaviour wherein mobile phones and internet connections have made nearly all Western children both participants and/or producer/directors in a filmed world. Children and young people may have started as being the object of filming by parents, usually for parents, but have now shifted to being the creators of videos for consumption by others.

With this in mind, you may have come across the idea of a generation gap. This is a term that was quite popular during the 1960s and 1970s. It referred to significant differences between young people and their parents' generation and could be seen in respect of fashion and music: children wore very different clothes to their parents and listened to different music. In some ways though it could be said that the idea of a generation gap disappeared to a large extent during the 1980s and 1990s when older people were seen to retain an interest in popular music and fashion in a way that was similar to the interests of younger people and children. However, when we consider those young people who are referred to as Generation Z – defined in Cervi (2021: 199) as those born between 1996 and 2010 – there is a key issue that distinguishes them from their parents. They are the first generation for whom the internet has always been a part of their lives (Cervi, 2021).

Cervi's interest is in dance, and she provides an interesting insight into how the video producing and sharing app TikTok influences behaviour. For Cervi, dance is integral to TikTok. She notes that in 2020 the most followed TikTok producer in the world, with 80 million followers, is someone who posts dance videos of themselves. However, what Cervi points out is that in respect of self-filming there is a key limitation. As the content creator has to remain on camera at all times, dance on TikTok is restricted to movement from the hips up. TikTok dances are copied widely but, in all cases, movement is only above the hips. In this way TikTok has changed what dance is for millions of people. For many children and young people, dance has become something that is done in bedrooms and to be filmed. Compare this to previous generations where dance was a social activity; children and young people went out to school discos and youth clubs from a young age and it didn't matter how you danced, no one was recording it.

Following from this what we might consider here is how social media such as Facebook or TikTok (other platforms are available) provide a platform upon which identity is shaped and manipulated. As such, social media can be used to construct social relationships and define social identities (Buckingham, 2009). So, instead of thinking about children being excluded from the media as per older media systems, it is important to consider how new technology provides many ways in which children can take part in the media and use this to explore their identity. This brings us back to the idea of structure and agency.

Consider though that when we talk about structure and agency, we can see how each might be insufficient alone to make sense of contemporary childhood. We may say that children have agency, as demonstrated by their engagement in media, but they have it within the structure that exists independently of them. In this case that structure is the technology of the media. At the same time new forms of technology, such as new apps, may subsequently change the structure and make new things possible. Not all new possibilities however are good, but equally they are not necessarily bad for children.

The dark side of social media: the trolls have come out from under the bridge

In one sense the development of new technologies which offer a platform for social media can be seen in a positive light, if we view them as providing opportunities for children and young people to engage in communal activities and in terms of how they foster the development of new, often creative, skills. The paper by Cervi provides one example of how young people may utilise new media in creative ways, sometimes in financially rewarding ways. In this way, social media offers possibilities to children.

It is also the case however that children and young people may encounter online content and/or online groups that is/are not at all welcome. Numerous news stories and cases around the world have linked children's deaths, including suicides, to engagement with online material. This ranges from so-called online challenges which have resulted in accidental deaths to pro-suicide websites which target young people and, it is argued, encourage young people to take their own life. It is also worth considering other ways in which children and young people can be exposed to ideas and beliefs that have a wider negative social impact. For example, children and young people with access to the internet are very likely to encounter material which could, or indeed aims to, influence their thinking in negative ways or radicalise them. This is evident in the social threat that arises from far-right groups promoting racism, often bound up with ideas about nationalism. It is also evident in relation to the rise of groups promoting sexism and misogyny.

Although we will say more about sexism and discrimination in the following chapter when we discuss gender, it is important to note that recently there appears to be a growth in sexism as displayed by boys and that this has been significantly influenced by online material (Bates, 2021). This is sometimes referred to as being bound up with the manosphere.

Note

The manosphere is an umbrella term referring to websites which foster ideas about what it means to be a man, and which promote anti-feminist or negative views about women.

These sites promote the idea that men's rights have been reduced because of women's rights and argue that there is a need to restore male supremacy.

Misogyny represents the idea that women are inferior to men. It contributes to a general contempt or even hatred for women and promotes negative treatment, even violence, towards women.

Incels are often self-labelled. The term refers to men who claim to be celibate against their will, that is, involuntary celibate. To be celibate is not to have sex and incels believe that women withhold sex from them because women's rights mean that they can, rather than because of any issues relating to their own behaviour or presentation. Incels claim that since the 1960s feminism has enabled women to gain social power and to control access to sexual activity. For incels this is a denial of a man's basic rights. This idea underpins the misogynistic views that they hold and supports their belief that it is reasonable to punish women for holding this imagined power over them.

The manosphere encompasses a wide range of websites and social media activity which promote misogynist ideas. Children may often encounter misogynistic groups who promote the idea that men in general are in some way under threat from women and/or feminist ideas. Such ideas contribute to making the lives of girls and women poorer in a range of ways, from general casual sexism to the real threat of violence. Crucially though these ideas do not just shape the thinking and values of boys, they also shape how girls both see themselves and understand their role in society.

As such, children are growing up in a world wherein internet and social media technologies have the capacity to increase the risks that young people face based upon sexual behaviour and the matter of consent. In this way it is pertinent to consider how the denial of consent, saying no to sex, may be challenged multiple times, whereas giving consent, saying yes, is inevitably accepted immediately. The ideas about what is expected of women (and girls) that are promoted online influence what boys and men understand as acceptable behaviour and how girls and women believe they should behave and what they can expect in relationships. Saying no is often seen as negotiable or subject to challenge; saying yes is rarely challenged or considered to be said under duress. Within the context of incel ideology however, women should not have the right to say no. All of this shapes childhood in terms of how from a young age gendered behaviour is shaped.

Is nothing private anymore?

In thinking about children's relationships with social media it is interesting to consider what this means for the ability of children to have or maintain privacy. Privacy itself is an interesting issue to consider in an era of individualism and it is useful to give some thought to how the ability to be private has changed over time, and why privacy is important. Privacy may be considered as a social issue in that it is essentially bound up with the extent to which your thoughts and behaviours are exposed, or made available, to others. A key part of this is the extent to which any individual can prevent thoughts and behaviours being made public. There may be a number of reasons why childhood is shaped by privacy or the lack of it. Although this may seem to be quite distinct from the media, it can be argued that media technologies can have a major influence upon the extent to which privacy can be, or should be, maintained for children.

Note

Privacy is one of those concepts that is often just taken at face value but is actually a very complex issue (Solove, 2002). With regards to our line of argument we feel that Kasper (2005: 76) is useful. Kasper provides a broad account of ideas about privacy, but by focusing upon how our privacy can be invaded she offers some key insights.

Following Kasper we can understand the invasion of privacy by another in relation to:

- the taking and or disclosing of an individual's personal information, identity, image or likeness without consent;
- the interception and/or surveillance of communication;
- intrusions upon or into an individual's body.

In each case the invasion of privacy should be seen as an act that is against the rights of the individual.

Note that privacy in childhood is linked to, but not solely about, child protection issues.

Alongside this, Baghai (2012) presents an argument about privacy which promotes the right to solitude in response to the growth of pressure from external sources. In other words, the right to be private. This can be seen as being more important to older children as they start to develop their own identity and ideas.

In considering our ability to be private, then, think about the factors that make privacy more or less possible. It is useful to start with something that is a part of everyone's life to indicate how changes over time have changed the experience of privacy: housing.

Think about the sort of housing that is available in contemporary UK society and focus on bedrooms and toilets, places where we might expect to be private. Now consider that housing can be said to embody ideas about families, which reflect notions of privacy. Contemporary ideas of housing both reflect and reinforce the idea that parents and children should have separate bedrooms and that children over a certain age should not have to share bedrooms with siblings of the opposite sex. However, think about the ideas which underpin a two-up, two-down terrace house. In this type of housing, children of both sexes and all ages are provided with one shared bedroom. Consider also that it is not so very long ago that such houses would have been unlikely to have an inside toilet, never mind a bathroom. Baths would have been taken in a portable tin bath in the kitchen/dining room.

You may appreciate then that children living in this sort of house would have had a very different experience of privacy when compared to children living in houses with three bedrooms or more. The widespread development of the three-bedroom house facilitates the segregation of children based on sex, but in doing so creates a further degree of privacy.

Now think about how in the UK very many new-build houses not only provide four bedrooms, but that en-suite toilets and/or bathrooms are very common. When we add to this the fact that children's centrally heated bedrooms will often contain a television and a networked computer, we can see that for many children home life in 2025 will be very different to previous generations and that this affords greater privacy.

In 2025, very many Western children will not share a bedroom, and their in-house leisure time will often be on their own as opposed to being a family activity in a shared space. Consequently, consider how developments in housing design along with new technologies have led to a more fragmented home experience compared to how families interacted in the past, but where this also increases the scope for privacy. Children in contemporary society then are more likely to have an early expectation and practical understanding of privacy. Contemporary childhood is shaped as part of the family but within its own space.

The reason for considering privacy within this chapter, however, is that the advent of social media seems to us to be a major influence upon the extent to which privacy has changed or how it can be hard to maintain. This seems a contradiction to the ideas of childhood having rights. That said, it may be important to state that ideas about what should be private are also subject to change.

Our experience

Sometime during the mid 2000s, one of our teenage children talked about being muddy or sweaty for the rest of the day if PE/Games was timetabled early. To us this seemed astounding, so we questioned why they hadn't showered after PE while at school. Our child was equally astounded by the thought of a communal shower at school taken in view of classmates and teachers. They questioned why we would think that was acceptable.

When we were at school it was perfectly normal and expected to have a communal shower after PE. One of us worked in heavy industry from the age of 16 and a communal shower was taken by all workers at the end of a shift. To us, public nudity for the purpose of showering was not at all unacceptable, it was the act of not showering that was unacceptable, but how does this sound to you?

Paradoxically, while the issue of communal showers or even changing in public has declined, other forms of exposing our bodies to others have increased. This is another way in which childhood has been changed by media. Think about the paradox that asserting rights to privacy, and our example of the decline of communal school showers, have occurred while activities such as sexting have increased. Sexting (Simpson, 2013), sending a sexual image of yourself, might be argued to be a choice, but we are all likely to be aware of a situation when sexting to a specific individual has resulted in a wider distribution of an image than the sender intended.

Sharenting and emotions

The example earlier regarding the declining experience of communal showers at school demonstrates what we mean by social change. Similarly, the advent of social media, facilitated by smartphones, has meant that new pressures are brought to bear upon privacy and that new tensions have emerged. The fact that young children are interacting with and are on social media is not in doubt (De Leyn et al, 2022), nor are we saying that this is altogether a bad thing. It is just part of the modern world. However, it is also worth considering that children are often drawn into social media by the actions of parents. As such, some consideration of what has come to be known as sharenting is relevant when we try to understand contemporary childhood, and of how the normalising of shared images shapes childhood.

Sharenting refers to the practice in which parents post photos and videos of their family life on social networks for a range of reasons, something which also covers the activity of parent-bloggers (Blum-Ross and Livingstone, 2017; Fox and Hoy, 2019; Lazard et al, 2019; Aydoğdu et al, 2023). This gives rise to concerns about the risks that may result from sharenting, such as revealing data and/or encouraging unwanted attention, but it is a reflection of online behaviour that has become normalised. However, the sharenting of images and videos of children can also be seen as an activity which infringes upon the rights of the child to privacy. This is particularly the case regarding the sharing of images without consent (Kasper, 2005) and in relation to solitude, by which we mean solitude as non-engagement with an online presence (Baghai, 2012). Children may not want their images to be online.

Although our focus here is on privacy, it is worth noting that concerns relating to children and solitude go back some time and are currently enjoying a resurgence of interest. One important aspect of this is in distinguishing between solitude and loneliness (Stern et al, 2022). Although children may be impacted negatively because of loneliness, times of solitude can be positive. Social media however can be seen as something which reduces the possibility of solitude.

As such, parental actions relating to their own self-representation can blur the boundary between parents' and children's selves, and rights as children become bound up in the practice of sharenting (Blum-Ross and Livingstone, 2017; Holiday et al, 2022; Walrave et al, 2022). The key issue for us here is not that there is one main reason for the fact that sharenting has become so commonplace, rather that the act of sharenting invades the children's privacy to a greater or lesser extent (Brosch, 2018). It also shapes childhood in a way that children are, in these instances, merely an extension of the parents' identity rather than individuals with their own rights.

It may be worth considering, then, that sharenting is simply one aspect of a much broader discourse regarding sharing. So, sharenting may be dismissed as just another way in which proud parents show off their children, in which case that is nothing new. Another way of looking at it would be that sharenting provides an opportunity to represent your parenting as good and there is certainly significant social pressure to be good parents. When we consider what we share and what we keep private, however, it is worth considering how there has been a significant move towards the sharing of thoughts and emotions in recent decades.

Social media can be seen as one method by which we can express our feelings and emotions, but this does not happen in a vacuum. Within contemporary society there are numerous systems that have been set up with the intention of facilitating the expression of emotions or which rest upon the expression of emotions. Because of this we can say that forms of confession have become deeply embedded within contemporary society (Besley, 2005; Elliott, 2009; Fejes and Dahlstedt, 2013; Macfarlane, 2017). Aspects of confession then have become part of children's lives in the 21st century.

Besley points to the growth in confessional type television shows such as Oprah Winfrey or Jerry Springer, whereas Fejes and Dahlstedt present reality type television shows such as Big Brother, alongside online communities such as Facebook, as examples of how confessional type presentation of the self has become an everyday practice. Confessional pressures affect children, also, as they will both observe and be drawn in to this practice. Practices such as circle time within schools exert force on children to share their thoughts and emotions (Hanafin et al, 2010; Leach and Lewis, 2013). You may have experienced circle time yourself; if so, would you consider that during circle time it may not have seemed acceptable to have nothing to share, or that children are encouraged to share things that might leave them vulnerable?

The idea of the confessional comes from the work of Foucault and underpins the idea of a therapeutic approach to society (Furedi, 2004; Ecclestone and Hayes, 2009; Fejes and Dahlstedt, 2013). Foucault's ideas about the social nature of the confessional were initially concerned with the role of the Catholic Church and its aims at social control but have gone beyond this towards an everyday process of sharing our thoughts and feelings. Confession is encouraged on the grounds that forms of confession are the ways in which we come to know ourselves. In this way, the act of confessing, irrespective of how, shapes our self-understanding and contributes to our sense of self.

The implications for children are that they now inhabit a world where emotional confession has become a normal part of their experience; following from this is the idea that therapy has been normalised. These ideas contribute to the way that children and young people will talk about mental health issues such as stress and anxiety and will activity seek or expect someone to be available to listen to their thoughts (Macfarlane, 2017). While this can be seen as a positive development for childhood, it is of concern that anxiety, when understood as something that is problematic, has appeared to reach endemic proportions and that this has led to a form of disabling for children who cannot attend school or engage in other social activities.

In thinking about emotions in a more general sense, though, compare how the move towards confessing emotions often foregrounds the revealing of unhappiness, stress or anxiety, and juxtapose this with the ubiquity of the sharing of photos or videos of people having a good time. The everyday world that we all inhabit is not a world in which we are always happy, or always having a good time, yet children today are growing up within a society where there is often significant pressure to project the image that life is always good. In this way the rise of social media technologies may be seen to intensify a sense that everyone else is having a better time and this may act to make our own unhappiness appear abnormal, so contributing to anxiety.

Being critical, making links and developing arguments

If you are tasked with an assignment that is concerned with the media it is important to recognise that the media represents a broad range of modes of communication which have changed, and do change, over time. What is also important, if we are to adopt the position that childhood is socially constructed, is that how we understand childhood will be influenced by the way that childhood is represented within the media as well as how children interact with or use media.

In the days of the mass media, before the internet, the media tended to represent innocence, risk or possibly threat. Images were produced by organisations and transmitted one-way. The mass media still exists, but its reach and influence are much smaller than was once the case. The most important development in relation to children and young people however is in the development of internet-enabled social media. The combination of mobile phone technologies, social media apps and easy access to online connectivity has transformed the media across the globe. This also means that children interact with media in a way that they didn't in the past and this has an altogether different influence on childhood. This is not to say this is always negative, as some might suggest, but that the influence of media is much more complex.

One thing to consider when it comes to your activities as a student is your ability to make links between the different things that you read and even the different aspects of your course. With that in mind you can make a clear link between the discussion that was offered in Chapter 6 about the development of a post-truth society and the nature of social media in respect of how this facilitates a post-truth society.

The key thing is that for companies engaged within the old mass media, such as newspapers or TV news, there are strict regulations in place regarding what can be said or reported. This provides for a degree of trust in that consumers may identify bias but still acknowledge a basic level of truth. Within the social media landscape there are few or no regulations. This means that individuals who engage with social media should be cautious in trusting what they see and read, but this is difficult if messages are continually repeated or presented in an engaging way, which they often are. The outcome is that misinformation, disinformation and a whole host of conspiracy theories are promoted and potentially believed. What is ironic is that although children are under pressure to be truthful, they are often interacting with a social world which is anything but truthful.

A further aspect of social media which can be said to have changed the lived experiences of children and young people is with regards to how privacy is understood and the ways in which sharenting by parents as well as posting by children creates different experiences compared to children before the internet. One particular aspect of posting and sharenting, however, is the way in which images are overwhelmingly of people having a good time and being happy. The reality of life for many people, however, is that good times are hard to come by and being happy seems out of reach. In some ways this is normal, our lives cannot always be good, we cannot be happy all the time. The problem arises when children and young people who are not happy come to assess themselves against the idea that everyone else is happy.

So, in thinking about some key points that summarise this chapter about the media and how an understanding of the media can help us understand contemporary childhood, consider that:

- Childhood is often represented in contradictory ways within the media.
- The old mass media was one-way, the internet and social media provides opportunities for participation.
- Images conceal as well as reveal.
- Social media provides a platform for spreading untruths as well as presenting children and young people with significant risks.
- Social media could be seen as being a platform for a post-truth society because it is unregulated.

One key thing that you might take away from this chapter is that to put yourself in a position whereby markers can have confidence in your assignments you would be well advised to ensure that the evidence that you draw upon when completing assignments comes from trusted sources (so perhaps not the internet!). It is expected that students will access material online but there is much that is online that is of little value.

Further thoughts

What does it mean to have a friend in an age of social media?

At the end of 2024 the Australian government approved legislation that is intended to prevent under-16s from accessing social media sites. This is obviously going to be a challenge to enforce, but consider if this is a positive or negative move in relation to children and young people's lives. What might be the negatives of banning social media for young people and children?

It is possible to access good quality reporting and unbiased news within the UK, and we would recommend the Guardian newspaper and website as a trusted source, but many adults and young people get their news from unregulated sources online. What we recommend is using more than one source of news and check who is saying what, and why they might be saying it, as well as what is not being revealed. In other words, be critical.

Further reading

Bates (2021) provides a good introduction to ideas about misogyny and incels which relate to the manosphere.

Cervi (2021) explores TikTok and Generation Z.

Holland (2004) is an interesting account of how children are presented within the media.

8

Gender

> **This chapter will help you to understand:**
> - how you can distinguish between sex and gender;
> - how gender is socially constructed and how we may be said to perform gender within social settings from an early age;
> - further ways in which sexism and misogyny impact upon the lives of women and girls;
> - how the umbrella term 'gender variance' reflects that gender has multiple forms rather than being a binary choice.

Do we have to have gender?

Let's start by repeating what we said in Chapter 7 about how children are faced with masses of information from a range of sources on a daily basis. The only way that we can cope with life is by making some sort of sense out of it all and sense making starts at a very early age. Think about everything that you see and hear, everything that you experience as well as the demands from others in your life. Sometimes we filter things out and take little, if any, notice of some things. However, to operate successfully within society we often need to recognise the differences that matter in our world and to make sense of them and develop a sense of how we fit into our world.

As such we can consider that we categorise the things that we experience. This doesn't mean that we are each required to create categories for things. In general, these categories are provided to us by the society that we live in; they often have a long history and are already established ways of understanding our society. Very often categories constitute dichotomies, such as rich or poor, north or south, Black or white. In considering these, though, you may well recognise that they exist as descriptions of relative positions.

In this chapter we are going to focus upon the categories of sex and gender. Traditionally these are understood in categories such as boy/male or girl/female and genders of masculine or feminine. Currently, in the West in the early 21st century, sex and gender are subject to some very volatile debates relating to sexual differences and gender categories in a way that is very relevant in understanding contemporary childhood.

Note

The starting point for understanding sex and gender in sociology is as follows:

- Sex refers to being male or female and is biological. In the first instance it is determined by nature. In general, this can be seen as fixed, though we will say more about this later.

- Gender means being masculine or feminine and is socially constructed. How gender is represented and understood can and does change. Therefore, what it means to be masculine or feminine can mean different things in different societies, different cultures and across different times.

The tensions that exist within contemporary society about trans rights arise from commentators foregrounding either sex or gender depending upon the position being taken.

The debate in relation to childhood is what and who we can be.

At this stage we have seen that childhood is shaped by elements of both nature and nurture. So, although we have argued that childhood is socially constructed, we recognise that it is shaped by natural processes such as biological differences and/or changes. A powerful factor with respect to gender is that it is socially constructed in relation to ideas about reproduction, even though in one sense this is irrelevant in that children's capacities for reproduction only exist in the future. As such the idea of children as becomings is reinforced by a focus upon their future biological position. As such, we can say that nature and nurture come together and overlap. So, nature determines the sex of a child, but nurture is how society creates genders, albeit often influenced by nature.

In relation to children, as soon as a pregnancy is announced it is not unusual for questions to be asked regarding the sex of the baby to be. This is then aided by technology which allows us to know the sex of an unborn foetus from as early as 12 weeks. From this we can see how biology, nature, is drawn upon in defining the child as a boy or girl. Consequently, this will have the effect of shaping the childhood that the child will experience.

It is also worth considering at this point that there is a biological condition (congenital adrenal hyperplasia) that results in a baby being born of indeterminate sex. This means that a decision is usually made as to whether the child is to be brought up as a boy or a girl, with medical intervention facilitating the choice made. Thus, we return to the position of having boys or girls.

What is evident is that childhood is gendered, that is, childhood is shaped differently depending on what sex a child is. As such, sex and gender play a significant part in how we experience childhood from an early age. It influences how we are expected to behave, what we do and how we think. We take on a particular gender through socialisation though that does not mean that this is a rigid and clearly defined process which leads to a particular version of gender being adopted. Gender is a lot more fluid than that. Boys can adopt feminine behaviours and attributes just as girls can adopt masculine ones.

So, as a first response to the question that the sub-heading posed, as to whether we have to have gender: we are going to say that it is not that we have to have it, but it is very hard to avoid it as our starting point to shaping childhood. Gender is applied to us by the society in which we live. However, we do have the ability to shape how we perform our gender, which in turn may impact upon how gender is seen in a broader social sense. Our power to shape our own gender can be seen in how children from an early age may do and say things about who they believe they are and how they want to be understood.

This takes us back to thinking about structure and agency, where gender, as a socially shared idea, exists at the time of our birth and operates as the structure, but as we grow up we can behave in ways that shapes and/or change our gender using our agency and, possibly, how gender is perceived in our society. In this way if we say that gender is a structure, we have to accept that it is always subject to the possibility of change.

So, is gender real or is it socially constructed?

So far, we have given an account of gender that is quite passive. The work of Judith Butler, however, gives much more weight to the idea of agency within an understanding of gender, especially the idea that gender is something that we do rather than just being something that we have. We said earlier that sex refers to biology and that gender refers to social or cultural understandings. Butler disagrees with this clear distinction on the grounds that even the biological nature of sex is embedded within social and cultural meanings.

The idea that we become a man or a woman from the starting point of being born a boy or a girl gives us a clue that these things are not wholly natural, because we then start to see that becoming a man or a woman is bound up with ideas about femininity or masculinity and what a man or a woman is. For Butler, gender is something that we construct and work on but it is not something that is an essential part of us (Butler, 2006). By 'work on', Butler suggests that we, individually as well as as a society, consider what gender is and what it can be. In turn this explains how gender can change.

To begin with, Butler rejects what has been called an essentialist position. This is the idea that there is some fixed essence that relates to sex and/or gender. Instead, she presents the argument that both sex and gender should be understood as being socially constructed to the extent that even biological sex is shaped by cultural and social norms. An example of this is how women, being born with a womb and the ability to carry a child, are then expected to carry a child; following from this expectation, childlessness is presented as abnormal. As such what we understand as male or female is mediated by language, culture and structures of power. So, even the assignment of the label male or female at birth is not a neutral act but is instead informed by social norms and expectations. A key concept used by Butler in presenting her ideas about sex and gender is the concept of performativity. This can be understood as presenting gender as a social script which we are aware of, and which shapes who we become; we are performing a role that is set out by society.

Note

Performativity is a common term in social science. In a simple sense it can be seen as the way that we perform, or behave, in ways which see us falling in line with discourses. These may be understood as social scripts representing the rules that society constructs, and which mean that we know how we should perform.

For Butler, then, it is not that gender exists as some essential aspect of us, instead gender exists as part of a cultural discourse that surrounds us and is revealed in how we act (Gérardin-Laverge, 2022)

In a simple sense, then, gender is something that is done (Ringrose and Rawlings, 2015).

However, because biological differences are strongly associated with the importance of reproduction it is easy for us to overlook the fact that gender is a social construct. Even so, the social perception and performing of these differences is embedded within culture. It is not the case that biological sex creates an essential need to behave in any particular way. The social practices and structures which influence how we behave, like all such social practices, may vary enormously, as is evident from anthropological and historical studies.

An example of this is play. When we look at toys aimed at girls there is a clear message being promoted regarding what a girl is. In suggesting girls play with dolls, for instance, we are focusing on the reproductive role of girls who we presume will become mothers and will be caring and nurturing. Boys, on the other hand, are typically encouraged in play reflecting physicality or work. We can see cultural expectations in how we relate to the ways in which children play which lead to us restricting what children may choose because they offend our sensibilities. It is important to recognise however that such approaches limit opportunities for both girls and boys.

Student task

Make a list of the various ways in which we treat boys and girls differently from birth to adulthood.

In doing this you might consider language, toys or clothes, and activities or games which act to reinforce and reproduce gender.

So, children are surrounded by information about gender, something that we raised at the start of this chapter. They are socialised to understand and respond to gender differences from an early age and soon come to learn adult views on what is appropriate (Schaffer, 1996). In respect of gender differences, then, children inevitably learn how to do gender. This does not mean that all adults act to keep children within accepted gender roles though. Some adults will encourage children to play across genders, offering a variety of activities regardless of the child's sex. Nurseries are actively encouraged to do this. However, if children are seen to resist this it may be presented as a demonstration of some essential aspect of gender corresponding to sex. It is important to recognise though that although children may resist toys and games which do not correspond with their gender, children are not simply passive recipients of socialising forces; they actively seek 'rules' which apply to behaviour according to gender. Children are often aware of the rules about gender, and these may come from sources other than parents or caregivers.

The worrying persistence of sexism and misogyny

We, the authors, both grew up in the 1960s and 1970s. We say this because to quote the novelist L.P. Hartley, 'the past is a foreign country, they do things differently there' (Hartley, 1958: 1). We would agree, the past really was different. During our lifetime it has been perfectly legal to pay men more than women for doing the same job and to restrict the subjects that girls could take at school on the basis that some subjects were not suitable or appropriate for them. There was a period in our lives when many women did not work outside the home and many employers barred women from certain jobs. It was acceptable to deny entry to women into clubs and/or bars or to refuse to serve them pints. In other words, everyday sexism was commonplace in a way that was not deemed offensive, but normal; common sense even.

During the 20th century the feminist movement had become more active, and women campaigned vigorously for greater equality. Because of actions taken by women a lot did change in respect of gender equality, and although we would not say that equality was ever really achieved, given that girls and women do still experience discrimination, things did get much better. However, we now worry that social changes are undermining the gains that were made, that equality is being challenged and that sexism exists in different but equally offensive ways.

Note

Sexism can be defined as discrimination or prejudice that is based on gender (Leaper and Brown, 2014). It is generally seen in attitudes and behaviours displayed by men and boys towards women and girls which assume or position women as subordinate to men (Ayala et al, 2021).

Misogyny refers to a hatred of women. Sexism can be considered as being one aspect of attitudes and behaviours, with misogyny a more extreme version of it. Both have a negative impact on women's lives. Neither sexism nor misogyny are ever acceptable forms of behaviour.

Patriarchy in a simple sense means male power. It refers to the social structures which act in a way that reduce the power of girls and women in society while privileging boys and men.

Discrimination and prejudice both reflect and reinforce an inequality in power when comparing two or more groups. Such discrimination and prejudice may operate at an informal level, such as in the telling of sexist 'jokes'; and which are often excused in contemporary society as 'banter', especially in response to objections. Referring to sexist joking as banter can be understood as an intention to dress up sexism as light-hearted, or something that was not really believed or meant by the speaker; it was just a joke. This acts to position the objector as having a problem, not the speaker. What this does though is to reinforce the possibility of discrimination. Discrimination and prejudice have also often operated at a formal level, though, in terms of providing a different curriculum for boys and girls and restricting, or even preventing, access to certain types of work based on sex or gender.

In spite of the inequalities that are bound up with discrimination it is not unusual to see sexism presented as common sense. By this we mean that some biological difference between types of people is used to act as the basis of a more wide-ranging explanation for social differences and inequalities. So, it is the case that women give birth and lactate. Because of this we can say that childbirth by women is natural but to then use this specific and short-term example to explain and support a whole range of social inequalities appears ludicrous. Apart from the actual breast-feeding of babies, we can be very confident in stating that childcare is social and is not dependent on the mother.

Furthermore, once we accept that there is nothing natural about childcare other than the matter of lactation in relation to feeding, we can begin to accept that the entire basis of gender divisions which go much further than childcare are themselves not natural but are the result of social processes which have led to men and women experiencing life in different ways. Note also that not all mothers breastfeed their children. In the contemporary world some babies are only fed milk formula, historically the use of wet nurses has been a solution to mothers not being able to breastfeed, and the wealthy often outsource childcare to nannies.

These ideas can be seen within the development of feminist theory in the 1970s. For example, in *The Dialectic of Sex*, Shulamith Firestone (1971) argues that women's particular physiology makes them weaker than men, which when taken together with the need for women to nurture the newborn child creates a situation where women rely upon men for physical security. Or it did in a very distant past. However, what has happened since is that men have constructed institutionalised structures of domination over women which act to subordinate all women and which place men in a superior role, even though the biological origins of this relationship have changed beyond recognition.

Although Firestone makes a good case she can be seen as giving some support to the idea that women are in some way naturally weaker. This argument however is overcome by the work of Mary Daly (1984). In *Gyn/Ecology* Daly argues that it is not female biology that has led to the subordination of women, it is male biology. Using suttee in India, genital mutilation (for example, female circumcision) in Africa, foot-binding in China and witch hunts in Europe, she argues that males are naturally aggressive and that this aggression is often channelled into the control of women. Susan Brownmiller's *Against Our Will* (1975) provides a similar argument based on male aggression, with a particular focus on the objectification of women within pornography.

We would point out here that Daly could be accused of falling into a deterministic trap in saying men are naturally aggressive. If she can explain male violence towards women on the basis of some innate, natural characteristic then critics will inevitably say that this supports the idea of natural difference. So, are men naturally violent, or are men socialised in a way that make it easy for some of them to be violent because of the structures of society? As not all men are violent then the latter argument is useful. For children growing up in a world in which violent and/or sexist behaviours are witnessed, then this may influence their childhood and their future selves.

Anti-feminism and masculinity: retreating to the past

In one sense it is easy to dismiss feminist arguments from the 1970s as history. The UK now is much more equal and some of the arguments about the exercising of male power seem to be no longer relevant. But is that really the case? Think about your own experiences of life in relation to the world that children and young people inhabit.

Consider how social media platforms have provided access to misogynistic views on a much broader scale than in previous generations and that 'influencers' are able to reach a much wider audience than was the case before the advent of accessible online social media platforms such as X, TikTok and so on. For young men in particular, social media contributes to many being drawn in to the misogynistic views put forward by influencers such as Andrew Tate and to holding negative views about feminism (Campbell et al, 2024).

Think also about the conspiracy type arguments being put forward within what has been termed the 'manosphere' by self-styled incel groups, as introduced previously (Ging, 2019; Glace et al, 2021; Sugiura, 2021; Helm et al, 2022). The rise of the incel phenomenon is embedded within a worldview that is characterised by specific ideas about sex and gender and the associated justification for violence against women which support ideas about the violent nature of men. Numerous studies demonstrate that incels associate violence with masculinity in a positive way and see this as a means by which domination over women not only can but should be achieved (Scaptura and Boyle, 2020; Glace et al, 2021; Helm et al, 2022; O'Donnell and Shor, 2022).

There is no doubt that the actions of anti-feminist groups have created a real problem for girls and women in the 21st century. In making sense of the resurgence of sexism, though, we want to reiterate the idea that gender is social. Remember, gender is not fixed and because of this it is subject to change. Now consider that many people either do not like change, or that some changes may have negative consequences for some. As such, the social position and experiences of boys and young men is also worth considering as part of this discussion about gender.

As pro-feminist ideas started to be accepted during the 1960s and 1970s, a parallel idea about men's liberation developed. This was initially aimed at self-critique and reflection with a view to changing ideas about masculinity (Messner, 2016; Ging, 2019). In other words, the concern was to be liberated from sexist and discriminatory ideas which limited men's role in society as well as women's. What Messner notes, however, is that the basic premise of feminism, that the social advantages that men have act against the interests of women, started to be seen as problematic by some. This led supporters of male liberation splitting into both a pro-feminist and an anti-feminist group.

This is relevant because it underpins ideas about masculinity. It involves reflecting upon what masculinity is and what masculinity means for both men and women. If we look back to the 1960s and 1970s, however, masculinity was often bound up with the industrial nature of work at the time. A central issue was that industrial work generally involved the demonstration and exercising of male strength and power. Think about the stereotypes of the Sheffield steelworker, the Birmingham foundryman, the Geordie miner and the Glaswegian shipbuilder. For boys in the 1970s and earlier, masculinity did not need to be worked for, masculinity often just came with the job and the job entailed hard physical work in difficult conditions. Those jobs have largely gone. For boys in contemporary society, what they are to become is less clear than it once was.

These industrial jobs disappeared through the 1980s as a consequence of what has been termed deindustrialisation (Greenstein, 2019). Although deindustrialisation can be seen as taking place over a long period of time (Nettleingham, 2019), the 1980s saw a rapid decline of industrial work and a major growth in service sector work. Service sector work was often portrayed as women's work. So, if industrial jobs are seen as men's jobs, and if masculinity is associated with such work, then deindustrialisation disrupts the path to masculinity. It is no longer straightforward. This reflects what we discussed about identity when we introduced post-modernism.

What also has to be considered is that the types of work that replaced industrial jobs during and after the 1980s were jobs that were often filled by women. As such, this intensified changes that can be traced to the 1960s. This change in the nature of the workforce is usually termed the feminisation of work (Rubery, 2015). Note that the feminisation of work is not limited to the UK, it has also taken place in other Western countries (Nolan, 1997; Hicks, 2000; Cooke-Reynolds and Zukewich, 2004).

Looking back over recent decades, then, it is possible to see social changes which mean that traditional forms of masculinity are no longer current. The world of work has changed to become more equal in gender terms and, in some ways, more sensitive to forms of behaviour that may be seen as oppressive. This is not to explain anti-feminism as simply a response to deindustrialisation; anti-feminists rarely call for the return of jobs involving physical labour and a harsh working environment. Instead, it is simply to demonstrate that a number of factors may combine in ways which change society. So, feminism seeks greater equality for women, and deindustrialisation has acted to change and/or reduce traditional men's jobs while more opportunities for women are being created. This leaves children and young people with less obvious ideas about what it is to be a man.

This has created a void that some anti-feminists are able to fill by calling for a return to so-called traditional forms of masculinity (Lawson, 2022; Sayogie et al, 2023), though such a response to social change is not new. In London in the 1960s, deindustrialisation was changing the nature of work that was available, while at the same time the hippie movement was changing Western culture (Clarke, 2006). This contributed to the emergence of skinhead groups in the East End of London at the end of the 1960s which can be understood as being a response by working-class boys aiming to recreate an image of a working-class culture that was rapidly disappearing. This is evident in the skinhead look – the shaved heads, braces and boots – which together with both an implicit and explicit air of aggression can be seen as the opposite of the middle-class or hippie image.

In a cultural sense the skinhead look operates to hold on to what is being lost by recreating a more stylised working-class identity. Given that commentators in the manosphere are preoccupied with the idea of a masculinity that has been lost then it could be argued that the lure of the manosphere for young boys today is in providing a way to recreate the past so as to magically regain what is being presented as lost power.

In one sense incels represent an extreme version of right-wing ideas which focus upon traditional gender roles, though more general anti-feminist ideas do represent a similar approach. In terms of politics and theory an intrinsic social conservatism locates anti-feminism on the right of politics. The right is always resistant to any form of change which they see as upsetting the natural order. As such, ideas about the natural basis of both sex and gender are drawn on by the right in response to what they see as developments which aim to increase equality or simply to accommodate changed positions regarding gender. Concerns with wokeness are relevant here in how wokeness promotes greater equality within society in a manner that many on the right resist. As such, it is now worth considering an even more contentious subject for many, that of transgender issues.

Is transgender another binary narrative?

At the beginning of this chapter, we presented some fairly traditional ideas regarding sex and gender by proposing that sex referred to biological matters and that gender referred to social matters. Following from this we made the traditionally accepted point that sex was a matter of being male or female and that gender was concerned with what it means to be masculine or feminine. We also stated that sex is relatively fixed or stable and that gender is much more fluid.

Consequently, descriptive terms about sex and gender have also come to be accepted as fixed or stable in what they refer to, such as male, female, man, woman, masculine and feminine. They are words that rest on, or represent, meanings that are widely shared and accepted. They are, or have been until very recently, uncontested words. However, as you will be aware, this simplistic binary thinking is now being challenged more openly. That is not to say that this is something new, gender roles have always been subverted. However, there is now much more open debate about this, and it has become more relevant to childhood.

So, it may be the case that even very recently labels relating to sex and gender were stable words, but by the 2020s it seems obvious that these words, and the meanings that they represent, have become unstable. Words such as masculine and feminine have become subject to interrogation and debate; they have become politicised and are up for grabs (Schiappa, 2021: 1). As such, we have moved to an era where gender is not binary but variant. We will come back to this idea.

Let us reiterate that politics is essentially about power. Politics is concerned with how one group with a set of shared ideas and values seeks to have its position accepted when compared to another group with different ideas and values. So, while binary thinking on gender is not a true reflection of people's lived experience, there are still many in society, and in power, who are uncomfortable with this.

Schiappa (2021) makes the point that with regards to issues concerning sex and gender, it is possible to describe two opposing positions:

- Biological determinism: this sees gender as corresponding to biology at birth (this is an essentialist position, sometimes referred to as natal sex).
- Autonomous nominalism: this presents gender as separate from biology, instead it is seen as a matter of self-identification.

This distinction is relevant to the issue of performativity in the work of Butler. For Butler, gender is located in how we act, rather than how we act being something that could reveal the gender that is an essential part of us. As such we can say that Butler presented an anti-essentialist position. An essentialist position claims that there is something that can be said to be located within us. This can be seen as the basis of a key philosophical conflict, as we will demonstrate later.

Note

You will often come across -ism's in social science and sometimes they seem complicated. Here are three -ism's that are particularly relevant to the debates about transgender issues:

- Essentialism is the idea that there is something that is the key factor. So, biological sex is often presented as the essential difference between men and women.
- Determinism refers to something being determined, or caused, by something else, in this case gender has usually been presented as being determined by sex.
- Nominalism refers to something being nominated, or named, as whatever it is rather than being seen as shaped by something else. So, if we accept the idea of personal authority, we can then accept that any person's gender is a consequence of what they say it is, irrespective of their biology.

In the three examples given here we are drawing attention to how arguments may be constructed from the different positions that may be adopted. Now consider a further two concepts that are often referred to when it comes to contemporary debates about sex and gender:

- Cisgender: this is where an individual conforms to the traditional gender image that corresponds to their sex at birth.
- Transgender: this is where an individual presents a different gender image, usually the traditional opposite, compared to their sex at birth.

When it comes to cisgender or transgender, we are drawing attention to the way that individuals choose to dress and/or act. As such it takes us back to Butler's idea regarding how we do gender, it is a matter of representation. To understand why it is that this simple matter of representation may result in extremely heated arguments, however, it is important to revisit two more positions, this time with regards to the extent to which individuals are more or less likely to accept or reject gender claims: social conservatism and social liberalism.

- Social conservatives will generally resist or reject the idea of being transgender and following from this they will resist or reject the need to accommodate or make adjustments for transgender people.
- Social liberals will be more willing to accept the idea of being transgender and more likely to support making changes to accommodate the needs of transgender people.

One thing that you may be thinking about by this stage is that in each of these descriptions we have presented a comparison between two positions. In other words, each of the positions represents a binary position, it's either one or the other. Someone who is transgender is not necessarily challenging gender roles, just adopting the opposite role to what their sex has previously determined. This fits neatly with the binary worldview that was established by the Enlightenment and is typical within modernity. However, not everyone fits neatly into a binary position. This is where the idea of non-binary comes in, or gender variant. Non-binary is a response to the dichotomy of masculine/feminine where neither position fits what a person, including a child, may be comfortable with. This is where gender variant as a term is helpful. It better represents how a person wants to behave, think and be seen, as neither one nor the other but something else.

So, be aware that transgender does not mean the same as non-binary, and as such gender variant is more useful a term. Non-binary is often presented as being the same as transgender, but it is not accurate to see them as the same. As Darwin (2020: 357) makes clear, 'although some nonbinary people certainly identify as transgender, others do not'. What Darwin is pointing to here is that there are lots of ways to be an individual.

In turn this reflects Butler's (2006) ideas about doing gender, as we stated earlier. As such we are reiterating the idea that as individuals, we each work on performing gender every day, but also that there are very many ways to do this, as is illustrated by a consideration of gender forms across the globe and in the past. In other words, gender should be understood as being very diverse and this gives rise to the idea that we might be better off seeing gender as an umbrella term, or even ignoring the concept of gender so as to allow males and females to choose how they want to act and be seen. If we accept the diversity of gender, then an alternative to gender variant is the concept of the transgender umbrella.

The concept of a transgender umbrella accommodates diversity and also operates as a much more useful approach compared to transgender alone, given that transgender restricts us to a binary model (Papoulias, 2006; Darwin, 2020; Schiappa, 2021). Be aware though that the idea of the transgender umbrella or of gender variant is often overshadowed by a narrative of transgender which reinforces the binary concept. As such, some individuals find that they are marginalised by discussions of what transgender is and what it means (Darwin, 2020; Vicente, 2021). This can be just as restrictive for children as having fixed ideas of what a boy is and what a girl is traditionally.

A good introduction to such ideas and issues is offered by Hinsliff (2021). This is accessible online. Read this and then read Vicente (2021) to consider how particular discourses of transgender may impact upon the trans individual's lived experience. Vicente also draws attention to the way in which the rise of transgender as a term has acted in a way to erase other terms such as transexual or transvestite. As Vicente puts it, the term transgender has 'become a sort of cloak that renders invisible all the nuances and multiple identities of trans people'. (2021: 437). Once again we can see how discourse shapes and limits ideas.

However, what can be seen in Vicente's work is that labels that are associated with deviance have become less influential. As such, transgender issues within sociological studies can be seen to have shifted from studies of transgender as deviance towards transgender as difference (Schilt and Lagos, 2017), though this is not to imply that society has become more accepting as this is not necessarily the case. In respect of how different understandings of transgender impact upon society it is always necessary to consider the idea of politics and power and how these shape the social position of transgender issues at any given time.

It can be argued, however, that the binary nature of the gender debate is something which is specifically Western and that looking beyond Western ideas reveals a much richer understanding of gender as a whole (Worth, 2008). One aspect of modernity as was discussed in Chapter 6 is the way in which the Enlightenment reinforced a worldview characterised by a binary understanding. This creates dualities such as are found within both sex and gender as male/female or masculine/feminine. Such a duality is not inevitable within a social and cultural world that is both rich and complex. This is illustrated by the example of fa'afafine within Samoan culture. Fa'afafine represents the cultural acceptance of a third gender involving males dressing and acting in a way that reflects females (Worth, 2008; Kanemasu and Liki, 2021). In India, being transgender is recognised in law, with the hijra community in particular representing a third gender. The hrija community has a long history in Indian culture.

The idea of a third gender, however, does not sit easily with the traditional Western binary approach and draws attention to the fact that within a post-modern world in which identity is important, gender may be both fixed and fluid. As such some individuals may adopt gender identities which do not neatly correspond with masculine or feminine versions of gender but be fixed, whereas other individuals may adopt much more fluid gender identities (Richards et al, 2016). Drawing from the latter scenario then it is best to see gender as a continuum, but where individuals are able to move throughout the continuum and, as such, gender variance is a much more useful term to understand this. Note that the idea of fluid gender identities corresponds to the use of the term genderqueer, which you may encounter. Genderqueer was a term used to resist the idea of gender being a binary distinction so as to accommodate diversity (Richards et al, 2017; Honkasalo, 2020).

How transgender matters

The issue of transgender is of relevance to this book if we acknowledge that in recent years there has been an increase in the number of children and young people identifying as transgender and who from an early age wish to be seen as the opposite gender to their sex. This expression of identity has increasingly become contentious, and it is useful to consider what this may mean in terms of the lived experiences of children and young people. Two issues in particular come to the fore. Firstly, there is the matter of how transgender issues are played out within what has been called the culture wars, and secondly what transgender issues mean in everyday life, especially in social institutions such as schools and colleges.

In social institutions overall, cis-normative approaches can be seen to act against the interests of children and young people who present as trans, and institutional change can be difficult to achieve even when the intentions behind attempts may be seen as positive. For example, Horton (2024) demonstrates how the Cass Review (2024) into addressing mental health provision for children and young people presenting as trans can be criticised as adopting a cis-normative position.

We suggested in Chapter 4 that gender is a key organising principle within UK schools and that how schools and colleges are organised will impact upon individual experiences, sometimes negatively. Even so, change is not always welcome and there is evidence of public hostility towards schools which have put measures in place that are explicitly accommodating or supportive of transgender pupils (Bower-Brown et al, 2023). Such hostility may come from parents with children at the school, or from sections of the media (Morgan and Taylor, 2019; Davy and Cordoba, 2020). Davy and Cordoba (2020) also note that parents who are supportive of their transgender children are also often subject to the same type of hostility. This means that the lived experiences of transgender children are often not very welcoming or supportive. Horton (2023) illustrates the lived experiences of many trans children, demonstrating how aspects of social isolation and personal harassment are routinely experienced.

Earlier we drew on Butler to claim that as individuals we do gender. Take this idea, but instead of focusing on individuals consider how organisations such as schools can also be seen to do gender in the way that they are organised and operate. Uniforms, toilets, changing rooms and sport are all examples of where gender is embedded within the school experience in a way that emphasises a traditional version of gender within schools (Bower-Brown et al, 2023). What this creates is a context or framework that is much more easily fitted into by cisgender pupils than it is by non-binary or transgender pupils.

Very often, the problems that trans children experience within schools centre around the homophobic assumptions and actions of others; the assumption is often that presenting as a different gender will lead to abusive behaviours towards others. This in turn can be seen to rest upon approaches that are what can be termed heteronormative (DePalma and Atkinson, 2009; Horton, 2024). When we say heteronormative, we simply mean that heterosexual or cisgender positions are put forward as the norm. What is unspoken here is a suggestion that not to be heterosexual is therefore to be not normal. This makes the negotiation of identity even more complex for some children. Importantly, though, transgender and homosexuality are not synonymous and being trans is often wrongly taken as an indication of not being heterosexual (Schiappa, 2021).

In relation to these issues the idea of gender critical feminism is pertinent. Gender critical feminism returns us to the positions regarding sex and gender that were set out earlier where the biological is seen as critical to understanding the social. From the perspective of gender critical feminism, the key issue is that biological sex cannot be changed. As such this can be seen to represent an essentialist position. This can be compared to transgender rights activists who adopt a nominalist position which aims to be trans-inclusive.

One aspect of this though is that gender critical feminism appears to undermine the more general feminist calls for equality and inclusive practices. This has led to gender critical feminism being said to be discriminatory (Shaw, 2023). Consequently, trans-rights supporters are often found using the term trans-exclusionary radical feminism (TERF) to categorise gender critical feminism

(Thurlow, 2022), but be aware that some commentators consider that the acronym TERF constitutes a misogynist slur (Pearce et al, 2020). For a short introduction to the complex situation relating to feminism and trans issues, Thurlow is highly recommended.

From the perspective of trans rights, though, the key issue is not biology. In practice this means that it is not sex that is the issue, it is gender. As such, each side in the argument is actually focused on something different, and it is this which points to why it is that trans issues reflect culture wars, especially where this is concerned with rights and the ways that society accommodates trans individuals. In this way the struggles that trans individuals face reflect the struggles that others have faced, such as women, the working class, ethnic minorities and homosexuals.

Note

At the end of 2022 a Scottish court had declared that sex is not limited to biology, so supporting the idea that having a Gender Recognition Certificate meant that a transgender individual identifying as a woman should be accepted as a woman. This ruling was challenged by a gender-critical group, For Women Scotland, and consequently the case was presented to the UK Supreme Court. In April 2025, the UK Supreme Court determined that for the purposes of the Equality Act 2010, the legal definition of sex as a protected characteristic established by the Equality Act rests upon biology. In making this judgement the UK Supreme Court emphasised that sex is a binary concept which is rooted within biology. This may have far-reaching consequences for the lives of trans individuals.

It is evident, then, that children and young people are growing up with an understanding of trans issues and with an awareness of the heated debates that surround them. They will be aware, then, that debates about transgender issues are often presented within highly exaggerated arguments which foreground social threat. At the same time we have already suggested that social media provides a platform for the spreading of untruths and that this is often accompanied by threats of real and imagined violence against individuals who are presenting unwelcome views (Wagner and Hayes, 2022). As such, even the possibility of being transgender represents another focus for culture wars (Pearce et al, 2020). In relation to children then there may be advantages in considering the whole spectrum of ways that we can present ourselves or live our lives, rather than restricting this to ideas about what it is to be a boy and what it is to be a girl.

In light of the debates that surround trans issues, though, we feel that there is a further aspect to be taken into account in relation to children and young people, particularly in relation to procedures associated with transitioning. This is that when it comes to the matter of the rights of children who may voice a desire to transition, or adopt an alternative identity to the norm, it is important that consideration is given to the fact that children and young people are often restricted and regulated in a significant range of activities and behaviours.

We have already raised the issue of the regulation of children and young people in ways that prevent certain behaviours. For example, society does not permit children, those under 18, to vote, to smoke tobacco or to drink alcohol. Under 17s are prohibited from driving, and regulated in terms of their freedom to leave education or even what they can wear while being educated in many cases. Under 16s are prohibited from engaging in sexual activity. We are sure that you can think of other restrictions based on age, all of which are presented as resting upon the idea that children either lack experience or the maturity to exercise their agency in a manner that is rational and reasonable. So, when we consider the numerous ways in which we regulate or restrict young people's behaviour, why should we not restrict or regulate their freedom to make changes in respect of their biological sex?

There is no doubt that matters about trans rights in relation to sex and gender evoke some extreme responses, but we feel that there is a further important question to ask in relation to this, and that is a question about the sort of world that we would want our children to live in. That question is centred on the extent to which we feel it is acceptable to threaten violence, including death threats, on the grounds that someone has put forward an opinion which we do not agree with. This has happened in relation to transgender issues. At the beginning of the book we stated that you do not have to agree with the things that we say, and we will reiterate it here, you don't. If you disagree with us though you can rest assured that we will not make threats against you. Of course, we hope that we will not be threatened for the positions that we take.

Making links

In respect of how the material from this chapter may be of use in your assignments, you could consider the following points as being important:

- Sex and gender are often seen as referring to the same thing but that is not the case.
- Sex is traditionally seen as relatively fixed as it reflects biology, but gender is social and this affords more scope for change.
- For writers such as Judith Butler, our social and cultural beliefs and understandings not only influence gender, they also influence how we conceptualise biology.
- Ideas about sex and gender have real consequences in respect of discrimination and disadvantage and are reflected in sexism and misogyny.
- In recent years sexism and misogyny can be understood as being located within culture wars.

These points are important, but as we start to move towards the end of the book we hope that you are recognising that in our attempt to make some sense of contemporary childhood we have considered a range of social, cultural and political influences and issues, and dealt with them individually. In a way this is maybe a little artificial but in our defence most texts that you read, and most courses on children and childhood, will do this. Childhood is complex. We could say that it is only by breaking things down into disparate issues that we are put in a position where we can really start to understand the issues. In turn this reinforces the idea that as students you really do need to read a wide range of reliable and academically rigorous books and articles if you are to develop your understanding of contemporary childhood. Sometimes that involves reading material that you may only see the value of quite a bit later. As we read more widely and develop our understanding then we start to see links.

As we considered gender, we hope that you started to recognise that issues which were raised previously can be useful to us in making sense of the issues and challenges which face children and young people in the contemporary Western world. For example, we suggested links between truth and the media previously. Chapter 7 also introduced the idea of the manosphere and the incel movement; though at the time we said little about gender, looking back on Chapter 8 we can see that these issues are relevant. Similarly, ideas such as modernity compared to post-modernity, or social media being a platform for promoting ideas were useful in this chapter, even though many books and articles that you will read about these issues will not foreground children and young people. This is where you use your reading when you develop arguments in your assignments.

Looking back at this chapter we feel that we have demonstrated that gender is a very contentious matter within contemporary society. It elicits some very heated disputes and creates many social tensions. We provided a fairly standard approach to sex and gender as our starting point by stating that sex is biological and gender is social. As such we also said that biology is somewhat fixed but that gender is subject to change. So, in biological terms we talk about being male or female but in terms of gender the concern is with masculinity or femininity. Biology can be changed to some degree but what it means to be masculine or feminine is much more fluid.

This is where we introduced Judith Butler, though because for Butler there is no essential biological truth to our bodies, we understand biology through a social lens. For Butler, a biological truth such as a womb does not define the person. Instead, she argues that individuals are drawn into a range of social acts which have the consequence that what it means to be a man or a woman is constructed within how we act. In other words, Butler's position is that we perform gender, we do gender.

Theorists such as Butler are useful in informing our understanding of gender. Given that we see empirical evidence illustrating different social positions and experiences that are based on gender, it is useful to consider that for the most part such differences result from how society organises itself and from the stories that societies tell about men and women, boys and girls.

One thing that is evident here, and is often used to justify social positions, is that men tend to gain advantages simply on the basis of being men, and women are often disadvantaged because they are women. This raises the issues of sexism, misogyny and patriarchy. This is where links to Chapter 7 can be made in relation to how sexism and misogyny as encountered on social media and how online platforms act to amplify the voices of those who would promote sexist messages. Children and young people are significant users of social media and online platforms so it would be wrong to think that they are in some way shielded from this. They are faced with this every day and it is not surprising that some children and young people start to accept sexism and misogyny as being in some way normal.

There are also similarities here with ideas that were raised when we discussed the emergence of post-modernity, especially the idea that within a post-modern world we have to engage in establishing our own identities. As societies have changed it is not surprising that some men turn backwards to lament a gendered position that has been lost. Socially conservative commentators commonly look backwards to some mythical golden age, but the golden age did not really exist, and gender has been diverse for all of humankind. What we have now though is a technological platform which provides numerous outlets for the spreading of claims about why we need to move backwards as a society, not forwards.

Maybe the most contemporary demonstration of the social concerns regarding sex and gender however is the issue of gender rights for those who wish to transition or vary their gendered behaviour. In assessing the charged atmosphere over trans rights we are drawn to conclude that at heart the key question is one of philosophy. Proponents that are both for and against trans rights can be seen as putting forward arguments which rest on quite different propositions. Maybe one way of addressing the tensions that this inevitably creates would be to shift attention on to children and young people, and instead of asking what makes a man a man or a woman a woman, instead ask what sort of world we would want for our children, one which is inclusive, or one which is exclusive.

Further thoughts

If the main focus of sex is the biological ability to reproduce, why might this matter to children, particularly young children?

How might rigid gender representation be helpful, and harmful?

Try and think about examples of the way in which children are expected to 'do' gender and how schools and other child-based settings reinforce gender. Consider whether this is necessary and if so why.

Further reading

Bates (2014) and David (2016) are both good books if you want to understand what girls and women experience as part of everyday life. Read chapter 4 of Bates in particular.

Pearce et al (2020), Wagner and Hayes (2022), Thurlow (2022) and Schiappa (2021) all provide useful accounts of sex and gender alongside issues relevant to transgender matters.

9

Thinking about outcomes and health

This chapter will help you to understand:
- outcomes from a critical perspective;
- why it may be difficult to achieve good outcomes;
- why some health risks, such as obesity, are difficult to address.

What do we mean when we talk about outcomes?

We have indicated previously that it can be quite hard to move away from seeing children as becomings, though as a society it could be argued that our key concern should be that we are not creating problems for children in the future. One of the things that reinforces the idea of children as becomings is a contemporary focus on outcomes. A concern with outcomes is to be found across a range of children's professions, and in this chapter we aim to adopt a more critical approach towards them.

We start by saying that the terminology of outcomes is yet another example of an idea that is seductive, especially when it is presented as a focus on good outcomes. It is seductive because who wouldn't want children to have good outcomes? It reminds us of the countless times that we read in student assignments that parents will always want the best for their children. Will they? If parents always wanted the best for their children, then a lot of social workers would be out of a job. Similarly, government spokespeople often talk about doing things that are in children's best interests or that will achieve the best outcomes for children, but we aren't too sure that they always mean it, or if they do, that they have the will to achieve it or the ways by which good outcomes can be achieved.

Student task

Take five to ten minutes to think about two things:

1. Think about the sort of good outcomes for children that you would expect to be generally agreed upon.

2. Try to think about policies or practice that promote the idea of good outcomes. These could be policies that the government is promoting or policies and/or practice that organisations such as nurseries, schools or health services put forward.

Consider whether there are any good outcomes for children that are not being achieved, as far as you can see.

The focus on outcomes in relation to children and young people can be seen as another consequence of the way in which neoliberal ideas have become embedded within society as a whole. Remember that we have said that neoliberalism promotes the idea of viewing society through the lens of business. This leads to a general understanding of social life as being competitive rather than cooperative and an understanding that individuals will tend to behave in ways that enhance personal gain. This positions children as becomings, who need to become successful in work when they are adults. Childhood in this sense is a period of preparation for adulthood.

Because of neoliberalism, ideas that may accurately describe and explain business practices come to be overlaid onto parts of society which have traditionally not been understood in this way. So, the world of business may be easily described in terms of investment, processing materials and/or generating value, and being accountable to financial regulations through accounting practices. Ideas about outcomes fit easily into this model. Ideas about outcomes do not sit so easily on public or social services such as childcare, health care or education, but neoliberal governments have sought ways by which such business descriptors will fit.

The use of the term outcomes in any discussion about children and young people then draws on the idea of a process that leads to a child's future state, and this is something that has increasingly become socially acceptable, fitting as it does with the notion of becomings. When we think about how influential developmentalism has been in shaping how we understand children then it is a small step to seeing children's development as being a process that continues to adulthood.

Note

To make sense of outcomes we can summarise and say that there is a discourse of outcomes that has been promoted by neoliberalism. This discourse fits easily with the idea of seeing children as becomings because it is focused on their future.

It means that rather than simply providing what children need, we promote the idea that we are investing in services for children so that children have the best opportunities to become successful adults. As soon as we have accepted the idea that we are investing we are drawn into establishing and defining the outcomes that we intend to achieve.

This then drives measurement to see what and how much children are achieving. It also means that we may choose not to invest if the projected outcomes don't seem worth it, because we cannot measure the outcome or because the cost is too high.

With this in mind, consider how many times governments, which can be termed policy makers, talk about investing in services or provision for children. This can be summarised as being an 'investment-outcomes discourse' (Cooke et al, 2023). As Hayes and Filipović (2018: 233) state though, 'because investment in early childhood education is seen as an investment in the future, policy makers consider it necessary to measure the value of such investment and the currency for such evaluation is the "measurable outcome".' However, this discourse of outcomes creates problems for practitioners as it is difficult to accurately measure outcomes relating to children. This is particularly the case when it comes to the value of play.

Alongside the neoliberal pressure to measure outcomes though is also a concern with accountability; those that are providing services are presented as needing to be held to account for the outcomes they should be achieving. So, the need for measurable outcomes which demonstrate the value of investment alongside the need for accountability gives us an understanding of how it is that practitioners end up spending a significant part of their time recording what children have done rather than actually interacting with, or providing for, children. This is taking us back to our discussion of data. It also means that childhood is shaped more by those activities that are believed to achieve the outcomes that are deemed to be important for adulthood.

Might outcomes be more complex than they first seem?

Up to this point we have been adopting a somewhat narrow definition of outcomes. By this we mean that we have done what most texts do, we have used the term outcomes to represent a position or situation that is located at some point in the future that is considered to have resulted from what has gone before. This reflects the idea of a process such as development and allows for the fact that providing or changing public services or provisions will impact upon the outcomes that will follow. In that sense, this is quite straightforward. We also ought to say that there is maybe a hint of determinism in saying this.

Note

Determinism can be summarised very simply in the formula X causes Y.

What this leads us to consider is the idea that something in a child's future will be determined by what has gone before. Maybe the best example of this is the idea of adverse childhood experiences. To experience adverse childhood experiences is often presented as leading to poor outcomes, but we have to be careful not to be deterministic; it is not a given that experiencing adverse childhood experiences will manifest as problems in later life. Adverse childhood experiences might not be what we would want for children, but children are remarkably resilient, and many children do get over adverse experiences.

So, what we want you to do now is to consider that if outcomes are positioned in the future, then we should also consider how far in the future we are talking about. That means that outcomes may be seen as being short-term, mid-term or long-term. This is something that is often left out of discussions about outcomes. The issue of when we might see the outcomes that we want is often lost within a somewhat vague idea about outcomes sometime in the future. And, if we are thinking about the future, how far in the future are we able to measure?

Consider also that the range of factors which occur in a child's life, and the experiences they have that can lead to poor outcomes, can be understood as being on a continuum that runs from simple to complex. The range of factors which may contribute to poor outcomes will not all be the same for each child, just as the range of factors which contribute to positive outcomes will also not all be the same. If we accept this idea about the factors which may influence our lives, then we can start to appreciate that introducing policies to improve outcomes may be more or less difficult. Following from this then we can appreciate that this provides us with an insight into how it is that some issues are tackled whereas other social issues may be ignored.

To illustrate what we mean here let us think about one particular issue relating to poor health outcomes: smoking tobacco or using tobacco substitutes, such as vaping. Smoking is harmful to health, the evidence on this is very clear and has been known for a long time. As such, we can confidently say that smoking leads to poorer health when compared to not smoking. In addition, we can confidently state that smoking is a social phenomenon. Taking up smoking is something that is affected by a range of social relationships and is associated with a number of social ideas such as image (MacFadyen et al, 2003; Wiltshire et al, 2005; Kmietowicz, 2008).

As a society we know that most smokers start to smoke at a young age but we also know that children are harmed by being in environments where smoking takes place, what is termed passive smoking. Governments have accepted this, and it is evidenced in the way that they have acted to improve health outcomes for adults by restricting the freedoms of children and young people to smoke alongside creating non-smoking laws which apply to particular environments. As such, there are laws prohibiting children from smoking and buying tobacco. There are further plans to restrict children's access to both tobacco products and vaping. In addition, there are places where smoking is prohibited and ongoing discussions about whether smoking should be prohibited in more public spaces.

This seems very reasonable; it is hard to argue against such restrictions given the dangers of smoking and the negative impact that it has on other people when someone smokes. As such this can be seen as a reasonable action being taken by governments who, when faced with the facts about something that is harmful to health, have done something about it. But we also know about the risks to health that arise from obesity. Whereas by 2018 fewer than 10 per cent of children smoked (RCPCH, 2020), by 2024 more than 20 per cent of four to five year old and over one third of ten to eleven year old children were classed as overweight or obese (AMS, 2024a, 2024b; OHID, 2024). Obesity poses risks not only to health but lifestyle. The question then has to be asked as to why obesity is not being addressed as decisively as smoking. Is it because tackling smoking addresses one, relatively simple factor, but tackling obesity requires addressing multiple and complex factors?

Obesity

In raising the question as to why smoking and/or vaping among children has been addressed decisively but obesity has not we are putting forward the idea that obesity is equally problematic. However, the claim that obesity is a problem may be challenged to a much greater extent than is the matter of children smoking and/or vaping. The issue of why children become obese can be seen to be more complex than the issue of smoking, which is a single action that is unnecessary and harmful. Body size is a contentious issue and although being slim is usually seen as healthier, as a society we have become more accustomed to larger bodies than say in the 1960s and 1970s when it was more normal to be very thin. It is also the case that size, shape and body weight are not easy subjects to address.

So, to begin with it may be useful to distinguish between obesity and being overweight. The National Institute for Health and Care Excellence and the NHS provide definitions of both overweight and of obesity based on Body Mass Index (BMI), where BMI is calculated by dividing a person's weight in kilograms by the square of their height in metres. Be aware, however, that even within the medical profession there are concerns with the usefulness of using BMI to represent health and there have been calls for the use of it to be revised (Rubino, 2025). That said it is regularly used as a reference point.

In measuring childhood obesity, NHS England adopts the National Child Measurement Programme for England (NCMP). The NCMP includes nearly all children in reception year (aged four to five) and year 6 (aged ten to eleven). BMI is calculated for each child but is adjusted for age and sex. This is recommended as a practical estimate of overweightness and obesity in children as it takes into account different growth patterns in boys and girls at different ages. To provide a base from which to work, NHS England use the British 1990 growth reference (UK90) to describe childhood overweightness and obesity and to distinguish between age and sex (NHS, 2020).

This is all very technical and gives an indication of the positivist approach to obesity that is rooted within a medical model in which weight is correlated with health. Some argue that a focus on children's health in this way is not helpful, and it is evident that for children being fat is a complex issue that is affected by a number of social issues including an ongoing debate about the privileging of being slim and a general negativity towards larger body shapes. This can be contrasted with the approach taken by fat rights activists who seek to move away from a focus on health (Cooper, 2010). Waite and Pritchard (2017) follow this approach in specifically focusing on the idea of the fat child. The term fat child is adopted to distinguish between the concerns with health that are associated with obesity and the social and environmental factors which may contribute to a child being fat. A concern with fatness is also useful in respect of accommodating a range of social concerns regarding fat bodies within societies which have tended to privilege being slim (Saguy and Ward, 2011; Sims-Schouten and Cowie, 2016).

Traditionally, concerns about obesity have been rooted in ideas about overeating, especially with a concern about the idea of being greedy (Waite and Pritchard, 2017). It is the case that overeating may lead to being overweight, but it is also important to consider other factors such as the nature of what is being eaten and the changing nature of childhood, which has seen children becoming much less active than in previous generations. This has led to a health and social problem that is complex, and which requires a much more nuanced solution than just banning something, as with the solution for addressing smoking.

There is widespread agreement that in the UK children are, in general, not as active as they once were. It is also accepted that there is a correlation between physical activity and weight (Raman, 2019). The place of screens in children's lives can be seen as a key factor in the increasingly sedentary lifestyle of children, though we have to be careful not to see this as just being a recent concern. We have indicated previously that concerns about children watching screens rather than going out to play have been common since televisions became features of Western households. In recent decades, however, a number of factors have combined in ways which mean that parents are now much more likely to encourage children to stay in whereas it is not so long ago that parents would have encouraged children to go out, thus children are more likely to use screens to amuse themselves in the absence of other activities (Creasy and Corby, 2019). They are also likely to take smartphones with them if they leave the home, restricting what they do when they go out.

Whereas these developments contribute to children being less active it is also important to consider how diets have changed over the past 50 years, as what children eat also contributes to weight and size. Childhood is a time when we are less likely to be in control of what we eat or have a real choice. However, two things stand out in relation to diet; a massive growth in fast-food outlets has led to an increased consumption of fast food, and there has also been a significant rise in ultra-processed foods that have hidden calories. The key issue here is a concern with what children are eating, with many foodstuffs that are now commonly consumed by children being categorised as unhealthy and/or junk food. Note though that this food is also often cheaper and easier to access.

Junk food is commonly described as being foodstuffs that are low in nutritional value with minimal levels of vitamins or minerals, and where calories are located in fats or sugars (Ertz and Le Bouhart, 2022). Alongside this, unhealthy foods are usually high in sugar, salts and saturated fats. What is without doubt then is that the modern food industry is not only producing significant amounts of poor-quality food, which is not conducive to good health, but that these foodstuffs are often packaged and marketed in ways which target children as consumers.

As with most aspects of the world that we live in, and, following from this, the world that children live in, food is not consumed in a vacuum; the consumption of food is social. This operates on a cultural level in terms of what different groups eat, and we can identify it on a social level in terms of how food can be both a marker of social position and be shaped by social positions. Children are likely to eat how their family eats.

Student task

Think about the ways in which unhealthy and/or junk foods may be packaged and/or marketed in ways which target children. Try to list four or five examples that you have come across.

In respect of how unhealthy foods are marketed at children, though, consider how parents may feel a degree of pressure in relation to what they allow their children to eat. We can also see that what parents feed their children or permit them to eat contributes to how parents understand their role and there is evidence that some parents feel that they take a harder approach compared to other parents with respect to what their children eat (Namie, 2011). That said, 'harder' parents may maintain a long-term approach towards restricting unhealthy and/or junk foods by the occasional relaxing of rules under the guise of special occasions, what has been called 'sometimes' food (Petrunoff et al, 2014). However, it is also the case that some parents may just provide food that they know their children will eat and which is affordable.

So, we began by asking how it is that a government can justify restrictions and/or outright bans on the sale of tobacco and vaping products on the grounds that this is in the best interests of children, yet do so little about foods which contribute significantly to childhood obesity. Sugar is known to have no nutritional value but is a significant contribution to the obesity crisis. There is no real attempt to restrict or ban sugar, although the sugar tax has gone some way to highlighting the problem of sugary drinks (Bridge et al, 2020; O'Sullivan et al, 2023). This returns us to the idea that in terms of outcomes for children, we may agree that we would want to promote good outcomes and work to prevent those things which lead to poor outcomes, but we can also recognise that something such as obesity is complex and difficult to address because of this.

That is not to say that governments have done nothing. In 2018 the government published the first chapter of a policy to tackle childhood obesity, including a tax on sugary drinks, as mentioned earlier. Further chapters soon followed (Griffin et al, 2021). However, although positive, the policy assumes a simple approach to childhood obesity, placing the relationship between activity and calories consumed at the centre and with a strong focus on making good food choices (Lancet, 2017).

The policy guides schools and parents to take simple actions, such as providing an hour of outdoor play, and encourages consumers to be more responsible when it comes to buying food and in terms of what is eaten, as has often been promoted by governments (Jebb and Aveyard, 2023). As Griffin et al point out, making good food choices tends to rely on having the economic resources to do so. It is also complex to understand what constitutes healthy food and cooking can be argued to be a skill that we need to learn. Because of this it may be argued that for good childhood outcomes it would be more effective for governments to restrict what food products are available to buy in a similar way to how tobacco is restricted.

Where are we with children's health?

The starting point in considering children's health is to recognise that health is a social phenomenon. Although there are some health issues which may have their causes in biological and/or genetic issues, the key thing to be clear about is that for the most part, health is a social matter. This means that issues relating to both good health and ill health are not simply a matter of chance. Health, whether that be good or bad, is shaped in large part by social factors. This may relate to the quality of sanitation that families experience or the quality of housing. It may be influenced by the quality of the air that we breathe and the quality of the diet that we have, or even the extent to which we are physically active.

There are some issues relating to health that individuals and families have more control over, such as diet, but there are also factors which the government has more control over, such as the provision of health services, or actions relating to improving the quality of the environment such as air pollution both inside (think of mould in damp housing) and outside the home (such as pollutants caused by traffic).

In considering the nature of childhood within the UK in the 2020s in relation to health and medical care, the Academy of Medical Sciences notes that:

> In recent years, progress on child health in the UK has stalled. Infant survival rates are worse than in 60% of similar countries and the number of children living in extreme poverty tripled between 2019 and 2022. Demand for children's mental health services surge and over a fifth of five-year-old children are overweight or obese, with those living in the most deprived areas twice as likely to be obese than in affluent areas. One-in-four is affected by tooth decay. Vaccination rates have plunged below World Health Organization safety thresholds, threatening outbreaks. Issues such as the COVID-19 pandemic, increased cost of living and climate change compound widespread inequality and are likely to make early years health in the UK even worse. (AMS, 2024a)

Similarly, AMS (2024b) is very useful when it comes to finding evidence for assignments along with commentaries in relation to health and children. For example, it provides a clear representation of many of the health problems that are experienced by children with a focus on the early years.

In making sense of the state of health within any society, then, we need to return to a point that was raised earlier. We must consider individuals and/or families on the one hand, and the role of a range of services on the other, including the wider environment in which people live. So, from the first position it is the case that some of the factors which increase or decrease instances of disease can be attributed to individual behaviours and the choices we make. On the other hand, we need to consider the range of services that impact upon health and the issues that are beyond the control of individuals. These are external to individuals and/or families. Health services in the UK are generally provided through the National Health Service (NHS) so they need to be seen as being shaped for the most part by the government. At the same time, services that are associated with sanitation such as the provision of clean water and the removal and treatment of sewage are also extremely important.

In respect of health we can confidently say that for the most part disease is not caused by individual biology but is instead better understood as a consequence of the ways in which humans interact with their environment (Mackenbach 2020; 2021). Maybe the most well-known social position with respect to health is the argument put forward by McKeown (1979). McKeown drew on empirical evidence in the form of health statistics over time to demonstrate that the incidences of most diseases had declined significantly in terms of infection before inoculations against particular diseases were made available (remember, empirical evidence is evidence that we can see; within sociology, statistics are often used as empirical evidence).

McKeown provides an interesting argument because it is often suggested that the development of inoculations was the breakthrough that led to the eradication of most diseases. This positions the decline in disease as the success of medical or health interventions. McKeown demonstrates that inoculation is important, but it cannot explain the massive reduction in infection that happened before inoculations were available. He gives further explanation of why disease has for the most part been eradicated. In the case of water-borne disease it was the development of effective sanitation which both provided clean drinking water and removed sewage. The building of drains and the laying of pipes in the Victorian era led to significant improvements in health. In respect of air-borne diseases, McKeown points to improved nutrition resulting from developments in agriculture and improving diets. So, from McKeown we can see how improving health in childhood depends on a number of things happening or changing as opposed to one simple change.

In emphasising the role of effective sanitation and public health matters, McKeown's work illustrates the extent to which the State, which in this case can be read as the government, can be seen as having a central role. It is important to note however that some governments will focus on some things and other governments will focus on other things. That is why some social services may be well supported, but others may be less well supported. It depends on what any government's priorities are or what evidence we have for the effectiveness of taking particular action.

Note

We have mentioned the State previously and it is easy to fall into the trap of seeing the State as being the government. The State is not limited to the government. The government is part of the State but the State is much broader than the government.

A good way to think about it is that the State includes the government, and that the government is a very important part of how the State operates. However, governments change and when they change, they will generally try to change the policies that are in place.

So, we often think about governments in terms of which political party is in power and then which prime minister is leading the government.

The key thing here then is the extent to which any particular government is concerned with supporting health services and to what extent they believe it is their responsibility rather than that of individual behaviour. Because of the scale of sanitation projects and/or public health programmes, governments are in a much better position than individuals to get things done. For example, the supply of clean drinking water and the treatment of sewage is something that is beyond the scope of individuals but is something that governments are able to address. In the UK, State-owned water services have been transferred to private companies (Helm, 2020), since which the quality of water in rivers, lakes and around the coast has deteriorated significantly (Adkins, 2022).

However, it would be wrong to consider that individuals have no part to play when it comes to health matters, especially when it comes to the health of children. We can see this by considering the provision of inoculation programmes aimed at protecting children from a range of diseases. The government provide this service but it relies on individual families taking up the service on offer. This is another example of how we might understand the ways in which structure and agency work. So, if we take the example of the childhood disease measles, we can see that governments have for a long time provided a public health programme to inoculate children against measles.

This programme had been so successful that measles had been considered as eliminated within the UK during 2016 and 2017 (Davis, 2023). By 2024, however, cases of measles had increased significantly. A key reason for this is that a growing number of parents have not had their children inoculated. So, if the inoculation programme represents the structure, the actions of parents represent agency. Parents are not compelled to have their children inoculated even though measles can be serious, including leading to death. The reasons for not taking up services are complex.

However, in terms of childhood, once again we can see how children's lives are shaped by the actions of adults and the information, or misinformation, that parents listen to.

A further example of the complexity of health issues is in the significant growth in mental health problems as experienced by children and young people. It is possible to see that both social structures, the childhoods created by society, and social actions, the way children and their parents are able to negotiate this childhood, combine in ways which have detrimental outcomes.

Anxiety as a social problem

The matter of children's mental health is a prominent theme in the 2020s. Many children report concerns about their mental health and within the UK children's mental health services have struggled to cope with increasing demand. This returns us to considering the priorities of governments and the services that they are willing to fund. Governments sometimes make general decisions that can seriously affect the services that are provided to children and families, and so shape childhood. An example of this is the decision made by the Conservative-led coalition government, elected in 2010, to implement an approach that has generally been referred to as austerity. Austerity involved the cutting of funds to services including services aimed directly at children.

This resulted in the underfunding of a range of services which had consequences into the 2020s. Underfunding results from two main causes; either increases in funding do not match the level of inflation year by year, or funding does not match an increase in demand. As such, by 2024, children's mental health services in the UK had seen significant growth in terms of demand for help but without sufficient funding to provide it. This resulted in long waits to get help by children and young people who were referred for help, and sometimes the help that was received was insufficient.

The number of children and young people who present with mental health problems has been increasing throughout the 21st century. The issue here though is that a concern with increasing demand for mental health services does little to explain why they are being needed. It seems obvious that something has changed in childhood that has led to children feeling less content and/or more anxious.

Unless we can establish that children within the 21st century are significantly different compared to children in previous generations then the things which are leading to the increase in mental health problems must be social. If children are biologically the same now as they were in previous generations then we have to consider that it is society that has changed. If we adopt a term that has been used previously, we could say that UK society can be seen as being toxic for childhood (Palmer, 2007; 2009; 2015). In other words, the society that we have created underpins and causes the mental illnesses that children experience (James, 2009). Anxiety is particularly relevant here in that it seems obvious that the way in which anxiety is experienced and understood within contemporary society demonstrates that anxiety is a matter for sociology (Crombez, 2021).

It is pertinent to consider then that a number of social changes which may seem unrelated, such as changed ways of parenting, the adoption of new technologies, new social concerns or practices, even the way education or school is provided, combine or overlap in ways that have created negative outcomes for children and young people in regards to their emotional wellbeing. So, consider some of the issues that we have already raised and think about how these contribute to the growth in the number of children who have mental health problems, or poor emotional wellbeing.

Note, we use the term both mental health problems and emotional wellbeing to reflect the range of experiences for children. While mental health as a term suggests the need for health interventions, emotional wellbeing reflects the everyday anxiety that children may experience that impoverishes childhood or, if unaddressed, can lead to more serious mental health concerns. It is also reasonable to suggest that anxiety as an issue has become subject to a changed understanding.

Within social theory of the 19th and early 20th centuries anxiety was linked either to the ways in which modern society had become increasingly impersonal (Wilkinson, 2001) or to the issue of uncertainty (Rebughini, 2021). Wilkinson provides a broad account drawing on many classical sociological studies to demonstrate that anxiety should be understood as a social phenomenon and, in doing so, to move focus away from a dominant clinical or mental health model. As such it may be argued that children have always experienced anxiety, but it has not always been understood as being a concern of mental health that adults needed to address.

Note

Anxiety is a normal experience for all people but an experience which may be increasingly portrayed as unwelcome, or which is debilitating for some.

Although most individuals feel anxious at times, a clear definition of anxiety is not so easy to arrive at. For Wilkinson (2001) the complexity of anxiety gives rise to a range of emotional, physiological and behavioural responses. In turn this means that definition is often vague and an understanding of causation unclear.

As a means of understanding anxiety, however, we draw from Wilkinson in suggesting that clinical or psychological responses to anxiety should be understood as dealing with symptoms rather than causes. It is not anxiety in itself that is an illness requiring treatment.

The causes of anxiety are best understood as being generated by social and cultural practices within modern society which engender feelings of insecurity, and which contribute to a sense of uncertainty that some individuals experience as threatening and difficult to deal with.

In terms of childhood, it is important that we consider anxiety as a normal condition, but where adult responses to anxiety in childhood have changed.

So, early studies presented anxiety as being rooted within social changes and the way that individuals were tasked with making decisions. However, for children decision making was likely to be limited and/or more straightforward. Within modern society the emphasis on individuals, including children, having control over their lives points to the way in which post-modern life may increase feelings of uncertainty and/or an inability to exert control or make good decisions within the context of a more complex world. This may contribute to a greater sense of being overwhelmed by events or demands that children are aware of but still feel they have no control over.

So, the key point we would make is that anxiety is a normal process of life. However, whereas in previous generations anxiety was likely to have been understood as apprehension about either situations or future events, it has since been transformed from being understood as a normal response to certain social situations or to new experiences into something that is seen as problematic and something that is difficult to overcome. As such, the experience of anxiety no longer seems to be limited to experiences which are uncomfortable but is instead an ongoing response to normal but perhaps challenging situations which are experienced as overwhelming.

This represents a change in the way in which we understand anxiety, but in trying to make sense of how social and cultural changes have contributed to this it may also be seen as corresponding to the way in which parenting has changed. When we consider the ways in which parenting had changed by the late 20th century, we start to see parents who have become very concerned that their children should not experience unhappiness, boredom or even failure (Stearns, 2003; Nelson, 2010; Creasy and Corby, 2019). This has seen the emergence of what has been called helicopter or snow-plough parents. These parents micromanage their children's lives in ways to prevent unhappiness, boredom and/or failure, but in doing so unwittingly create the preconditions of anxiety by removing opportunities for children to learn how to negotiate and navigate new situations, so dealing with small-scale anxiety in a way that builds resilience to deal with bigger issues as they get older.

Similarly, Haidt (2024) provides a good account of the way in which child-led, or free play has become much less of a feature of children's lives and how parental supervision or education (for example in nursery care) has come to dominate children's experiences. Children's lives have become much more structured and organised as parents have become preoccupied with risk and learning. Alongside this change in parenting, though, Haidt argues that screens have become a key feature of the child's world.

The dominance of screens though needs to be considered alongside what Haidt refers to as selfie-culture, together with the importance within social media of 'likes'. This is because of the ways in which this changes our understanding of self and the way in which we engage with others. Similarly, Hill (2015) suggests that social media platforms may actually operate to reduce anxiety for individuals in terms of self-expression while online, in that we can consider what we are saying or doing before posting, so removing the risk to some extent of making social mistakes. However, this is associated with a changed understanding of friendships, where friends are not necessarily people we spend time with in the same physical space but only communicate with online. The nature of contemporary childhood, then, may underpin a rise in anxiety about social settings as a consequence of the ways in which communication has often shifted online and as children draw away from engaging with others and towards screens. Screens are a contentious issue though and they are often blamed for the problems in society. This is another seductive idea that masks the complexity of contemporary childhood.

In addition, although it may be said that children and young people have easier lives in comparison with previous generations, particularly in a material sense, the vast number of choices that children are faced with contributes to greater pressures (Bell et al, 2019). Alongside material choices, children are presented with options that are seen to define them as well as facing pressures to be successful. As a consequence, we may consider that within recent decades the self has become much more central and that this increases anxiety for children and young people in relation to the decisions that they take and their actions.

To take a simple approach, the way in which decision making has increasingly been undertaken by parents alongside an education system that increasingly emphasises a 'correct' answer and within a post-modern, neoliberal society where success and failure are individualised, it is maybe not surprising that children and young people experience greater levels of pressure than their parents may have done. We encounter this in our classes where students are reluctant to answer questions or make comments for fear of saying the wrong thing and where student support workers advise against putting students on the spot even when students know what classes will be focused on. Similarly, it is also evident in how students often find negotiating the physical space of college or higher education difficult. Children and young people do appear to find things much more stressful and do report more anxiety, but they did not create the world that they live in.

Don't take things for granted

Although we have tended to emphasise health issues in discussing outcomes, the general discourse of outcomes can be understood as being central to how childhood is understood in contemporary society. For example, Hayes and Filipović (2018) note that the current approach towards early years education is dominated by a market-based approach within a discourse of outcomes. The early years has shifted from being about the provision of care to the provision of early education. As such a concern for the care of children is lost and this does not act in children's best interests. To change this, it will be necessary for early years care and education to move away from outcomes and to focus upon an approach which promotes a concern with capabilities.

Within this chapter we have repeated the idea that certain ideas can be understood as representing something that may be seen as seductive. We have used this term a lot and think that it is a useful way of looking at the types of terms and phrases which we often come across which on the face of it seem very reasonable and easy to go along with. One of the problems that we see with ideas which are seductive is that in being seduced we don't stop to question what is meant. In one sense then the idea of seeking positive outcomes for children may act to close debate down about what we are doing for children and how this shapes childhood. Sometimes it is maybe more important to look at what an organisation or government does, rather than to listen to what they say.

In one sense a focus on outcomes can be useful with respect to giving an account of the landscape of childhood, or the context within which children live their lives. We have argued that a concern with outcomes draws upon neoliberal ideas and you should recognise that it fits easily with some of the points that were raised regarding datafication earlier. This follows from the need to be accountable in that service providers are often called upon to demonstrate, through data, that they are meeting outcomes in a way that is acceptable.

A focus on outcomes, then, is another issue which enables us to promote criticality. Remember that with regards to assignment marking schemes it is common for students to be assessed in respect of criticality and to be rewarded for being critical. As an example, the term 'outcomes' is often taken for granted, so, if you are writing about outcomes, it will be useful for you to comment upon timescale and to comment upon the extent to which outcomes may be seen as simple or complex.

The example that we presented here was a comparison of policies restricting tobacco use among children and usefully juxtaposed with the dangers inherent within many contemporary foodstuffs and/or children's diets. In general, then, some of the key issues that we have raised within this chapter that may be of use in assignments reflect the following points:

- Outcomes fit well with a neoliberal approach to understanding processes but less well in relation to children's futures.
- Outcomes should be understood as short-term, medium-term and long-term, as well as being on a continuum that ranges from simple to complex.
- Be careful not to be deterministic when thinking about how childhood experiences may influence children's future lives.
- Policies which aim to improve outcomes for children are likely to focus on simple issues such as reducing smoking and vaping and less likely to address complex issues such as obesity.
- Health is social and there is a strong correlation between poverty and ill-health.
- Children's mental health can be seen to be a product of changed social conditions and experiences, such as new forms of parenting and the development of online experiences.

Further thoughts

The issue of diet is a good example of the tension between a nanny state and individual freedoms. (The nanny state is a term used to denigrate too much involvement by the State and the government in people's lives.) Given that junk food and ultra-processed food is undoubtedly bad for children and young people's health, should governments restrict foodstuffs that can be sold, in a similar way to restricting tobacco and alcohol, or should it be up to individuals as to what foodstuffs they buy?

In thinking about anxiety and stress, can you identify social developments which may put more pressure on children and young people within contemporary society when compared to previous generations?

Further reading

AMS (2024b) would be a good introduction to health issues relating to children and useful if writing assignments.

Haidt (2024) provides a good account of how the contemporary world has changed the context of childhood.

Hayes and Filipović (2018) are useful for considering the context of early years care and education when it comes to outcomes. This is also a good example of how discourse operates within society.

10

Children's futures and future childhoods

This chapter will help you to understand:
- how environmental changes might impact upon children;
- why the economy matters to children;
- the relevance of ideas about post-humanism.

Would we really do anything to make things better for our children?

It is common to hear parents say that they would do anything for their children and that they want them to have a better life. Similarly, politicians often talk about policies as being in the best interests of children. Neither claim stands up to scrutiny. In this chapter we consider a broad approach to the landscape of childhood and the possibilities that may come to shape future childhoods. In doing this we are particularly concerned with the idea that the world has changed. One thing which indicates a changed world when we compare children now with previous generations is the move into what has been called the Anthropocene. Having an understanding of the Anthropocene is important not only in terms of contemporary childhood, but also in regarding childhoods that may be experienced in the future.

The issue that underpins the Anthropocene is that human activity has fundamentally changed the ecological nature of the earth and that this change is experienced by humans and non-humans alike (Hamilton et al, 2015; Barla and Von Verschuer, 2022). The changes that have led to the Anthropocene are particularly associated with the industrial revolution and the effect this has had on the environments in which we live, especially in relation to pollutants.

The Anthropocene is not just the consequence of the development of industry though. It can also be seen as arising from the consequences of widespread colonisation and the population changes that resulted from this, such as humans moving to live in cities. Colonisation has involved the global spread of diseases such as from Europe to the Americas (Lewis and Maslin, 2015), along with the transfer of plants, animals and insect species around the globe (Frankopan, 2023).

In respect of children and childhood it is important to consider two key issues: the extent to which the conditions of the Anthropocene may be seen in various types of pollution, and the reality of climate change which is generally accepted as the climate crisis. As with many aspects of the world, however, we do not all face these problems in the same way, or to the same extent. Pollution affects all of us but not necessarily to the same extent. It may be harder to avoid for poor families and in poorer countries, and it can be understood as a parenting matter when parents are faced with the consequences of their decisions regarding where they live and how they live their lives in respect of how pollution may affect their children (Laird, 2017; Laville, 2020).

Maybe the key feature of the Anthropocene though is the climate crisis in that this is truly global. The climate crisis is the result of human activity that has affected the climate, leading to global heating, rising sea levels and a range of ecological problems. The climate crisis is fundamentally changing the world that our children live in and has consequences which go beyond changes in climate and weather, such as the extent to which it affects crop yields or contributes to both droughts and flooding.

Although the impact of climate change leading to the climate crisis has been demonstrated over a number of decades, it is important to be aware that there are some commentators and politicians that deny it and/or see the problem as something they do not need to worry about as it does not affect them. The denial of climate change is associated with culture wars as discussed earlier, in that it is essentially a right-wing argument which seeks to resist the changes that are required if we are to halt global heating. Changes such as moving away from using fossil fuels are needed to lessen the effects of climate change, and to reduce the potential for future harms, but many see this as unreasonable because this would require changes based upon how they live their lives. This can be seen as ignoring the future that children are inheriting. In essence the denial of climate change demonstrates that humans across the globe do not share the same social and economic position in terms of what climate change means (Lakind and Adsit-Morris, 2018).

There are evidently some irrational responses to the issue of climate change. For example, in the UK developments aimed at encouraging more people to cycle instead of drive often result in verbal, and sometimes physical, attacks on cyclists, even though individuals who are choosing to cycle rather than drive contribute to reducing congestion on the roads, so making driving easier and not contributing to the overall problem of pollution.

Similarly, proposals which lessen the need to drive have also been criticised. The idea of 15-minute cities promotes the wholly reasonable aim of making services such as schools, doctors and shops easier to access so as to make towns and cities better places to live by cutting down on car use and reducing the time we waste on travel. This would be advantageous for children. However, conspiracy theories about the concept of the 15-minute city put forward by some on the political right suggest that it forms part of a global strategy of control which aims to not only restrict our ability to travel but to form the basis of curfews as to when we might travel, or when we might undertake activities, such as going shopping (Loader, 2023).

Although such arguments may be far-fetched, they have had consequences. In the UK the Conservative government led by Rishi Sunak in 2023 drew on conspiracy theories relating to 15-minute cities to justify significant cuts to funding for sustainable, or active, transport, such as walking and cycling, while favouring the use of cars (Walker, 2024). This also ignores how cars also present risk to children in terms of car accidents and the issue of children trying to negotiate traffic when walking to and from school and other activities. To put this in context, 2023 was the hottest year on record (Copernicus, 2024), yet during 2023 Sunak's Conservative government also either scrapped or watered down a number of important environmental policies which had previously been introduced with the aim of addressing the climate crisis (Crerar et al, 2023).

Note

'Conspiracy theory' is the term given to claims that are made which suggest either that there is some ulterior or additional motive when governments introduce policies, or that some undefined group is able to exert pressure on governments such that they will introduce policies which will be against the best interests of the population. In the US this is typified by concerns relating to 'the deep state'.

Conspiracy theories by right-wing groups have been prominent in Western countries in recent decades, typified by spurious claims made during the COVID-19 health pandemic and by claims that tragedies such as mass shootings in schools are staged using 'crisis actors'.

Although they are often fanciful and unfounded, the growth of social media means that conspiracy theories can be influential.

In assessing the climate crisis alongside the limited pace of changes that are necessary to address it we return to questioning whether or not we would do anything for our children and whether there is real concern about how childhood is experienced across the world. In thinking about this, though, we return once again to thinking about how individuals and households may be confined to making small changes to their lives but where the State, in the form of government, may be able to make much larger changes. This brings us to the question of who shapes childhood. It also reiterates the idea that was introduced earlier in asking us to focus on what the priorities of any government might be and what they may see as being in the best interests of the population as a whole, and for childhood in particular. We do know that human activity is changing the world, and we do know that this will be detrimental to children.

Doughnuts and how they may help children thrive

Having stated that the climate crisis is problematic for children, this section will focus on something that may be of benefit for all children by considering the work of Kate Raworth. Raworth (2017) argues that a key aim of any society should be the aim of establishing the social conditions under which children can thrive. In one sense, this is another of those seductive arguments in that it is easy to say that we want a society in which children can thrive and not so easy to say that we don't. What tends to happen in practice is that we may all agree that we want a society within which our children will thrive, but we then resist making any changes to our lives which may be necessary to achieve this, sometimes because we just don't like change, but often because these changes feel too complex.

Creating a society where children will thrive will inevitably mean that we have to change some of our existing beliefs and practices. Economic practices related to natural resources such as fossil fuels are central to this. Raworth argues that we cannot keep growing the economy if growth means consuming more and more natural resources. In making this claim, though, she asks us to recognise that in the natural world creatures do not keep growing. When we look at animals, including humans, we experience a period of growth, which in humans we refer to as childhood and adolescence, and then we experience a period of maturity. For Raworth this is the period of thriving. As such, Raworth is arguing that it is perfectly reasonable for societies to move away from a need for growth.

Of course, you may be thinking what all this has to do with doughnuts. Well, Raworth presents her ideas as having two important limits. The first is what she refers to as the ecological ceiling. Activity beyond this ceiling is harmful to the ecology of the planet, and, following this, what is harmful to the planet is harmful to us in that it degrades our quality of life, and consequently childhood. The second is what she refers to as the social foundation. This is a baseline of what is considered a good life experience, below which we experience some form of deprivation.

Raworth presents this as a model that looks like the sort of doughnut that has a hole in the middle, where the space in the centre represents deprivation but where going beyond the doughnut represents ecological harm. Meanwhile the doughnut itself is ideal, what Raworth refers to as a 'safe and just space for humanity' (2017: 11). Raworth refers to the space below the social foundation as the shortfall, and the space above the ecological ceiling as the overshoot. Both a shortfall and an overshoot are not good for us, and she provides a lot of detail regarding the issues that relate to problem areas caused by a shortfall or an overshoot.

Note

Examples provided by Raworth of both shortfalls and overshoots include the following:

Problems caused by a shortfall	Problems caused by an overshoot
Food and/or water shortages	Climate change
Decline in health and/or education services	Oceans becoming acidic
Decline in incomes and/or work	Chemical pollution
Increased social inequalities	Air pollution
Housing problems	Loss of biodiversity

So, let us return to the issue of children again and maybe reconsider that classic statement that 'I would do anything for my kids'. The climate crisis requires people to change their behaviours, like driving their car less or reducing their consumption of meat. Will people change? Will they do something to address the sorts of problems that Raworth is saying will only increase unless we adopt a new approach towards managing the economy and the environment? If childhood is to be good for all children, and continue to be good, then these are the issues that governments and parents need to address.

Economics without growth to help children thrive

The first thing to say here is that economic growth is deeply embedded in political ideas about how we should see success, so changing this is unlikely to be easy. Growth simply means that we make more things, buy more things and use more things. Central to Raworth's idea of doughnut economics is that economic growth must be dropped on the basis that it is unsustainable, though Raworth is certainly not the first to suggest this. For example, European governments had considered the negative consequences of continued growth over 50 years ago (Döring and Aigner-Walder, 2022). A more critical approach is provided by Shiva (2016), who illustrates how the British colonisation of India changed agricultural production in a way that was both ecologically harmful and damaging, especially to women's lives, and children's lives as a result.

One reason why growth has come to dominate thinking can be seen as the combination of ideas from the Enlightenment together with the development of capitalism. Within capitalism the pursuit of profit dominates business thinking. This is embedded within neoliberal politics. Alongside this concern with generating profit, however, is the way that the Enlightenment introduced the idea of a rational approach to understanding the world. The emphasis on rationality reflects an ordered or structured approach to doing things in a manner that is seen as logical, but where the logic of capitalism is in producing profit. The paradox is that an approach which is effectively destroying the planet upon which we depend for survival cannot really be seen as rational (Thornton et al, 2019). As such, for Shiva the Enlightenment is neither rational nor enlightened (Hayward, 1995). An accessible summary of Shiva's ideas can be found in Shiva (2013). Similarly, throughout the 1980s James Robertson was arguing that we need a future model of society and economics which he called 'Sane, Humane and Ecological' if we are to avoid ecological disaster (Robertson, 1983; 1985; 1990).

What we could suggest, then, is that what we have is childhood being shaped by the macrosystem as Bronfenbrenner discusses, but in a way that disregards children and their future. So, when we think about the world that children inhabit, we can see that there have been warnings for some time that we are creating ecological problems that will be detrimental to them. However, it is important to recognise that it is a world that is being created by the actions of adults and that those actions are never inevitable. Adults do have choices. When we consider the world in a more general sense the words of C.P. Snow (1993), originally published in 1959, crop up in many books. Richards (1983:181) summarises a key part of Snow's argument in the following observation: 'it does not require one additional scientific discovery to alleviate the worlds suffering; lack of knowledge is no longer the problem. What is still lacking is a sure means of enabling humankind to discriminate between that knowledge which is worth having and that which is largely superfluous.'

So, what is being presented in these arguments is really the idea that it is how adults see the world that is important, especially those adults who have positions of power and influence. Currently it is evident that there is little political will to make the sort of changes that are necessary to address the climate crisis. If the world of the future is to be better for children, then it will have to change in some ways. As such a more holistic perspective which considers humanity as more ecologically aware is necessary, as will be considered in the following section.

A post-human view of childhood

Earlier we raised the issue of how the philosophical developments of the 18th century resulted in what has come to be referred to as the Enlightenment, and how the changes that were brought about as a consequence of the Enlightenment shaped the period in human history, especially in the West, that is referred to as modernity. Now we know that in some ways this seems to be moving away from a concern with children and childhood, and you only picked up this book to read about children, but stay with us, at least for a while; modernity has had some real consequences for childhood.

This is particularly relevant when we consider the interplay between humans and the material world. Remember that what became known as the new sociology of childhood emphasised children's agency in a way that moved away from just considering material issues (Malone et al, 2020). When we say material issues, we mean the real world, the world of things, environments, biological bodies and so on. As such, the material world is the world of the things that we live in. The climate crisis is a material reality. This can be compared to the abstract world of ideas.

Now we want you think that modernity reinforced a way of understanding the world that puts humans at the centre of our concerns. Think of this as humanism. In this approach it is human activity, community and culture that is the prime focus. This is also at the heart of sociology. If we return to the beginning of the book and use the analogy of Bronfenbrenner's socio-ecological model, it is humans that are at the centre. Agency is directed outward from humans. Humans become seen as the sole source of agency. Humans shape the world that we live in.

What post-humanism encourages you to do is to take a much broader picture when considering the world that we live in. So, consider the idea that agency flows not only from humans, but that it flows from non-human things too (Pickering, 2000). That might seem a big claim, especially when we have already said that in sociology agency refers to our capacity to act, to exert our will. However, although Pickering is not saying that non-human things have free will, he is arguing that the material world that we live in shapes us just as we shape the material world.

Pause for reflection

Let us give you a trivial example to show what we mean here. We have children, and one thing that we often complained about is how they seemed to lack the ability to make arrangements with friends, such as times and places to meet, as we would expect to do.

But they grew up in a world of mobile phones. Because of this they never really needed to make arrangements in terms of when and where to meet. Their arrangements are vague because the detail can be sorted out later via phone.

We were both 18 when we had a phone installed in our houses, and in our thirties when we first got mobile phones. We grew up having to make firm arrangements with friends when we were with them as we had no means of contacting them later.

Can you see how the material world that our children, and you probably, have grown up in means that they think and behave in a different way compared to us?

Pickering provides a somewhat objective view of post-humanism in emphasising how the material world shapes us. Others are more concerned with how the humanism that is central to modernity had the effect of seeing human wants and needs becoming the primary concern but, ironically, how this led to the ecological problems that the world now faces. We introduced these problems earlier when we discussed the Anthropocene. What post-humanism considers is how the non-human world or post-human world shapes us, and how it shapes childhood, and this cannot be ignored.

In considering the welfare of children, though, we need to be more ecologically aware and take action (Jansen van Vuuren, 2023). The consequences of not taking action, what Robertson referred to as business as usual or a hyper-industrial future, will have negative consequences for our children. As such the emergence of a post-human focus within a range of academic disciplines creates a position where we become more concerned with seeing humans in a broader context. So, where Pickering gives us the idea that modernity made humans the central focus of the world, and then suggests that it ignores how the world that we have made generates feedback which shapes us, other aspects of post-humanism propose the idea that we need to see humans as merely one part of a complex and interrelated world.

Note

This is sometimes referred to as decentring humans (Nichols and Campano, 2017).

Decentring simply means a shift in how we understand position. Instead of seeing humans as the most important concern, or as seeing humans as the only thing of consequence, we start to see humans as part of a broader landscape which includes the natural, the technological and the social.

To understand the post-human perspective, though, it is also important to recognise that modernity constructed a way of seeing the world in terms of dualities, and then to accept that we have to move beyond that.

We have referred to some of these dualities already, such as rich and poor, black and white, male and female. To add to this, we can say a key duality is that of human compared to non-human, or nature. What post-humanism does, then, is promote a way of understanding the world where the human–nature duality is replaced by a worldview in which humans are not separate from nature, but are a part of nature (Margulies and Bersaglio, 2018; Fagan, 2019). Maybe one way of starting to understand a post-humanist view of the world is to think about the position of dogs as pets, within families (Charles, 2016). Dogs have been domesticated for a long time, but if you have a dog for a pet to what extent is the dog a family member? If the dog is treated as a family member, does that signify the breaking down of the human/nature duality? Can you recognise that in a lot of households the dogs' needs are as important as the human needs?

We could then move on from this example of dogs as pets and think about how animal rights in general provides us with a way of looking at post-humanism. A claim for animal rights also breaks down the duality between humans and non-humans or humans and nature by applying some of the principles that apply to human rights to other species (Stucki, 2023). In turn, this demonstrates that how we understand the world always influences rights.

The view of understanding the world that was shaped by modernity positioned human wants as central to an understanding of rights. As such, what humans want often becomes more important than considerations about non-humans or the natural world. It is important, however, to recognise that modernity is a specifically Western perspective and that it has certain limitations. For example, the Western practice of colonisation demonstrates that the Western view of human rights never applied to all humans (Lindgren and Sjöstrand Öhrfelt, 2017). We also see this within societies around the world which have used, or do use, various reasons and explanations for denying rights to certain groups based on characteristics such as sex, gender, skin colour and sexuality. We may also consider that certain rights are routinely denied to children and young people all over the world.

The post-human perspective then is a view of the world which sits more easily with diversity. It is inevitably bound up with promoting equality and respect not only for all people but for nature as well. In this way, post-humanism is inevitably bound up with a more ecological perspective. At the same time post-humanism will inevitably be criticised or rejected by individuals who adopt a more conservative view of what society should be like, and do not want to change their behaviours, even if it means a better future for children, or improved childhoods now.

Sustainability, inclusion and diversity

It can be argued that certain ideas which reflect post-humanism are gaining traction within Western societies. As is always the case, this is rarely a smooth process and sometimes ideas get a little changed as they are adopted, but progress is still evident. As such it may be seen that one of the implications of a move towards post-humanism is also a move towards embedding ideas about sustainability, inclusion and diversity within education. In this section we will say a bit more about how sustainability, inclusion and diversity can be seen within education by focusing on two issues, Forest Schools and decolonisation. These may seem very different issues, but consider how we described post-humanism as a move towards consideration of all things human and non-human.

Forest Schools originated within Denmark and can be seen as a development which reflects a move towards post-human education (Lindgren and Sjöstrand Öhrfelt, 2017). It should be noted however that the development of Forest Schools in the UK often represents a somewhat limited version of Danish practices. Different ideas in relation to social philosophy (ideas about how society should be) in the UK compared to Denmark means that although Forest Schools may be based upon Danish practices, there are significant differences (McLeod, 2019). A basic distinction is that outdoor learning is much more embedded within the Danish education system (Williams-Siegfredsen, 2017). This can be compared to the experiences of UK children, where the Forest School is usually experienced as something that is bolted on to the normal school experience, it is not integral to it (Waite et al, 2016; McLeod, 2019). This could be seen to reflect how we in the UK are less inclined to allow children outside in what is seen as poor weather such as rain or cold, but it is also a concern that children being outside and engaged in what might appear to be playing has limited educational opportunities that align to the UK national curriculum.

In one sense, however, it is not surprising that a practice which has developed in Denmark spontaneously, and led by teachers (Bentsen et al, 2013; Williams-Siegfredsen, 2017; McLeod, 2019), takes on a different feel when introduced to the UK. The cultural attitudes to both the outdoors and to education differ in each country. However, within the context of the discussion earlier about the climate crisis and in terms of more general moves towards post-humanism, Forest Schools can be seen as a start in respect of developing an educational system which would support post-humanism. Forest Schools are argued to give children a better sense of nature and the environment. However, the limitations of this approach towards education in the UK reflect a wider concern about how far we are prepared to change to improve childhood.

A further aspect of the post-humanist approach that has value is that of decolonisation. This seems far removed from children's everyday lives when taken at face value, so it is important to establish what we mean by this. Colonisation generally refers to the practices of European countries taking over, or colonising, other countries and changing their cultures. For example, many European nations used military power to support the colonisation of lands across the globe irrespective of the wishes of the peoples who already lived there. In some of those countries, such as the US, Australia and Canada, the position of indigenous peoples is now very limited. In other countries, including countries in Asia and Africa, indigenous peoples were able to mobilise resistance to European rule so as to gain independence. However, it would be fair to say that their way of life has been permanently affected by colonisation even if they now have independence.

Colonisation has impoverished some countries and has often led to the establishment of views which denigrate people from different backgrounds. As such, ideas relating to equality and to accepting diversity can be difficult to achieve because of long-standing views overhanging from colonisation which undermine knowledge held by indigenous groups or which position other cultures as inferior. Underpinning this, however, are ideas which emerged within the Enlightenment which suggested that human races could be identified and that these races were not equal. In this way European nations were able to justify colonisation.

Similarly, ideas about combating the climate crisis through environmental education should be seen as being entwined with decolonisation (Thornton et al, 2019). This is on the basis that the knowledges that have been negated or lost because of the colonial mindset often have important and relevant insights into developing a sustainable future. This reflects Shiva's concerns as were introduced earlier regarding how colonial forces had a negative impact upon agriculture in India (Shiva, 2016). This is because colonialism involved the displacement or replacement of existing ideas and beliefs in those countries that were colonised. Consequently, the existing knowledge that was held by indigenous groups became ignored and seen as inferior to Western ideas. The value in decolonisation within education then fits with ideas about sustainability, inclusion and diversity by promoting the idea that all cultures have value.

Note

Where we said earlier that post-humanism involves decentring humans by appreciating that humans are part of nature rather than being above nature, we need to see ideas about decolonisation as decentring Western ideas and values and moving towards recognition of all humans being equal.

In this way we can start to see all ideas as having equal validity and an equal right to be heard. As such, decolonisation is a project which seeks to recognise imbalances of power and achieve parity.

With this in mind, the early years education approach within New Zealand, *Te Whāriki,* may be seen as an example of how decolonising can be embedded within education. *Te Whāriki* is an approach to the curriculum which sets out to encompass both indigenous and external cultures as being of equal value in a way that is explicitly bicultural (Lee, 2013; Delaune, 2019; Giardiello et al, 2019; Malone et al, 2020). Such approaches become important to childhood as globalisation has led to multicultural environments in which children live and learn.

Making use of ecological ideas and issues

We hope that this chapter is useful in encouraging you to think beyond children themselves and to start to consider the world within which children live. This could enable you to develop your work by offering arguments which draw upon the landscape of childhood in a broader sense. One thing that could be seen as framing this chapter is the idea that the world as a whole has entered a new phase, the Anthropocene. In focusing upon the Anthropocene, we are positioning childhood within an ecological network. The Anthropocene represents a world that has been fundamentally changed by human activity and has resulted in a wide range of pollutants which have degraded the environment and culminated in the climate crisis.

We have said previously that the idea of framing an argument is a useful skill for students to develop. In its most basic sense, think about how a picture frame creates a boundary for a painting or photograph. The frame contains the painting or photograph and in doing so it imposes a sense of focus. Now think that frames can come in different styles and colours. Within this chapter, the ecological aspects of the Anthropocene act as the frame in that they act to establish the boundary for the chapter. What is discussed within the chapter is always in some way restricted to ecological matters. In a similar way, the frame for the book as a whole is the issue of childhood and children. So, when it comes to producing assignments, you may benefit from establishing a frame and then keeping within it. This can provide a better structure to your work and keep you focused.

In considering the Anthropocene and what it means for the ecology of the planet, what is evident is that changes will have to be made if the climate crisis is to be addressed. If the climate crisis has resulted from human activity, then it is not unreasonable to suggest that changing human activity will help to lessen the impact of the problems which now face us. Raworth's ideas of doughnut economics are useful here, especially her concern that society should seek to ensure that it provides the conditions under which children can thrive. After all, parents are fond of saying that they would do anything for their children, so it does not seem unreasonable to make changes to how we live if this benefits us all in the long run. If we are concerned about providing good childhoods, we need to consider this.

So, if you are tasked with producing an assignment which places an understanding of childhood within ecological concerns, then this chapter can be very useful. We have demonstrated that any discussion of ecology really needs to make mention of the Anthropocene. We have also shown how you might consider the ways in which economic growth that uses even more natural resources may compound the problem. Following from this, framing an assignment around establishing the conditions under which children can thrive will be useful. It is unlikely that children will thrive in the future if these issues are not addressed.

There is also scope, however, to demonstrate how more recent ideas about post-humanism work to decentre humans and that this acts to counter the ways in which the Enlightenment, which ushered in the period that is referred to as modernity, placed humans and human concerns at the centre of our thinking. Where the Enlightenment established a way of seeing the world in terms of dualities, the decentring that is integral to post-humanism acknowledges a broader world of relationships that accommodates nature and technologies alongside humanity. The relevance for childhood is that this perspective is more likely to avoid some of the environmental mistakes of the past. We suggested that Forest Schools fit with this approach, but this will require changes in thinking about what we want children to learn, and how learning can take place in childhood.

In tackling an assignment that covers ecological issues, then, it seems reasonable to suggest that the following bullet points reflect some key issues that may be drawn upon or referred to:

- The Anthropocene is the ecological backdrop to childhood.
- The climate crisis is likely to disrupt childhoods around the globe.
- A focus on enabling children to thrive could improve children's lives.
- Post-humanism decentres the place of humans in a way that facilitates a more holistic approach towards ecological issues.
- Forest Schools represent one move towards post-human ideas.

Further thoughts

Consider the statement made by parents, 'I would do anything for my kids'. What are the limitations to this and why might parents resist doing things that would benefit their children?

Might Raworth's ideas about doughnut economics and economic growth have consequences for some of the other issues that have been raised within the book, such as the increase in anxiety as experienced by children and young people?

What do you see as the future for childhood?

Further reading

With respect to the relationship between the economy and the environment, Raworth (2017) is well worth reading.

An accessible summary of Shiva's ideas can be found in Shiva (2013), and most works by Robertson are available online at www.jamesrobertson.com.

In relation to education and ecology, Buckles (2018) provides a good account.

For a bit more on post-humanism, try Jansen van Vuuren (2023).

11

Tips to get higher grades

> **This chapter will:**
> - discuss the role of artificial intelligence (AI) in assignments;
> - say more about the things that you can do to get a higher grade.

There's really no need to have read this book, not when we have artificial intelligence and essay mills

We spent a long time writing this book and read lots of books, journal articles and various other sources so as to be able to make claims with confidence. We aren't sure if we would have been able to do it without using word-processing software and without an internet connection to access online sources. In one sense this book is an extended version of the types of assignment task that we have regularly asked students to engage with; reading, thinking and writing about a topic in response to a question. But we know that writing assignments, and/or books, is challenging and there is always the temptation to get AI to do it for us. Students are in the same position, AI can write assignments.

Well, OK, artificial intelligence might write your assignment for you, but that doesn't mean that it will be any good. In the UK many students use AI to assist them in their studies (Freeman, 2024). Although very few seem to claim that it is acceptable to get AI to actually write, or should we say generate, assignments, many see it as a valid and useful tool for providing explanations of concepts and ideas. In fact, a good number of respondents thought that universities should provide AI facilities for students.

So, given that part of our concern in this book is to provide advice and guidance that students can use to produce stronger assignments, and of course by that we mean guidance on how students can improve their grades, it is maybe worth giving a bit of space to the use of AI. If AI can generate an assignment that will receive a high mark it is obviously going to be attractive. What could possibly go wrong?

Firstly, your university may throw you off your course if you are found to have used AI to generate an assignment that you submit as being all your own work. In addition to this, though, there is one key danger in using AI to generate your assignments: AI systems often hallucinate (Anghelescu et al, 2023; McGowan et al, 2023). To hallucinate when used in the context of AI we mean that AI will generate something that looks right but is false.

The most obvious issue in relation to academic assignments is with respect to references, or citations. So, an assignment that has been generated by AI may look good, but a check of the reference list is likely to find that many are simply made up. This is illustrated by McGowan et al (2023), who asked two freely available AI tools to do a literature search. Thirty-five sources were provided by the AI. Of the 35, only two were real. The rest were just made up, they were hallucinations.

That said, it is also fair to say that before AI was available students could turn to several businesses who, for a fee, would provide an essay on any given topic. This is still possible. Such essays would ostensibly be provided to the student as a guide to what they should produce, but it is fair to say that many students would submit the bought essay. A quick internet search will reveal very many sites offering such services. These are generally referred to as 'essay mills', (Medway et al, 2018; Sweeney, 2023).

Using essay mills or using AI to generate assignments, and submitting said work, means that a student is guilty of either academic dishonesty or plagiarism. Having sat on very many academic misconduct boards we can confirm that students have been thrown off courses for academic dishonesty. Most higher education (HE) providers will use software such as Turnitin to routinely check student assignments. Plagiarism detection software such as Turnitin will identify text that replicates other works, including other students work. Such plagiarism detection software is increasingly providing AI detection also.

Sweeney (2023) is interesting in that he offers a strategy to staff which makes it harder for students to use AI, which can be adopted by students to improve their work. Here's point one regarding improving your grade: the approach that Sweeney suggests involves insisting that assignments are focused on the readings that are recommended within the module. As markers we recognise that in spite of the effort that we go to in order to point students towards useful and relevant readings, including direct online links to many readings, we find that we mark assignments where the student has ignored these readings in favour of some very obscure, and often not very useful, texts.

Study tip

Take the easy route when it comes to producing assignments and make sure that the readings that have been provided or recommended are used within your work.

Within the UK it is normal practice to set up Virtual Learning Environments such as Blackboard or Moodle to provide direct links to module readings such as books and journal articles.

If you want a good mark, then you want the marker to have confidence in what you have done. A good strategy is to make sure that you read and use the texts that have been recommended.

Make it easy for yourself but take care

The sources that you use for writing assignments are important as this is the platform that your assignments rest on, so it is important to make sure that your sources have validity. Not all sources are the same. Think of them as being located on a continuum which represents better or poorer resources. This could be read as more or less academic. One criterion for ascertaining where a resource fits could be the extent to which the reader is required to have greater knowledge and understanding in the first place. Think about journal articles in highly ranked journals. Articles in highly ranked journals are not written for students, they are written for other academics, that is why they are often difficult to read. They require the reader to have a decent understanding in the first place.

That said, we know that very many tutors in HE are more likely to look upon student assignments favourably if they have used journal articles. So, play the game and use them. As a simple rule of thumb about making decisions regarding which sources to use, think about sources as being in a league table and note the following:

- At the top are journal articles from a highly respected peer-reviewed journal.
- Next come books which are deemed to be monologues. Not textbooks. Creasy and Corby (2019) is a monologue.
- Then come textbooks such as Creasy and Corby (2023). These are aimed at students and make sense of journal articles and monologues for students.

Now it becomes less clear but still useful:

- Articles on publishers' websites such transformingsociety.co.uk or *The Conversation* are reliable.
- Newspapers such as *The Guardian* or *The Times* are reliable, but not all newspapers are reliable.
- Government websites such as the ONS will provide good quality, up-to-date statistics. Charity websites or websites such as the Joseph Rowntree Foundation are good.

Now we come to sources to steer clear of:

- General websites or blogs are very unreliable. Avoid them.
- Tabloid newspapers, and their associated websites.
- Any website that will charge you for an essay-style document, or provide a sample essay, is going to be risky. Such sources will undermine your work.
- Online video sources are not going to be the most reliable sources. Avoid them.

When searching for sources you may come across organisations with websites which sound very useful, but we urge you to be a little sceptical. For example, during the Brexit referendum the European Research Group (ERG) was often referred to and did much to promote their agenda. What is important, however, is to recognise that the agenda that the ERG was promoting was that the UK should leave the European Union (EU) (Murray and Armstrong, 2021). So, although they may be engaged in carrying out research with regards to the EU, it was aimed at achieving a particular outcome. A similar example concerns the Centre for Social Justice (CSJ). The CSJ produces numerous reports concerning social issues and concerns and any student searching for material relating to social justice would inevitably conclude that the CSJ must be a relevant source of information. However, as Slater (2014: 950) argues:

> emotive terms, phrases and concepts have been strategically deployed by a conservative think tank (the Centre for Social Justice) to manufacture doubt with respect to the structural causes of unemployment and poverty, and to give the impression that 'welfare' is a lifestyle choice made by dysfunctional families despite the fact that considerable social scientific evidence shatters that impression.

One way of considering the integrity of organisations such as the Centre for Social Justice is to try to find out how they are funded. This is because the funders of any organisation will have an intention and an organisation that is transparent about where they receive funding from is making it possible to assess their intentions. To do this visit the website of Who Funds You. Who Funds You is a part of an organisation called openDemocracy. It investigates how organisations and pressure groups or research bodies get their funding and scores them in terms of transparency. A high score is good, a low score is not good. Who Funds You scores the Centre for Social Justice very low.

The two examples that we have offered are quite straightforward in that they are both organisations which pursue a particular agenda. One other concern to be aware of, however, is false balance, as introduced earlier. The problem here is when a concern to provide both sides of an argument gives the impression that the evidence in support of each side is equal. So, if any particular position is supported by evidence from, say, 99 researchers, but an opposite position is offered by one, then to broadcast both positions gives a false impression that each position is valid when this is not the case.

So, at this point we are urging you to give some thought to the sources that you use for your assignments. That said, we don't want to give the impression that the key thing is content. It isn't. By focusing on content, we are more likely to make the mistake of thinking that assignment marks represent the extent to which an assignment is correct or not.

So, be aware, the marker of your assignments does not start with a potential mark of 100 and then proceeds to deduct a mark for every mistake. At the same time, the mark that you get is not a percentage of 100. For example, a mark of 57 does not mean that you are 57 per cent right and 43 per cent wrong. We know that it is common to say that the mark is a percentage and that you might even receive a mark with a percentage attached, but trust us, it's just not logical in written assignments to say this. This is relevant though because we want to shift your focus away from the idea of getting the content correct and start you thinking about assignments more holistically.

So, what we want you to think about here is what is important with respect to an assignment, noting that this is bound up with a particular way of looking at assignments which may differ to some extent from what you have been used to before you started in HE.

On university open days we would often ask potential students if it was the case that in A-levels and BTEC, students would generally be presented with a model answer for an assignment which emphasised content. The consequence being that if they were to reproduce the model and cover the same content, they would then get a good mark. They generally agreed that achieving a high mark was dependent upon putting the right content into an assignment, no thinking required. This can create problems in terms of the transition to HE in that it means that students come to HE with the understanding that the content of assignments is the most important thing. Because of this, tutors in HE are often asked about what to put in to assignments. In social science courses this doesn't apply all that well. It has some relevance in that you need to be writing about relevant issues, but we want you to start to change how you look at assignments so that presentation, style and application of ideas and theories come to be seen as more important than content.

It is important to state at the outset, then, that the mark that you receive for an assignment represents a judgement about the overall quality of the work. That is important because it means that correcting or improving any one particular issue with your work is not going to see your mark jump from, say, 45 to 65. Remember, the mark is simply an indicator of the overall quality of that assignment.

Your university should provide you with guidance on how marks are awarded in relation to different aspects of the assignment and these marking guides are well worth reading. Universities are also very likely to have staff whose role is to assist students in doing better. Use these staff. Library staff are very useful but often under-used. In addition, there will often be study-support staff that can help with improving writing. Seek them out and use them.

To reiterate what we have said earlier, though, your aim is to avoid the mistakes or practices which will hold your mark down and to incorporate some of the approaches that will lift your mark up. Some of this advice will be easy to follow. Some of it will be obvious. Some of the advice however will mean that you have to take further advice and work on it. If you start to put these ideas into practice, though, we are confident that you will be able to avoid a low grade and you are likely to see your grades improve.

Please note that terms and conditions apply. You can write a brilliant assignment with no errors, an engaging style, perfect referencing and have evidenced lots of reading but still fail if it is not what you were asked to do. We know because we have failed this assignment. Always read the assignment brief carefully and seek advice from tutors if necessary. If there is a word limit, then stick to it. Many universities will apply a penalty to work which exceeds word limits. Some universities will also apply a penalty to work which is too short, though not always. Always meet the deadlines that are set. Penalties usually apply to assignments that are late, no matter how good they are. Check your university's regulations about not submitting work carefully. Sometimes not submitting at all means you won't get a second chance in the way that a failed assignment submitted as a first attempt will nearly always be able to be reworked.

How your reference list can support a good mark

Finally then, as a consequence of the growing concerns about the possibility that assignments have been generated by AI, many markers will start their assessment of an assignment by reading the reference list, sometimes referred to as the citation list. The reason for this is that it gives the marker a good idea as to how the student has approached the task. Following from this it will be quite useful to give a little thought to why it is necessary to reference assignments and then to guide you, the reader, into producing better assignments. There are three good reasons regarding why we are required to reference:

1. Because we will lose marks if we don't and may even be automatically failed.
2. To demonstrate that we have not plagiarised (copied) someone else's work.
3. So that we can relocate the sources that we used to write the assignment.

Luckily, referencing is the one part of your assignment that is always straightforward and logical. It is also something that will come with a clear guide as to how to do it. Most social science type courses will use the Harvard referencing system, though there are two things to say about this. Firstly, that there are different versions of Harvard. Secondly, that because there are different versions you must make sure that you use the system that you have been directed to use.

Note

The Harvard system is widely used, probably because it is simple and logical. There are two parts to referencing using Harvard: inserting a reference where you write (in-text citations) and providing a list of the sources that you used (the reference, or citation, list). What is crucial is that the in-text reference has a corresponding entry in the reference list.

Always make sure that all in-text references (citations) match an entry in the reference (citation) list. If you reference Creasy and Corby (2023) in the assignment the marker must be able to find Creasy and Corby (2023) in the reference list!

One solution is to start using referencing software. In writing this book we used Endnote, but we could have chosen to use others such as Refworks or Mendeley. Each takes a bit of getting used to but if your university provides any of them for free, they are well worth it. Basically, when you write your assignments you use the software to insert the in-text reference. What the software then does is to build a reference list at the end of your assignment. You don't have to write the reference out and you can change the style very easily. What's more, once the source reference has been used once it remains within the system and you don't have to input it again. Even better, most library systems, or on-line access systems for books and journals, will have a link which means that you can download all the required details for a reference at the click of a button. For those of us who had to write everything out by hand, this is just magical!

Student task

Check if your college or university provides you with referencing software. If it does, then either access online guides and learn how to use it or go to your university and speak to a librarian about getting help to use it.

Library staff are always very helpful but are often under-used by students.

So, what we want to end up with in an assignment is illustrated in the following example.

> What seems obvious then is that children face many more restrictions in relation to what they can do or where they can go when compared to 50 years ago. This is partly explained by a growing concern about the risks that children face (Creasy and Corby, 2019).

Here, (Creasy and Corby, 2019) is the in-text reference. This means that there has to be a corresponding entry in the reference list. There is. In the reference list we find the following:

Creasy, R. and Corby, F. (2019). *Taming Childhood?: A Critical Perspective on Policy, Practice and Parenting,* Palgrave Macmillan.

We have ended with a short section on referencing because it just seemed to fit given that this is what comes next. At this stage we just want to say that we hope that you have found some of the material within the book interesting and that some of it will be useful. Readers will have approached the book for a range of reasons, and we never expected that all sections will have equal value for all readers but on the whole we are confident that it will provide most of you with something to think about.

References

Adams, R. and C.A. García (2023) 'Rise in school absences since Covid driven by anxiety and lack of support, say English councils', *The Guardian*, [online] 23 April, Available from: https://www.theguardian.com/education/2023/apr/23/rise-in-school-absences-since-covid-driven-by-anxiety-and-lack-of-support-say-english-councils [Accessed 14 July 2025].

Adkins, F. (2022) 'Raw deal: discontent is rising as water companies pump sewage into UK waters', *The Guardian*, [online] 13 November, Available from: https://www.theguardian.com/environment/2022/nov/13/raw-deal-discontent-is-rising-as-water-companies-pump-sewage-into-uk-waters [Accessed 14 July 2025].

African Union (1990) *African Charter on the Rights and Welfare of the Child*, [online], Available from: https://au.int/sites/default/files/treaties/36804-treaty-african_charter_on_rights_welfare_of_the_child.pdf [Accessed 20 July 2025].

Ainsworth, M.D.S. and S.M. Bell (1970) 'Attachment, exploration, and separation: illustrated by the behavior of one-year-olds in a strange situation', *Child Development*, 41(1): 49–67.

Albertson, K. and P. Stepney (2020) '1979 and all that: a 40-year reassessment of Margaret Thatcher's legacy on her own terms', *Cambridge Journal of Economics*, 44(2): 319–42.

Alston, P. (2019) 'Visit to the United Kingdom of Great Britain and Northern Ireland: Report of the special rapporteur on extreme poverty and human rights', United Nations.

AMS (2024a) '"Urgent action" needed on failing child health', The Academy of Medical Sciences, [online] 5 February, Available from: https://acmedsci.ac.uk/more/news/urgent-action-needed-on-failing-child-health [Accessed 6 February 2024].

AMS (2024b) *Prioritising Early Childhood to Promote the Nation's Health, Wellbeing and Prosperity*. The Academy of Medical Sciences.

Anghelescu, A., I. Ciobanu, C. Munteanu, L.A.M. Anghelescu and G. Onose (2023) 'ChatGPT: "To be or not to be" … in academic research. The human mind's analytical rigor and capacity to discriminate between AI bots' truths and hallucinations', *Balneo and PRM Research Journal*, 14(4): 614.

Anning, A. and M. Ball (2008) *Improving Services for Young Children: From Sure Start to Children's Centres*. Sage.

Aras, S. (2016) 'Free play in early childhood education: a phenomenological study', *Early Child Development and Care*, 186(7): 1173–84.

Archard, D. (2015) *Children: Rights and Childhood*. Routledge.

Aries, P. (1962) *Centuries of Childhood: A Social History of Family Life*. Vintage Books.

Aronowitz, S. (1988) *Science as Power: Discourse and Ideology in Modern Society*. University of Minnesota Press.

Arthur, J. (2019) 'Christianity and the character education movement 1897–1914', History of Education, 48(1): 60–76.

Ayala, A., C. Vives-Cases, C. Davó-Blanes, C. Rodríguez-Blázquez, M.J. Forjaz, N. Bowes, et al (2021) 'Sexism and its associated factors among adolescents in Europe: Lights4Violence baseline results', *Aggressive Behavior*, 47(3): 354–63.

Aydoğdu, F., B.Ş. Güngör and T.A. Öz (2023) 'Does sharing bring happiness? Understanding the sharenting phenomenon', *Children and Youth Services Review*, 154: 107122.

Baghai, K. (2012) 'Privacy as a human right: sociological theory', *Sociology*, 46(5): 951–65.

Barla, J. and F. Von Verschuer (2022) 'Anthropocene', *Matter: Journal of New Materialist Research*, 6: 137–43.

Basford, J. (2019) 'The early years foundation stage: whose knowledge, whose values?', *Education 3–13*, 47(7): 779–83.

Bates, A. (2019) 'Character education and the "priority of recognition"', *Cambridge Journal of Education*, 49(6): 695–710.

Bates, L. (2014) *Everyday Sexism*. Simon and Schuster.

Bates, L. (2021) *Men Who Hate Women: From Incels to Pickup Artists, the Truth About Extreme Misogyny and How It Affects Us All*. Simon and Schuster.

Bateson, P. and P. Martin (2013) *Play, Playfulness, Creativity and Innovation*. Cambridge University Press.

Bauman, Z. (1997) *Postmodernity and its Discontents*. Polity.

BBC (2017) 'Posing as a schoolgirl to expose online groomers', [online] 5 December, Available from: https://www.bbc.co.uk/news/av/uk-42243733 [Accessed 17 April 2024].

Beer, D. (2016) *Metric Power*. Palgrave Macmillan.

Bell, J., M. Reid, J. Dyson, A. Schlosser and T. Alexander (2019) 'There's just huge anxiety: ontological security, moral panic, and the decline in young people's mental health and well-being in the UK', *Qualitative Research in Medicine & Healthcare*, 3(2): 8200.

Bennett, T. (2003) 'Culture and governmentality', in J.Z. Bratich, J. Packer and C. McCarthy (eds), *Foucault, Cultural Studies, and Governmentality*. State University of New York Press, pp 47–64.

Bentsen, P., J. Schipperijn and F.S. Jensen (2013) 'Green space as classroom: outdoor school teachers' use, preferences and ecostrategies', *Landscape Research*, 38(5): 561–75.

Berlant, L. (2011) *Cruel Optimism*. Duke University Press.

Besley, A.C. (2005) 'Self-denial or self-mastery? Foucault's genealogy of the confessional self', *British Journal of Guidance & Counselling*, 33(3): 365–82.

Biesta, G.J.J. (2010) 'Learner, student, speaker: why it matters how we call those we teach', *Educational Philosophy and Theory*, 42(5/6): 540–52.

Biesta, G.J.J. (2013) *The Beautiful Risk of Education*. Paradigm Publishers.

Billingham, K., J. Morrell and C. Billingham (1996) 'Reflections on the history of health visiting', *British Journal of Community Health Nursing*, 1(7): 386–92.

Blacker, D.J. (2019) *What's Left of the World*. Zero Books.

References

Blacker, D.J. (2013) *The Falling Rate of Learning and the Neoliberal Endgame*. Zero Books.

Blatchford, P. (1989) *Playtime in the Primary School: Problems and Improvements*. NFER-Nelson.

Blum-Ross, A. and S. Livingstone (2017) '"Sharenting", parent blogging, and the boundaries of the digital self', *Popular Communication*, 15(2): 110–25.

Bodrova, E. and D.J. Leong (2015) 'Vygotskian and post-Vygotskian views on children's play', *American Journal of Play*, 7(3): 371–88.

Bodrova, E. and D.J. Leong (2019) 'Making play smarter, stronger, and kinder: lessons from tools of the mind', *American Journal of Play*, 12(1): 37–53.

Bourquin, P., R. Joyce and D. Sturrock (2021) *Inheritances and Inequality over the Life Cycle: What Will They Mean for Younger Generations?* Institute for Fiscal Studies.

Bower-Brown, S., S. Zadeh and V. Jadva (2023) 'Binary-trans, non-binary and gender-questioning adolescents' experiences in UK schools', *Journal of LGBT Youth*, 20(1): 74–92.

Bradbury, A. (2019) 'Datafied at four: the role of data in the "schoolification" of early childhood education in England', *Learning, Media and Technology*, 44(1): 7–21.

Bradley, S., R. Crouchley, J. Millington and J. Taylor (2000) 'Testing for quasi-market forces in secondary education', *Oxford Bulletin of Economics and Statistics*, 62(3): 357–90.

Bramoullé, Y. and C. Orset (2018) 'Manufacturing doubt', *Journal of Environmental Economics and Management*, 90: 119–33.

Bridge, G., S.W. Flint and R. Tench (2020) 'An exploration of the portrayal of the UK soft drinks industry levy in UK national newspapers', *Public Health Nutrition*, 23(17): 3241–9.

Brogaard Clausen, S. (2015) 'Schoolification or early years democracy? A cross-curricular perspective from Denmark and England', *Contemporary Issues in Early Childhood*, 16(4): 355–74.

Bronfenbrenner, U. (1979) *The Ecology of Human Development: Experiments by Nature and Design*. Harvard University Press.

Brooks, R. and J. Timms (2024) 'Institutional constraints to higher education datafication: an English case study', *Higher Education*. https://doi.org/10.1007/s10734-024-01363-2

Brosch, A. (2018) 'Sharenting – why do parents violate their children's privacy?', *The New Educational Review*, 54(4): 75–85.

Brown, F. (2008) 'The fundamentals of playwork', in F. Brown and C. Taylor, *Foundations of Playwork*. McGraw-Hill Education, pp 7–13.

Brown, F. (2015) 'The principles of playwork', in J.E. Johnson, S.G. Eberle, T.S. Henricks and D. Kuschner, *The Handbook of the Study of Play*. Rowman & Littlefield Publishers, pp 319–32.

Brownmiller, S. (1975) *Against Our Will: Men, Women and Rape*. Secker and Warburg.

Bruzzone, D. (2023) 'Rediscovering the meaning of education: the aims of teaching in an era of "learnification"', *Encyclopaideia*, 27(1S): 1–8.

Buckles, J. (2018) *Education, Sustainability and the Ecological Social Imaginary: Connective Education and Global Change*. Palgrave Macmillan.

Buckingham, D. (2009) 'New media, new childhoods? Children's changing cultural environment in the age of digital technology', in M.J. Kehily, *An Introduction to Childhood Studies*. Open University Press, pp 124–40.

Burns, S. (2023) 'Merseyside school girls anxious as teachers measure pupils skirts', [online] 27 February, Available from: https://hellorayo.co.uk/city/local/news/merseyside-school-girls-anxious-as-teachers-measure-pupils-skirts [Accessed 14 July 2025].

Butler, J. (2006) *Gender Trouble: Feminism and the Subversion of Identity*. Routledge.

Calder, G. (2018) 'What would a society look like where children's life chances were *really* fair?', *Local Economy*, 33(6): 655–66.

Cammaerts, B. (2022) 'The abnormalisation of social justice: The "anti-woke culture war" discourse in the UK', *Discourse & Society*, 33(6): 730–43.

Campbell, R., B. Duffy, G. Gottfried, K. Hewlett, G. May and G. Skinner (2024) *Emerging Tensions? How Younger Generations are Dividing on Masculinity and Gender Equality*. Kings College and Ipsos.

Casey, R. and V. Koshy (2013) 'Gifted and talented education: the English policy highway at a crossroads?', *Journal for the Education of the Gifted*, 36(1): 44–65.

Cass, H. (2024) *Cass Review: Independent Review of Gender Identity Services for Children and Young People*. NHS England.

Cassidy, C. (2012) 'Children's status, children's rights and "dealing with" children', *The International Journal of Children's Rights*, 20(1): 57–71.

Cervi, L. (2021) 'Tik Tok and generation Z', *Theatre, Dance and Performance Training*, 12(2): 198–204.

Charles, N. (2016) 'Post-human families? Dog-human relations in the domestic sphere', *Sociological Research Online*, 21(3): 83–94.

Chicken, S. (2022) '"Doing Reggio?" Exploring the complexity of "curriculum" migration through a comparison of Reggio Emilia, Italy and the EYFS, England', *Global Studies of Childhood*, 13(4): 322–40.

Chinn, C.A., S. Barzilai and R.G. Duncan (2021) 'Education for a "post-truth" world: new directions for research and practice', *Educational Researcher*, 50(1): 51–60.

Choonara, J. (2019) *Insecurity, Precarious Work and Labour Markets: Challenging the Orthodoxy*. Springer International Publishing.

Clarke, J. (2006) 'The skinheads and the magical recovery of community', in S. Hall and T. Jefferson (eds), *Resistance Through Rituals: Youth Subcultures in Post-War Britain*. Routledge, pp 80–3.

Clow, D. (2013) 'An overview of learning analytics', *Teaching in Higher Education*, 18(6): 683–95.

Coen, S. (2016) 'Sorry Michael Gove, we really do need experts – here's why', *The Conversation*, [online] 5 July, Available from: https://theconversation.com/sorry-michael-gove-we-really-do-need-experts-heres-why-62000 [Accessed 14 July 2025].

References

Coleman, J. and A. Hagell (2007) *Adolescence, Risk and Resilience: Against the Odds*. John Wiley.

Colliver, Y. and N. Veraksa (2021) 'Vygotsky's contributions to understandings of emotional development through early childhood play', *Early Child Development and Care*, 191(7–8): 1026–40.

Cooke-Reynolds, M. and N. Zukewich (2004) 'The feminization of work', *Canadian Social Trends*, Spring(72): 24–9.

Cooke, E., Z. Zheng, S. Houen, K. Thorpe, A. Clarke, C. Oakes and S. Staton (2023) 'Discursive tensions: outcomes and rights in educators' accounts of children's relaxation', *Contemporary Issues in Early Childhood*, 24(1): 70–81.

Cooper, C. (2010) 'Fat studies: mapping the field', *Sociology Compass*, 4(12): 1020–34.

Copernicus (2024) 'Copernicus: 2023 is the hottest year on record, with global temperatures close to the 1.5°C limit', *Copernicus Climate Change Service*, [online] 9 January, Available from: https://climate.copernicus.eu/copernicus-2023-hottest-year-record [Accessed 11 January 2024].

Corsaro, W. (2015) *The Sociology of Childhood*. Sage.

Courcy, I. and C. des Rivières (2017) '"From cause to cure": A qualitative study on contemporary forms of mother blaming experienced by mothers of young children with autism spectrum disorder', *Journal of Family Social Work*, 20(3): 233–50.

CPAG (2023) 'Poverty: facts and figures', *Child Poverty Action Group*, [online], Available from: https://cpag.org.uk/child-poverty/child-poverty-facts-and-figures [Accessed 29 November 2023].

Creasy, R. (2018) *The Taming of Education*. Palgrave.

Creasy, R. and F. Corby (2019) *Taming Childhood?: A Critical Perspective on Policy, Practice and Parenting*. Palgrave Macmillan.

Creasy, R. and F. Corby (2023) *Children, Family and the State: A Critical Introduction*. Policy Press.

Crerar, P., F. Harvey and K. Stacey (2023) 'Rishi Sunak announces U-turn on key green targets', *The Guardian*, [online] 20 September, Available from: https://www.theguardian.com/environment/2023/sep/20/rishi-sunak-confirms-rollback-of-key-green-targets [Accessed 14 July 2025].

Crombez, J.M. (2021) *Anxiety, Modern Society, and the Critical Method: Toward a Theory and Practice of Critical Socioanalysis*. BRILL.

Cronin, J.E. and T.G. Radtke (1987) 'The old and the new politics of taxation', *Socialist Register*, 23: 263–96.

Cunningham, H. (2021) *Children and Childhood in Western Society Since 1500*. Routledge.

Daly, M. (1984) *Gyn/ecology: The Metaethics of Radical Feminism*. Women's Press.

Darwin, H. (2020) 'Challenging the cisgender/transgender binary: nonbinary people and the transgender label', *Gender & Society*, 34(3): 357–80.

Davey, C. and L. Lundy (2011) 'Towards greater recognition of the right to play: an analysis of Article 31 of the UNCRC', *Children and Society*, 25(1): 3–15.

David, M.E. (2016) *Reclaiming Feminism: Challenging Everyday Misogyny*. Policy Press.

Davis, N.K. (2023) 'Measles cases on the rise in England, say public health experts', *The Guardian*, [online] 4 May, Available from: https://www.theguardian.com/society/2023/may/04/measles-cases-on-the-rise-in-england-say-public-health-experts [Accessed 14 July 2025].

Davy, Z. and S. Cordoba (2020) 'School cultures and trans and gender-diverse children: parents' perspectives', *Journal of GLBT Family Studies*, 16(4): 349–67.

De Bellaigue, C. (2019) 'Great expectations? Childhood, family, and middle-class social mobility in nineteenth-century England', *Cultural and Social History*, 16(1): 29–46.

De Leyn, T., R. De Wolf, M. Vanden Abeele and L. De Marez (2022) 'In-between child's play and teenage pop culture: tweens, TikTok & privacy', *Journal of Youth Studies*, 25(8): 1108–25.

Dean, M. (2010) *Governmentality: Power and Rule in Modern Society*. Sage.

Delaune, A. (2019) 'Moral philosophy, Te Whāriki and gender', *Educational Philosophy and Theory*, 51(7): 721–30.

DePalma, R. and E. Atkinson (2009) '"No outsiders": Moving beyond a discourse of tolerance to challenge heteronormativity in primary schools', *British Educational Research Journal*, 35(6): 837–55.

Detmer, D. (2003) *Challenging Postmodernism: Philosophy and the Politics of Truth*. Humanity Books.

DfE (2023) *Statutory Framework for the Early Years Foundation Stage: Setting the Standards for Learning, Development and Care for Children from Birth to Five*, [online] Available from: https://dera.ioe.ac.uk/id/eprint/39980/1/EYFS_framework_from_September_2023.pdf [Accessed 20 July 2025].

Dickerson, A. and G. Popli (2018) 'The many dimensions of child poverty: evidence from the UK millennium cohort study*', *Fiscal Studies*, 39(2): 265–98.

Dickinson, M. J. and D.A.G. Dickinson (2015) 'Practically perfect in every way: can reframing perfectionism for high-achieving undergraduates impact academic resilience?', *Studies in Higher Education*, 40(10): 1889–903.

Di Paolantonio, M. (2016) 'The cruel optimism of education and education's implication with "passing-on"', *Journal of Philosophy of Education*, 50(2): 147–59.

Dobson, C. (2015) 'Parents urged to get more children walking to school', *Manchester Evening News*, [online] 8 November, Available from: https://www.manchestereveningnews.co.uk/news/greater-manchester-news/parents-urged-more-children-walking-10409076 [Accessed 20 July 2025].

Donetto, S. and J. Maben (2015) '"These places are like a godsend": a qualitative analysis of parents' experiences of health visiting outside the home and of children's centres services', *Health Expectations*, 18(6): 2559–70.

Dorey, P. (2015) 'A farewell to alms: Thatcherism's legacy of inequality', *British Politics*, 10(1): 79–98.

Döring, T. and B. Aigner-Walder (2022) 'The limits to growth – 50 years ago and today', *Intereconomics*, 57(3): 187–91.

References

Duffell, N. (2000) *The Making of Them: The British Attitude to Children and the Boarding School System London*. Lone Arrow Press.

Dyvik, E.H. (2023) 'Proportion of children living in poverty in the OECD countries in 2022', Statista, [online], Available from: https://www.statista.com/statistics/264424/child-poverty-in-oecd-countries/ [Accessed 29 November 2023].

Ecclestone, K. and D. Hayes (2009) *The Dangerous Rise of Therapeutic Education*. Routledge.

Edwards, R., V. Gillies and N. Horsley (2015) 'Brain science and early years policy: hopeful ethos or "cruel optimism"?', *Critical Social Policy*, 35(2): 167–87.

Elkin, S. (2013) 'Only 25 per cent of children walk to school alone compared to 86 per cent in 1971. What went wrong?', *The Independent*, [online] 15 January, Available from: https://www.independent.co.uk/voices/comment/only-25-per-cent-of-children-walk-to-school-alone-compared-to-86-per-cent-in-1971-what-went-wrong-8452266.html [Accessed 14 July 2025].

Ellerton, P. (2016) 'Post-truth politics and the US election: why the narrative trumps the facts', *The Conversation*, [online] 9 October, Available from: http://theconversation.com/post-truth-politics-and-the-us-election-why-the-narrative-trumps-the-facts-66480 [Accessed 5 March 2017].

Elliott, A. (2009) *Contemporary Social Theory: An Introduction*. Routledge.

Ertz, M. and G. Le Bouhart (2022). 'The other pandemic: conceptual framework and future research directions of junk food marketing to children and childhood obesity', *Journal of Macromarketing*, 42(1): 30–50.

Exley, S. (2014) 'Are quasi-markets in education what the British public wants?', *Social Policy & Administration*, 48(1): 24–43.

Fagan, M. (2019) 'On the dangers of an Anthropocene epoch: geological time, political time and post-human politics', *Political Geography*, 70: 55–63.

Fattore, T., J. Mason and E. Watson (2007) 'Children's conceptualisation(s) of their well-being', *Social Indicators Research*, 80: 5–29.

Fejes, A. and M. Dahlstedt (2013) *The Confessing Society: Foucault, Confession and Practices of Lifelong Learning*. Routledge.

Fergusson, D.M. and L.J. Horwood (2003) 'Resilience to childhood adversity: results of a 21-year study', in S.S. Luthar (eds), *Resilience and Vulnerability: Adaptation in the Context of Childhood Adversities*. Cambridge University Press, pp 130–55.

Ferrari, F., A.M. Lorusso, S. Moruzzi and G. Volpe (2023) 'Perspectives on post-truth', *Social Epistemology*, 37(2): 141–9.

Firestone, S. (1971) *The Dialectic of Sex: The Case for Feminist Revolution*. Cape.

Fisher, J. (2022) 'To play or not to play: teachers' and headteachers' perspectives on play-based approaches in transition from the Early Years Foundation Stage to Key Stage 1 in England', *Education 3–13*, 50(6): 803–15.

Fox, A.K. and M.G. Hoy (2019) 'Smart devices, smart decisions? Implications of parents' sharenting for children's online privacy: an investigation of mothers', *Journal of Public Policy & Marketing*, 38(4): 414–32.

Frankopan, P. (2023) *The Earth Transformed: An Untold History London*. Bloomsbury.

Freeman, J. (2024) *Provide or punish? Students' Views on Generative AI in Higher Education*. Higher Education Policy Institute, Policy Note 51.

Frydenberg, E. (2008) *Adolescent Coping: Advances in Theory, Research, and Practice*. Routledge.

Furedi, F. (2001) 'Paranoid parenting', *The Guardian*, [online] 26 April, Available from: https://www.theguardian.com/education/2001/apr/26/highereducation.socialsciences [Accessed 14 July 2025].

Furedi, F. (2004) *Therapy Culture: Cultivating Vulnerability in an Uncertain Age*. Routledge.

Garrett, P.M. (2022a). 'Bowlby, attachment and the potency of a "received idea"', *The British Journal of Social Work*, 53(1): 100–17.

Garrett, P.M. (2022b) 'Social work and the "social doctor": Bowlby, social reproduction and "common sense"', *The British Journal of Social Work*, 53(1): 587–603.

Gérardin-Laverge, M. (2022) 'Realistic approach to the performativity of gender', *Nordic Wittgenstein Review*, Special Issue: 150–62.

Gerrard, J. (2017) *Precarious Enterprise on the Margins: Work, Poverty, and Homelessness in the City*. Palgrave Macmillan US.

Giardiello, P., G. Leydon and A. Hargreaves (2019) 'Te Whāriki', in N. McLeod and P. Giardiello (eds), *Empowering Early Childhood Educators*. Routledge, pp 155–74.

Giesinger, J. (2017) 'The special goods of childhood: lessons from social constructionism', *Ethics and Education*, 12(2): 201–17.

Gill, M. (2024) 'Millennials will be the richest generation ever, but who gets that wealth is down to luck', *The Observer*, [online] 3 March, Available from: https://www.theguardian.com/commentisfree/2024/mar/03/millennials-will-be-the-richest-generation-ever-but-who-gets-wealth-is-up-to-luck [Accessed 14 July 2025].

Gill, T. (2007) *No Fear: Growing Up in a Risk Averse Society*. Calouste Gulbenkian Foundation.

Gillespie, J. (2013) 'Being and becoming: writing children into planning theory', *Planning Theory*, 12(1): 64–80.

Gillis, J. (2009) 'Transitions to modernity', in J. Qvortrup, W.A. Corsaro and M.-S. Honig, *The Palgrave Handbook of Childhood Studies*. Palgrave, pp 114–26.

Ging, D. (2019) 'Alphas, betas, and incels: theorizing the masculinities of the manosphere', *Men and Masculinities*, 22(4): 638–57.

Gittins, D. (1998) *The Child in Question*. Macmillan Education UK.

Gittins, D. (2009) 'The historical construction of childhood', in M.J. Kehily (ed), *An Introduction to Childhood Studies*. Open University Press, pp 35–49.

Glace, A.M., T.L. Dover and J.G. Zatkin (2021) 'Taking the black pill: An empirical analysis of the "incel"', *Psychology of Men & Masculinity*, 22(2): 288–97.

Glasper, A. (2011) 'Improving public health through health visitor services', *British Journal of Nursing*, 20(6): 362–3.

References

Goldberg, R.F. and L.N. Vandenberg (2021) 'The science of spin: targeted strategies to manufacture doubt with detrimental effects on environmental and public health', *Environmental Health*, 20: 33, https://doi.org/10.1186/s12940-021-00723-0

Greenstein, J. (2019) 'Development without industrialization? Household well-being and premature deindustrialization', *Journal of Economic Issues*, 53(3): 612–33.

Gregory, A. (2024) 'UK regulator to apologise to gay doctors struck off because of sexuality', *The Guardian*, [online] 22 February, Available from: https://www.theguardian.com/world/2024/feb/22/uk-regulator-to-apologise-to-gay-doctors-struck-off-because-of-sexuality [Accessed 14 July 2025].

Griffin, N., S.M. Phillips, F. Hillier-Brown, J. Wistow, H. Fairbrother, E. Holding, et al (2021) 'A critique of the English national policy from a social determinants of health perspective using a realist and problem representation approach: the "Childhood Obesity: a plan for action" (2016, 2018, 2019)', *BMC Public Health*, 21: 2284, https://doi.org/10.1186/s12889-021-12364-6

Gross, S.-A., G. Musgrave and L. Janciute (2018) *Well-being and Mental Health in the Gig Economy: Policy Perspectives on Precarity*. University of Westminster Press.

Grunfled, N. (2018) 'What age can children walk to school alone?', *Country & Town House*, [online], Available from: https://www.countryandtownhouse.com/school-house/age-children-walk-to-school-alone/ [Accessed 14 July 2025].

Guldberg, H. (2009) *Reclaiming Childhood: Freedom and Play in an Age of Fear*. Routledge.

Gunnarsdottir, B. (2014) 'From play to school: are core values of ECEC in Iceland being undermined by "schoolification"?', *International Journal of Early Years Education*, 22(3): 242–50.

Hadland, S.E. (2022) 'Professionals as targets in the culture wars', *The New England Journal of Medicine*, 387(7): 584–5.

Haidt, J. (2024) *The Anxious Generation: How the Great Rewiring of Childhood is Causing an Epidemic of Mental Illness*. Allen Lane.

Hall, J., N. Eisenstadt, K. Sylva, T. Smith, P. Sammons, G. Smith, et al (2015) 'A review of the services offered by English Sure Start children's centres in 2011 and 2012', *Oxford Review of Education*, 41(1): 89–105.

Hamilton, C., F. Gemenne and C. Bonneuil (2015) 'Thinking the Anthropocene', in C. Hamilton, C. Bonneuil and F. Gemenne (eds), *The Anthropocene and the Global Environmental Crisis: Rethinking Modernity in a New Epoch*. Routledge, pp 1–13.

Hanafin, J., T. O'Donoghue, M. Flynn and M. Shevlin (2010) 'The primary school's invasion of the privacy of the child: unmasking the potential of some current practices', *Educational Studies*, 36(2): 143–52.

Handberg, C., P. Myrup and A.L. Højberg (2022) '"I was worried about not being good enough". Experiences and perspectives on pregnancy, childbirth and parenthood when living with a neuromuscular disorder – an exploration of everyday life challenges', *Disability and Rehabilitation*, 44(10): 1821–9.

Hanvey, C. (2019) *Shaping Children's Services*. Taylor & Francis.

Harper, N.J. (2017) 'Outdoor risky play and healthy child development in the shadow of the "risk society": A forest and nature school perspective', *Child & Youth Services*, 38(4): 318–35.

Hart, P. (2022) 'Reinventing character education: the potential for participatory character education using MacIntyre's ethics', *Journal of Curriculum Studies*, 54(4): 486–500.

Hartley, L.P. (1958) *The Go-Between*. Penguin.

Hartog, J. and H. Oosterbeek (2007) 'What should you know about the private returns to education?' in J. Hartog and H. Maassen van den Brink (eds), *Human Capital: Advances in Theory and Evidence*. Cambridge University Press, pp 7–20.

Hasinoff, A.A. (2017) 'Where are you? Location tracking and the promise of child safety', *Television & New Media*, 18(6): 496–513.

Hayes, K.N. and L.A. Turner (2021) 'The relation of helicopter parenting to maladaptive perfectionism in emerging adults', *Journal of Family Issues*, 42(12): 2986–3000.

Hayes, N. and K. Filipović (2018) 'Nurturing "buds of development": from outcomes to opportunities in early childhood practice', *International Journal of Early Years Education*, 26(3): 220–32.

Hayward, T. (1995) *Ecological Thought: An Introduction*. Polity.

Helm, B., R. Scrivens, T.J. Holt, S. Chermak and R. Frank (2022) 'Examining incel subculture on Reddit', *Journal of Crime & Justice* (ahead-of-print): 1–19.

Helm, D. (2020) 'Thirty years after water privatization – is the English model the envy of the world?', *Oxford Review of Economic Policy*, 36(1): 69–85.

Hendrick, H. (2005) 'Children and social policies', in H. Hendrick (ed), *Child Welfare and Social Policy: An Essential Reader*. Policy Press, pp 31–50.

Henricks, T.S. (2015) *Play and the Human Condition*. University of Illinois Press.

Heywood, C. (2018) *A History of Childhood*. Polity Press.

Hick, R.O.D. and A. Lanau (2018) 'Moving in and out of in-work poverty in the UK: an analysis of transitions, trajectories and trigger events', *Journal of Social Policy*, 47(4): 661–82.

Hicks, H.J. (2000) 'Postindustrial striptease: the full monty and the feminization of work', *Colby Quarterly*, 36(1): 48–59.

Hill, D.W. (2015) *The Pathology of Communicative Capitalism*. Palgrave Macmillan.

Hill Collins, P. and S. Bilge (2016) *Intersectionality*. Polity.

Hinsliff, G. (2021) 'Finn Mackay: the writer hoping to help end the gender wars', *The Guardian*, [online] 5 October, Available from: https://www.theguardian.com/lifeandstyle/2021/oct/05/finn-mackay-the-writer-hoping-to-help-end-the-gender-wars [Accessed 14 July 2025].

Hirsch, D. (2018) 'The "living wage" and low income: Can adequate pay contribute to adequate family living standards?', *Critical Social Policy*, 38(2): 367–86.

Holiday, S., M.S. Norman and R.L. Densley (2022) 'Sharenting and the extended self: self-representation in parents' Instagram presentations of their children', *Popular Communication*, 20(1): 1–15.

Holland, P. (2004) *Picturing Childhood: The Myth of the Child in Popular Imagery*. I.B. Tauris.

Honkasalo, J. (2020) 'Genderqueer', *lambda nordica*, 25(1): 57–63.

Horton, C. (2023) 'Institutional cisnormativity and educational injustice: trans children's experiences in primary and early secondary education in the UK', *British Journal of Educational Psychology*, 93(1): 73–90.

Horton, C. (2024) 'The Cass Review: cis-supremacy in the UK's approach to healthcare for trans children', *International Journal of Transgender Health*: 1–25, https://doi.org/10.1080/26895269.2024.2328249

Howard, J. and K. McInnes (2013) *The Essence of Play: A Practice Companion for Professionals Working with Children and Young People*. Taylor & Francis.

Hughes, F.P. (2010) *Children, Play, and Development*. Sage.

Hughes, M., F. Wikely and T. Nash (1994) *Parents and their Children's Schools*. Blackwell.

Hughson, T.A. (2021) 'Learnification and the outcomes-focused curriculum: The case of secondary school English in Aotearoa New Zealand', *The Curriculum Journal*, 32(4): 652–66.

Humphries, J. (2010) *Childhood and Child Labour in the British Industrial Revolution*. Cambridge University Press.

Hyndman, B.P. and A. Telford (2015) 'Should educators be "wrapping school playgrounds in cotton wool" to encourage physical activity? Exploring primary and secondary students' voices from the school playground', *Australian Journal of Teacher Education*, 40(6): 60–84.

Inglis, D. and C. Thorpe (2019) *An Invitation to Social Theory*. Polity.

James, A. (2009) 'Childhood matters: is children's wellbeing a high enough priority', *Mental Health Today*, 2009 (June): 18–21.

James, A. and A. Prout (1997) *Constructing and Reconstructing Childhood: Contemporary Issues in the Sociological Study of Childhood*. Falmer Press.

James, C. and I. Oplatka (2015) 'An exploration of the notion of the "good enough school"', *Management in Education*, 29(2): 77–82.

Jansen van Vuuren, E. (2023) 'Early childhood in the era of post-humanism: lending an ear to nature', *Journal of Curriculum Studies Research*, 5(1): 171–80.

Jaser, Z. (2016) 'Post-truth leaders are all about their followers', *The Conversation*, [online] 24 November, Available from: http://theconversation.com/post-truth-leaders-are-all-about-their-followers-69020 [Accessed 5 March 2017].

Jebb, S.A. and P. Aveyard (2023) '"Willpower" is not enough: time for a new approach to public health policy to prevent obesity', *BMC Medicine*, 21(1): 89.

Jenkins, H., R. Purushotma, M. Weigel, K. Clinton and A.J. Robison (2009) *Confronting the Challenges of Participatory Culture: Media Education for the 21st Century*. MIT Press.

Jenkins, N.E. (2006) '"You can't wrap them up in cotton wool!" Constructing risk in young people's access to outdoor play', *Health, Risk & Society*, 8(4): 379–94.

Jones, P. and L. Bradbury (2018) *Introducing Social Theory*. Polity.

JRF (2024) *UK Poverty in 2024: The Essential Guide to Understanding Poverty in the UK*. Joseph Rowntree Foundation.

Judge, D. (2022) '"Would I lie to you?": Boris Johnson and lying in the House of Commons', *The Political Quarterly*, 93(1): 77–86.

Kanemasu, Y. and A. Liki (2021) '"Let fa'afafine shine like diamonds": Balancing accommodation, negotiation and resistance in gender-nonconforming Samoans' counter-hegemony', *Journal of Sociology*, 57(4): 806–24.

Kasper, D.V.S. (2005) 'The evolution (or devolution) of privacy', *Sociological Forum*, 20(1): 69–92.

Kingdon, Z. (2020) *A Vygotskian Analysis of Children's Play Behaviours: Beyond the Home Corner*. Taylor & Francis.

Kmietowicz, Z. (2008) 'BMA calls for ban on smoking images that "keep the habit cool" among children', *The BMJ*, 337(7661): a713, doi: 10.1136/bmj.a713.

Knight, S. and S. Buckingham Shum (2017) 'Theory and learning analytics', in C. Lang, G. Siemans, A. Wise and D. Gasevic (eds), *Handbook of Learning Analytics*. Society for Learning Analytics Research, pp 17–22.

Knowles, G. and R. Holmstrom (2013) *Understanding Family Diversity and Home-School Relations: A Guide for Students and Practitioners in Early Years and Primary Settings*. Routledge.

Koch, I. (2017) 'What's in a vote? Brexit beyond culture wars', *American Ethnologist*, 44(2): 225–30.

Koshy, V., C. Pinheiro-Torres and C. Portman-Smith (2012) 'The landscape of gifted and talented education in England and Wales: how are teachers implementing policy?', *Research Papers in Education*, 27(2): 167–87.

Kotzee, B. (2019) 'Intellectual perfectionism about schooling', *Journal of Applied Philosophy*, 36(3): 436–56.

Laird, S. (2017) 'Learning to live in the Anthropocene: our children and ourselves', *Studies in Philosophy and Education*, 36(3): 265–82.

Lakind, A. and C. Adsit-Morris (2018) 'Future child: pedagogy and the post-Anthropocene', *Journal of Childhood Studies*, 43(1): 30–43.

Lambert, E.B. (2000) 'Questioning Vygotsky's 'theory' of play', *Early Child Development and Care*, 160(1): 25–31.

Lambie-Mumford, H. and M.A. Green (2017) 'Austerity, welfare reform and the rising use of food banks by children in England and Wales', *Area*, 49(3): 273–80.

Lancet (2017) 'The UK's inadequate plan for reducing childhood obesity', *The Lancet*, 390(10097): 822.

Larner, W. (2000) 'Neo-liberalism: policy, ideology, governmentality', *Studies in Political Economy*, 63(1): 5–25.

Laville, S. (2020) 'Air pollution a cause in girl's death, coroner rules in landmark case', *The Guardian*, [online] 16 December, Available from: https://www.theguardian.com/environment/2020/dec/16/girls-death-contributed-to-by-air-pollution-coroner-rules-in-landmark-case [Accessed 14 July 2025].

References

Lawson, R. (2022) 'Andrew Tate: how the "manosphere" influencer is selling extreme masculinity to young men', The Conversation, [online] 27 October, Available from: https://theconversation.com/andrew-tate-how-the-manosphere-influencer-is-selling-extreme-masculinity-to-young-men-192564 [Accessed 13 December 2023].

Lazard, L., R. Capdevila, C. Dann, A. Locke and S. Roper (2019) 'Sharenting: pride, affect and the day-to-day politics of digital mothering', *Social and Personality Psychology Compass*, 13(4): e12443.

Le Grand, J. and W. Bartlett (eds) (1993) *Quasi-Markets and Social Policy*. Macmillan.

Leach, T. and E. Lewis (2013) 'Children's experiences during circle-time: a call for research-informed debate', *Pastoral Care in Education*, 31(1): 43–52.

Leaper, C. and C.S. Brown (2014) 'Sexism in schools', in L.S. Liben and R.S. Bigler (eds), *Advances in Child Development and Behavior*, vol 47. Academic Press, pp 189–223.

Lee, W. (2013) *Understanding the Te Whāriki Approach: Early Years Education in Practice*. Routledge.

Lemish, D. (2015) *Children and Media: A Global Perspective*. Wiley-Blackwell.

Leverett, S. (2011) 'Children's spaces', in P. Foley and S. Leverett (eds), *Children and Young People's Spaces: Developing Practice*. Palgrave Macmillan, pp 9–24.

Lewis, J., R. Cuthbert and S. Sarre (2011) 'What are children's centres? The development of CC services, 2004–2008', *Social Policy & Administration*, 45(1): 35–54.

Lewis, S.L. and M.A. Maslin (2015) 'Defining the Anthropocene', *Nature*, 519(7542): 171–80.

Lindgren, T. and M. Sjöstrand Öhrfelt (2017) 'Fabricating the posthuman child in early childhood education and care', *Philosophy of Education*, 73: 264–73.

Loader, I. (2023) '15-minute cities and the denial(s) of auto-freedom', *IPPR Progressive Review*, 30(1): 56–60.

Locke, J. (2000) *An Essay Concerning Human Understanding*. Batoche Books.

Loebach, J.E. and J.A. Gilliland (2016) 'Free range kids? Using GPS-derived activity spaces to examine children's neighborhood activity and mobility', *Environment and Behavior*, 48(3): 421–53.

Lundy, L. (2007) '"Voice" is not enough: conceptualising Article 12 of the United Nations Convention on the Rights of the Child', *British Educational Research Journal*, 33(6): 927–42.

Lupton, D. (2016) *The Quantified Self*. Polity.

Lupton, D. and B. Williamson (2017) 'The datafied child: The dataveillance of children and implications for their rights', *New Media & Society*, 19(5): 780–95.

Lyotard, J.-F. (1984) *The Postmodern Condition: A Report on Knowledge*. Manchester University Press.

MacDonald, R. and A. Giazitzoglu (2019) 'Youth, enterprise and precarity: or, what is, and what is wrong with, the "gig economy"?', *Journal of Sociology*, 55(4): 724–40.

MacFadyen, L., A. Amos, G. Hastings and E. Parkes (2003) '"They look like my kind of people" – perceptions of smoking images in youth magazines', *Social Science & Medicine*, 56(3): 491–9.

Macfarlane, B. (2017) *Freedom to Learn: The Threat to Student Academic Freedom and Why it Needs to be Reclaimed*. Routledge.

MacInnes, T., H. Aldridge, S. Bushe, P. Kenway and A. Tinson (2013) *Monitoring Poverty and Social Exclusion 2013*. Joseph Rowntree Foundation.

Mackenbach, J.P. (2020) *A History of Population Health: Rise and Fall of Disease in Europe*. Brill.

Mackenbach, J.P. (2021) 'The rise and fall of diseases: reflections on the history of population health in Europe since ca. 1700', *European Journal of Epidemiology*, 36(12): 1199–205.

Main, M. and J. Solomon (1990) 'Procedures for identifying infants as disorganized/disoriented during the Ainsworth strange situation', in M.T. Greenberg, D. Cicchetti and E.M. Cummings (eds), *Attachment in the Preschool Years: Theory, Research, and Intervention*. University of Chicago Press, pp 121–60.

Malone, K. (2007) 'The bubble-wrap generation: children growing up in walled gardens', *Environmental Education Research*, 13(4): 513–27.

Malone, K., M. Tesar and S. Arndt (2020) *Theorising Posthuman Childhood Studies*. Springer.

Manyukhina, Y. (2022) 'Children's agency in the National Curriculum for England: a critical discourse analysis', *Education 3–13*, 50(4): 506–20.

Margulies, J.D. and B. Bersaglio (2018) 'Furthering post-human political ecologies', *Geoforum*, 94: 103–6.

Marsh, J. and J. Bishop (2014) *Changing Play: Play, Media and Commercial Culture from the 1950s to the Present Day*. McGraw-Hill Education.

Mavoa, J., S. Coghlan and B. Nansen (2023). '"It's about safety not snooping": parental attitudes to child tracking technologies and geolocation data', *Surveillance & Society*, 21(1): 45–60.

Mayall, B. (2000) 'The sociology of childhood in relation to children's rights', *The International Journal of Children's Rights*, 8(3): 243–59.

Mayall, B. (2008) 'Conversations with children', in P.M. Christensen and A. James (eds), *Research with Children: Perspectives and Practices*. Routledge, pp 109–22.

McBride, J., A. Smith and M. Mbala (2018) '"You end up with nothing": the experience of being a statistic of 'in-work poverty' in the UK', *Work, Employment & Society*, 32(1): 210–18.

McDonald, B., K.J. Lester and D. Michelson (2023) '"She didn't know how to go back": School attendance problems in the context of the COVID-19 pandemic – A multiple stakeholder qualitative study with parents and professionals', *British Journal of Educational Psychology*, 93(1): 386–401.

McDowall-Clark, R. (2020) *Childhood in Society for the Early Years*. Sage.

McGowan, A., Y. Gui, M. Dobbs, S. Shuster, M. Cotter, A. Selloni, et al (2023) 'ChatGPT and Bard exhibit spontaneous citation fabrication during psychiatry literature search', *Psychiatry Research*, 326: 115334.

References

McGrath, R.E., H. Han, M. Brown and P. Meindl (2022) 'What does character education mean to character education experts? A prototype analysis of expert opinions', *Journal of Moral Education*, 51(2): 219–37.

McIntyre, L. (2018) *Post-Truth*. MIT Press.

McKeown, T. (1979) *The Role of Medicine: Dream, Mirage or Nemesis?* Blackwell.

McLeod, N. (2019) 'Danish outdoor nature pedagogy', in N. McLeod and P. Giardiello (eds), *Empowering Early Childhood Educators*. Routledge, pp 175–200.

McLuhan, M. (2013) *Understanding Media: The Extensions of Man*. Gingko Press.

Medway, D., S. Roper and L. Gillooly (2018) 'Contract cheating in UK higher education: A covert investigation of essay mills', *British Educational Research Journal*, 44(3): 393–418.

Messner, M.A. (2016) 'Forks in the road of men's gender politics: men's rights vs feminist allies', *International Journal for Crime, Justice and Social Democracy*, 5(2): 6–20.

Michaels, D. (2008) *Doubt Is Their Product: How Industry's Assault on Science Threatens Your Health*. Oxford University Press.

Miller, P.P.D. and N.S. Rose (2007) *Governing the Present: Administering Economic Social and Personal Life*. Polity.

Morgan, E. and Y. Taylor (2019) 'Dangerous education: the occupational hazards of teaching transgender', *Sociology*, 53(1): 19–35.

Moss, P., J. Dillon and J. Statham (2000) 'The "child in need" and "the rich child": discourses, constructions and practice', *Critical Social Policy*, 20(2): 233–55.

Moyles, J. (2001) 'Passion, paradox and professionalism in early years education', *Early Years: An International Journal of Research and Development*, 21(2): 81–95.

Mulryan-Kyne, C. (2014) 'The school playground experience: opportunities and challenges for children and school staff', *Educational Studies*, 40(4): 377–96.

Murray, C.R.G. and M.A. Armstrong (2021) 'A mobile phone in one hand and Erskine May in the other: the European Research Group's parliamentary revolution', *Parliamentary Affairs*, 75(3): 536–57.

Namie, J. (2011) 'Public displays of affection: mothers, children, and requests for junk food', *Food, Culture & Society*, 14(3): 393–411.

NCB (2023) 'Number of children in poverty living in working households on the rise', *National Children's Bureau*, [online], Available from: https://www.ncb.org.uk/about-us/media-centre/news-opinion/number-children-poverty-living-working-households-rise [Accessed 20 July 2025].

Nelson, M. (2010) *Parenting Out of Control: Anxious Parents in Uncertain Times*. New York University Press.

Nettleingham, D. (2019) 'Beyond the heartlands: deindustrialization, naturalization and the meaning of an "industrial" tradition', *British Journal of Sociology*, 70(2): 610–26.

Neumann, E. (2021) 'Setting by numbers: datafication processes and ability grouping in an English secondary school', *Journal of Education Policy*, 36(1): 1–23.

Newstead, S. and P. King (2021) 'What is the purpose of playwork?', *Child Care in Practice:* 30(3): 261–73.

NHS (2020) 'Statistics on obesity, physical activity and diet, England, 2020', [online] 5 May, Available from: https://digital.nhs.uk/data-and-information/publications/statistical/statistics-on-obesity-physical-activity-and-diet/england-2020/part-4-childhood-obesity-copy [Accessed 9 February 2024].

Nichols, T.P. and G. Campano (2017) 'Post-humanism and literacy studies', *Language Arts*, 94(4): 245–51.

Nolan, M. (1997) 'The white blouse revolution: heroic and anti-heroic interpretations of the feminisation of work', *Journal of Australian Studies*, 21(52): 54–66.

O'Donnell, C. and E. Shor (2022) '"This is a political movement, friend": why "incels" support violence', *The British Journal of Sociology*, 73(2): 336–51.

O'Hara, M. (2020) *The Shame Game: Overturning the Toxic Narrative of Poverty*. Policy Press.

O'Hara, M. and M. Thomas (2014) *Austerity Bites: A Journey to the Sharp End of Cuts in the UK*. Policy Press.

O'Sullivan, T., E. Daniel and F. Harris (2023) 'Media and the staging of policy controversy: obesity and the UK sugar tax', *Critical Policy Studies*, 17(4): 599–618.

OHID (2024) *Patterns and Trends in Child Obesity*. Office for Health Improvement & Disparities.

Palmer, S. (2007) *Detoxing Childhood: What Parents Need to Know to Raise Happy, Successful Children*. Orion.

Palmer, S. (2009) 'What is toxic childhood?', in R. House and D. Loewenthal (eds), *Childhood, Well-Being, and a Therapeutic Ethos*. Karnac Books, pp 53–69.

Palmer, S. (2015) *Toxic Childhood: How the Modern World is Damaging our Children and What We Can Do About It*. Orion.

Papastephanou, M. and K. Drousioti (2023) 'On learning and unlearning', *Policy Futures in Education*, 22(3): 352–68.

Papoulias, C. (2006) 'Transgender', *Theory, Culture & Society*, 23(2–3): 231–3.

Pearce, R., S. Erikainen and B. Vincent (2020) 'TERF wars: An introduction', *The Sociological Review*, 68(4): 677–98.

Peckover, S. (2013) 'From "public health" to "safeguarding children": British health visiting in policy, practice and research', *Children & Society*, 27(2): 116–26.

Peregrine, P.N. (2017) 'Seeking truth among "alternative facts"', The Conversation, [online] 24 February, Available from: https://theconversation.com/seeking-truth-among-alternative-facts-72733 [Accessed 20 September 2023].

Peterson, A. (2020) 'Character education, the individual and the political', *Journal of Moral Education*, 49(2): 143–57.

Petrunoff, N.A., R.L. Wilkenfeld, L.A. King and V.M. Flood (2014) '"Treats", "sometimes foods", "junk": a qualitative study exploring "extra foods" with parents of young children', *Public Health Nutrition*, 17(5): 979–86.

Pickering, A. (2000) 'Practice and post-humanism: social theory and a history of agency', in K. Knorr Cetina, T.R. Schatzki and E. von Savigny (eds), *The Practice Turn in Contemporary Theory*. Routledge, pp 140–57.

References

Pike, J. (2008) 'Foucault, space and primary school dining rooms', *Children's Geographies*, 6(4): 413–23.

Pike, J. and P. Kelly (2014) *The Moral Geographies of Children, Young People and Food; Beyond Jamie's School Dinners*. Palgrave Macmillan.

Play Commission (2025) *The Play Commission's Interim Report: A Watershed Moment for Play Policy*. UK, Raising_the_Nation_Play_Commission.

Playwork Foundation (2005) 'The Playwork Principles', [online], Available from: https://playwork.foundation/principles/ [Accessed on 27 September 2024].

Postman, N. (1994) *The Disappearance of Childhood*. Vintage.

Powell, D. (2014) 'Childhood obesity, corporate philanthropy and the creeping privatisation of health education', *Critical Public Health*, 24(2): 226–38.

Powell, J. (2020) 'The struggle for the heart of the early years', *The Times Educational Supplement*, [online] 2 October, Available from: https://www.tes.com/magazine/archived/struggle-heart-early-years [Accessed 14 July 2025].

Powell, S. and K. Smith (2017) *An Introduction to Early Childhood Studies*. Sage.

Qvortrup, J., M.-S. Honig and W.A. Corsaro (2009) *The Palgrave Handbook of Childhood Studies*. Palgrave.

Radnor, H., V. Koshy and A. Taylor (2007) 'Gifts, talents and meritocracy', *Journal of Education Policy*, 22(3): 283–300.

Raman, L. (2019) 'Do children recognize the impact of physical and sedentary activities on weight?', *Journal of Child and Family Studies*, 28(11): 3161–9.

Ramdass, D. and B.J. Zimmerman (2011) 'Developing self-regulation skills: the important role of homework', *Journal of Advanced Academics*, 22(2): 194–218.

Raworth, K. (2017) *Doughnut Economics: Seven Ways to Think Like a 21st-Century Economist*. Penguin.

RCPCH (2020) *State of Child Health in the UK*. Royal College of Paediatrics and Child Health.

Rebughini, P. (2021) 'A sociology of anxiety: Western modern legacy and the COVID-19 outbreak', *International Sociology*, 36(4): 554–68.

Richards, C. (2012) 'Playing under surveillance: gender, performance and the conduct of the self in a primary school playground', *British Journal of Sociology of Education*, 33(3): 373–90.

Richards, C., W.P. Bouman and M.-J. Barker (2017) *Genderqueer and Non-Binary Genders*. Palgrave Macmillan.

Richards, C., W.P. Bouman, L. Seal, M.J. Barker, T.O. Nieder and G. T'Sjoen (2016) 'Non-binary or genderqueer genders', *International Review of Psychiatry*, 28(1): 95–102.

Richards, S. (1983) *Philosophy and Sociology of Science: An Introduction*. Blackwell.

Ring, E. and L. O'Sullivan (2018) 'Dewey: a panacea for the "schoolification" epidemic', *Education 3–13*, 46(4): 402–10.

Ringrose, J. and V. Rawlings (2015) 'Posthuman performativity, gender and "school bullying": exploring the material-discursive intra-actions of skirts, hair, sluts, and poofs', *Confero*, 3(2): 80–119.

Rist, R. C. (2000) 'HER classic: Student social class and teacher expectations: the self-fulfilling prophecy in ghetto education', *Harvard Educational Review*, 70(3): 257–301.

Roberts-Holmes, G. (2015) 'The "datafication" of early years pedagogy: "if the teaching is good, the data should be good and if there's bad teaching, there is bad data"', *Journal of Education Policy*, 30(3): 302–15.

Roberts-Holmes, G. and A. Bradbury (2016a) 'The datafication of early years education and its impact upon pedagogy', *Improving Schools*, 19(2): 119–28.

Roberts-Holmes, G. and A. Bradbury (2016b) 'Governance, accountability and the datafication of early years education in England', *British Educational Research Journal*, 42(4): 600–14.

Roberts-Holmes, G. and P. Moss (2021) *Neoliberalism and Early Childhood Education: Markets, Imaginaries and Governance*. Taylor & Francis.

Robertson, J. (1983) *The Sane Alternative: A Choice of Futures*. J. Robertson.

Robertson, J. (1985) *Future Work: Jobs, Self-employment and Leisure After the Industrial Age*. Gower/Maurice Temple Smith.

Robertson, J. (1990) *Future Wealth: A New Economics for the 21st Century*. Cassell.

Rubery, J. (2015) 'Change at work: feminisation, flexibilisation, fragmentation and financialisation', *Employee Relations*, 37(6): 633–44.

Rubino, F., D.E. Cummings, H. Eckel, R.V. Cohen, J.P.H. Wilding, W.A. Brown, et al (2025) 'Definition and diagnostic criteria of clinical obesity', *The Lancet Diabetes & Endocrinology*, 13(3): 221–62.

Russell, W., S. Lester and H. Smith (2017) *Practice-Based Research in Children's Play*. Bristol University Press.

Sagi, A., M.H. Van Ijzendoorn and N. Koren-Karie (1991) 'Primary appraisal of the Strange Situation: A cross-cultural analysis of preseparation episodes', *Developmental Psychology*, 27(4): 587–96.

Saguy, A.C. and A. Ward (2011) 'Coming out as fat: rethinking stigma', *Social Psychology Quarterly*, 74(1): 53–75.

Sayogie, F., M. Farkhan, Z. Zubair, H.P. Julian, H.S.F. Al Hakim and M.G. Wiralaksana (2023) 'Patriarchal ideology, Andrew Tate, and Rumble's Podcasts', *Journal of Language Teaching, Linguistics, and Literature*, 29(2): 1–12.

Scaptura, M.N. and K.M. Boyle (2020) 'Masculinity threat, "incel" traits, and violent fantasies among heterosexual men in the United States', *Feminist Criminology*, 15(3): 278–98.

Schaffer, H.R. (1996) *Social Development*. Blackwell Publishing.

Schiappa, E. (2021) *The Transgender Exigency: Defining Sex and Gender in the 21st Century*. Routledge.

Schilt, K. and D. Lagos (2017) 'The development of transgender studies in sociology', *Annual Review of Sociology*, 43(1): 425–43.

Schouten, L. (2015) 'Ban on 'Tag': Are school children getting the right playtime?', *Christian Science Monitor*, [online] 26 September, Available from: https://www.csmonitor.com/USA/Society/2015/0926/Ban-on-Tag-Are-school-children-getting-the-right-playtime [Accessed 20 July 2025].

References

Schubak, A. (2020) 'Read the stories of 40 incredible kids who have changed the world', Good Housekeeping, [online] 8 October, Available from: https://www.goodhousekeeping.com/life/inspirational-stories/g5188/kids-who-changed-the-world/ [Accessed 27 November 2024].

Shaw, D. (2023) 'A tale of two feminisms: gender critical feminism, trans inclusive feminism and the case of Kathleen Stock', *Women's History Review*, 32(5): 768–80.

Shelton, L.G. (2019) *The Bronfenbrenner Primer: A Guide to Develecology*. Routledge, Taylor & Francis Group.

Shiva, V. (2013) 'How economic growth has become anti-life', *The Guardian*, [online] 1 November, Available from: https://www.theguardian.com/commentisfree/2013/nov/01/how-economic-growth-has-become-anti-life [Accessed 14 July 2025].

Shiva, V. (2016) *Staying Alive: Women, Ecology and Development*. North Atlantic Books.

Simpson, B. (2013) 'Challenging childhood, challenging children: Children's rights and sexting', *Sexualities*, 16(5–6): 690–709.

Simpson, B. (2014) 'Tracking children, constructing fear: GPS and the manufacture of family safety', *Information and Communication Technology Law*, 23(3): 273–86.

Sims-Schouten, W. and H. Cowie (2016) 'Ideologies & narratives in relation to "fat" children as bullies, "easy targets" and victims', *Children & Society*, 30(6): 445–54.

Siraj, I. and A. Mayo (2014) *Social Class and Educational Inequality: The Impact of Parents and Schools*. Cambridge University Press.

Sismondo, S. (2017) 'Post-truth?', *Social Studies of Science*, 47(1): 3–6.

Slater, T. (2014) 'The myth of "broken Britain": welfare reform and the production of ignorance', *Antipode*, 46(4): 948–69.

Smith, K. (2012) 'Producing governable subjects: Images of childhood old and new', *Childhood*, 19(1): 24–37.

Smith, K.M. (2014) *The Government of Childhood: Discourse, Power and Subjectivity*. Palgrave Macmillan.

Smith, M.J. (1998) *Social Science in Question*. Sage.

Smith, R.S. (2010) *A Universal Child?* Palgrave Macmillan.

Snow, C.P. and S. Collini (1993) *The Two Cultures*. Cambridge University Press.

Soler, J. and L. Miller (2003) 'The struggle for early childhood curricula: a comparison of the English Foundation Stage Curriculum, Te Whāriki and Reggio Emilia', *International Journal of Early Years Education*, 11(1): 57–68.

Solove, D.J. (2002) 'Conceptualizing privacy', *California Law Review*, 90(4): 1087–155.

Sonu, D. and J. Benson (2016) 'The quasi-human child: how normative conceptions of childhood enabled neoliberal school reform in the United States', *Curriculum Inquiry*, 46(3): 230–47.

Stern, J., C.A. Sink, M. Watejko and P.H. Wong (eds) (2022) *The Bloomsbury Handbook of Solitude, Silence and Loneliness*. Bloomsbury Academic.

Stearns, P.N. (2003) *Anxious Parents: A History of Modern Childrearing in America*. New York University Press.

Stevenson, H. (2017) 'The "datafication" of teaching: can teachers speak back to the numbers?', *Peabody Journal of Education*, 92(4): 537–57.

Stewart, W. (2006) 'New register for the gifted and talented', *TES: Times Educational Supplement,* [online] 14 July, Available from : https ://www.tes.com/magazine/archive/new-register-gifted-and-talented [Accessed 31 July 2025].

Stucki, S. (2023) *One Rights: Human and Animal Rights in the Anthropocene.* Springer Nature.

Sturrock, S. (2022) 'Primary teachers' experiences of neo-liberal education reform in England: "Nothing is ever good enough"', *Research Papers in Education*, 37(6): 1214–40.

Sudarsan, I., K. Hoare, N. Sheridan and J. Roberts (2022) 'Giving voice to children in research: the power of child-centered constructivist grounded theory methodology', *Research in Nursing & Health*, 45(4): 488–97.

Sugiura, L. (2021) *The Incel Rebellion: The Rise of the Manosphere and the Virtual War Against Women.* Emerald.

Sutton-Smith, B. (2008) 'Beyond ambiguity', in F. Brown and C. Taylor (eds), *Foundations of Playwork.* McGraw-Hill Education.

Sweeney, S. (2023) 'Who wrote this? Essay mills and assessment – considerations regarding contract cheating and AI in higher education', *The International Journal of Management Education*, 21(2): 100818.

Thomson, S. (2003) 'A well-equipped hamster cage: the rationalisation of primary school playtime', *Education 3–13*, 31(2): 54–9.

Thomson, S. (2007) 'Do's and don'ts: children's experiences of the primary school playground', *Environmental Education Research*, 13(4): 487–501.

Thornton, S., M. Graham and G. Burgh (2019) 'Reflecting on place: environmental education as decolonisation', *Australian Journal of Environmental Education*, 35(3): 239–49.

Thoutenhoofd, E.D. (2018) 'The datafication of learning: data technologies as reflection in the system of education', *Studies in Philosophy and Education*, 37(5): 433–49.

Thurlow, C. (2022) 'From TERF to gender critical: A telling genealogy?', *Sexualities*, 27(4): 962–78.

Turkle, S. (2012) *Alone Together: Why We Expect More From Technology and Less From Each Other.* Basic Books.

UNICEF (1989) *UN Convention of the Rights of the Child*, [online] Available from: https://www.unicef.org/child-rights-convention/convention-text [Accessed 20 July 2025].

van Bakel, H.J.A. and R.A.S. Hall (2018) 'Parent–child relationships and attachment', in M.R. Sanders and A. Morawska (eds), *Handbook of Parenting and Child Development Across the Lifespan.* Springer International Publishing, pp 47–66.

Vicente, M.V. (2021) 'Transgender: a useful category?: Or, how the historical study of "transsexual" and "transvestite" can help us rethink "transgender" as a category', *Transgender Studies Quarterly*, 8(4): 426–42.

Voce, A. (2016) *Policy for Play.* Policy Press.

References

Wagner, W. and N. Hayes (2022) 'Repressive moralism: world making and petty fascism in transgender politics', *Integrative Psychological and Behavioral Science*, 56(3): 573–89.

Waite, L. and E. Pritchard (2017) 'The fat child', in A. Owen (ed), *Childhood Today*. Sage, pp 125–38.

Waite, S., M. Bølling and P. Bentsen (2016) 'Comparing apples and pears?: A conceptual framework for understanding forms of outdoor learning through comparison of English Forest Schools and Danish udeskole', *Environmental Education Research*, 22(6): 868–92.

Walker, P. (2024) 'Ministers prioritised driving in England partly due to conspiracy theories', *The Guardian*, [online] 10 January, Available from: https://www.theguardian.com/uk-news/2024/jan/10/shift-from-15-minute-cities-in-england-partly-due-to-conspiracy-theories [Accessed 14 July 2025].

Walkerdine, V. (2009) 'Developmental psychology and the study of childhood', in M.J. Kehily (ed), *An Introduction to Childhood*. Open University Press, pp 71–82.

Walrave, M., K. Verswijvel, G. Ouvrein, L. Staes, L. Hallam and K. Hardies (2022) 'The limits of sharenting: exploring parents' and adolescents' sharenting boundaries through the lens of communication privacy management theory', *Frontiers in Education*, 7: 803393.

Watson, K. (2022) '"I am big; he is little": interrogating the effects of developmental discourses among children in inclusive early childhood classrooms', *International Journal of Early Years Education*, 30(2): 448–62.

Wells, K. (2018) *Childhood Studies*. Polity.

Whalley, M. and P.G. Centre (2007) *Involving Parents in their Children's Learning*. Paul Chapman.

Wheway, R. (2008) *Not a Risk Averse Society*. Fair Play for Children.

Wheway, R. (2015) 'Opportunities for free play', *International Journal of Play*, 4(3): 270–4.

Whitebread, D., M. Basilio, M. Kuvalja and M. Verma (2012) *The Importance of Play: A Report on the Value of Children's Play with a Series of Policy Recommendations*. Toy Industries of Europe.

Wilkes, S. (2011) *The Children History Forgot*. Robert Hale.

Wilkinson, I. (2001) *Anxiety in a Risk Society*. Routledge.

Williams-Siegfredsen, J. (2017) *Understanding the Danish Forest School Approach: Early Years Education in Practice*. Routledge.

Williams, A. and J. May (2022) 'A genealogy of the food bank: historicising the rise of food charity in the UK', *Transactions of the Institute of British Geographers*, 47(3): 618–34.

Wilson, A., C. Watson, T.L. Thompson, V. Drew and S. Doyle (2017) 'Learning analytics: challenges and limitations', *Teaching in Higher Education*, 22(8): 991–1008.

Wiltshire, S., A. Amos, S. Haw and A. McNeill (2005) 'Image, context and transition: smoking in mid-to-late adolescence', *Journal of Adolescence*, 28(5): 603–17.

Wood, D., J.S. Bruner and G. Ross (1976) 'The role of tutoring in problem solving', *Journal of Child Psychology & Psychiatry*, 17(2): 89–100.

Wood, E. and H. Hedges (2016) 'Curriculum in early childhood education: critical questions about content, coherence, and control', *Curriculum Journal*, 27(3): 387–405.

Woodhead, M. (2009) 'Child development and development of childhood', in J. Qvortrup, W. Corsaro and H.H. Michael-Sebastian (eds), *The Palgrave Handbook of Childhood Studies*. Palgrave Macmillan, pp 46–61.

Woodin, T., G. McCulloch and S. Cowan (2013) 'Raising the participation age in historical perspective: policy learning from the past?', *British Educational Research Journal*, 39(4): 635–53.

Worth, H. (2008) 'Bad-assed honeys with a difference: South Auckland Fa'afafine talk about identity', in M. Fran, P.A. Jackson, M. McLelland and A. Yue (eds), *AsiaPacifiQueer: Rethinking Genders and Sexualities*. University of Illinois Press, pp 149–62.

Wrigley, T. (2009) 'Rethinking education in the era of globalization', in D. Hill (ed), *Contesting Neoliberal Education: Public Resistance and Collective Advance*. Routledge, pp 356–77.

Wyness, M.G. (2012) *Childhood and Society*. Palgrave Macmillan.

Yates, E. (2018) 'Play', in J. Johnston, L. Nahmad-Williams, R. Oates and V. Wood (eds), *Early Childhood Studies: Principles and Practice*. Taylor & Francis Group.

Index

15-minute cities 171
1988 Education Reform Act 68

A

academic sources 184
added value *see* potential
adverse childhood experiences 33, 156
age regulation 151
age restrictions 41, 42
agency 17–20, 126, 138
    interplay with structure 18–19
ages and stages 6, 13, 16, 34, 37
Ainsworth, Mary 31
alternative facts 114
alt-right movements 116
Anthropocene 170–1, 180
anti-feminism 143–4
anxiety 165–6
Aries 43–4, 56
artificial intelligence 182–3
    hallucinations 183
assignment marks 185
attachment 29
austerity 16, 55, 85, 164
autonomous nominalism 145

B

becomings or beings 5, 33–5
bedrooms 105
binary thinking 145
biological determinism 145
Bowlby 29–31
Brexit 113, 115
Bronfenbrenner *see* socio-ecological model

C

Cass Review (2024) 148
character building/education 73–5
child poverty 81–4
child's voice 36–9
children's health 161–2
circle time 132
cisgender 146
Clause 28 116
climate change/crisis 170–5, 180
colonisation 177–9
confession 132

confinement 105
conspiracy theories 172
critical understanding 117
culture wars 114–7, 148, 150, 171

D

datafication 91
decentring 176–7
decolonisation 179
deindustrialisation 143
determinism 146, 156
dictionary definitions 4
diet 159–61, 168–9
discourse 25–7, 41
disease 162
Don't say Gay laws 117
doughnuts 173
dualities 177

E

economic growth 174
education 60
embodiment 3–4
emotional wellbeing 165
empiricism 108
enculturation 28
Enlightenment, the 108, 174–5
epistemology 43–4, 108
Equality Act 2010 150
essay mills 183
essentialism 146

F

fa'afafine 148
false balance 114
feminisation of work 143
Forest Schools 178
free markets 67
friendships 167
Further and Higher Education
    Act 1992 68

G

gender 136–8
    gender critical feminism 149
    gender variant 145
    genderqueer 148

heteronormative 149
non-binary 147
as socially constructed 138–40
third gender 148
trans-exclusionary radical feminism (TERF) 149
transgender 146–7
transitioning 110, 150
gifted and talented 92–3
good enough 71
good food choices 161
good universities 92
governmentality 95, 97
grammar schools 92

H
Harvard referencing 187
Head Start 16
hegemony 116
helicopter parenting 70, 166
heteronormative 149
human capital theory 66
humanism 175
hypothetico-deductive method 108, 111, 113

I
idealism 62, 64, 65
incel 127–8, 142, 144
   see also manosphere, misogyny
individuation 28
industrialisation 106
innocence 122
inoculation programmes 163
instrumentalism 62
interpretivism 12
intersectionality 5
investment-outcomes discourse *see* outcomes

J
junk playgrounds 54

L
learnification 61, 64, 77, 78
learning analytics 90
Leave campaign *see* Brexit
living conditions 105

M
male aggression 142
manosphere 127–8, 135, 142, 144, 152
manufactured doubt 113

masculinity 142–4
measurable outcomes 156
mental health services 164
misogyny 127, 140–1, 142

N
Narnia 74
National Curriculum 61
neoconservatism 116
neoliberalism 66–7, 75, 78, 83, 116, 155
and education 55, 68, 74, 78
and inequality 83–4
and welfare 85–6
and work 76, 79, 84
nominalism 146

O
obesity 158–60
ontology 43–4, 108
othering 21
outcomes 154, 155
over-protective parents 72

P
parental supervision 166
patriarchy 141
perfectionism 69, 70
performativity 63, 139
play 46–52, 139, 156
   play as inefficient 63
   play work 53–4
playgrounds 51–2
plurality 110
pollution 170
positionality 20
positivism 12
post-humanism 175–8
post-industrial society 110
post-modern theory 110
post-modern turn 109
post-structuralist theory 110
post-truth 114
potential 89
poverty 80
previous experiences 5
privacy 128–31
privatisation of public services 67, 163
public spaces 106

Q
quasi-markets 68

Index

R
reading lists 183
reference lists 187
referencing software 187–8
Reggio Emilia 62
rights 18–19, 22, 35–6, 57, 177
risk 107

S
sanitation and public health 162
scaffolding 50
school leaving age 10, 45, 86
school readiness 63
school uniform 10, 96
schoolification 63–4, 78
scientific method 108
screen time 123
self 167
selfie-culture 166
self-regulation 97
self-tracking 90–1
sex 137
sexism 140–1
  see also misogyny
sexting 130
sharenting 131–2, 134
Sheffield Wednesday 92
skinhead 144
smoking 157
social conservatives 146
social construct 6, 139
social constructionism 1, 11, 12, 21
social engineering 8
social liberals 146
social media 107, 123–8, 130–4, 142, 150, 166
socio-ecological approach 14
sources 184
stages of development 6
Sure Start 16
surveillance of children 104

T
Te Whāriki 62, 179
therapy 132
thriving 173
trans-exclusionary radical feminism (TERF) 149
transgender *see* gender (sub-entry)
tripartite system 67
truth 109–10

U
unhealthy foods 159–60
  see also diet
United Nations Convention of the Rights of the Child 19
utilitarian 55
utilitarianism 64–5

V
verstehen 117
vocationalism 62
vulnerability 27

W
Who Funds You 185
woke 114–6, 144

Z
Zone of Proximal Development 49–50

www.ingramcontent.com/pod-product-compliance
Lightning Source LLC
Chambersburg PA
CBHW080214040426
42333CB00044B/2669